AF594052

Practicing Democracy

Practicing Democracy

Local Activism and Politics in France and Finland

Eeva Luhtakallio
University of Helsinki, Finland

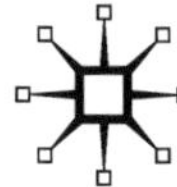

© Eeva Luhtakallio 2012

All rights reserved. No reproduction, copy or transmission of this publication may be made without written permission.

No portion of this publication may be reproduced, copied or transmitted save with written permission or in accordance with the provisions of the Copyright, Designs and Patents Act 1988, or under the terms of any licence permitting limited copying issued by the Copyright Licensing Agency, Saffron House, 6–10 Kirby Street, London EC1N 8TS.

Any person who does any unauthorized act in relation to this publication may be liable to criminal prosecution and civil claims for damages.

The author has asserted her right to be identified as the author of this work in accordance with the Copyright, Designs and Patents Act 1988.

First published 2012 by
PALGRAVE MACMILLAN

Palgrave Macmillan in the UK is an imprint of Macmillan Publishers Limited, registered in England, company number 785998, of Houndmills, Basingstoke, Hampshire RG21 6XS.

Palgrave Macmillan in the US is a division of St Martin's Press LLC, 175 Fifth Avenue, New York, NY 10010.

Palgrave Macmillan is the global academic imprint of the above companies and has companies and representatives throughout the world.

Palgrave® and Macmillan® are registered trademarks in the United States, the United Kingdom, Europe and other countries.

ISBN 978–0–230–30929–6

This book is printed on paper suitable for recycling and made from fully managed and sustained forest sources. Logging, pulping and manufacturing processes are expected to conform to the environmental regulations of the country of origin.

A catalogue record for this book is available from the British Library.

Library of Congress Cataloging-in-Publication Data
Luhtakallio, Eeva.
Practicing democracy: local activism and politics in France and Finland/
Eeva Luhtakallio, University of Helsinki, Finland.
pages cm
Includes bibliographical references.
ISBN 978–0–230–30929–6 (hardback)
1. Democracy—France. 2. Democracy—Finland. 3. Politics, Practical—France. 4. Politics, Practical—Finland. 5. Political participation—France. 6. Political participation—Finland. 7. France—Politics and government. 8. Finland—Politics and government.
9. Comparative government. I. Title.

JN2916.L85 2012
320.944—dc23 2011049325

10 9 8 7 6 5 4 3 2 1
21 20 19 18 17 16 15 14 13 12

Printed and bound in the United States of America

To my grandparents

Contents

List of Illustrations

List of Tables

Preface

This book has made me travel a great deal, and share the road with a number of memorable people. The traveling companions to whom I owe the most in accomplishing this work are the activists, politicians, and civil servants in Lyon and Helsinki who gave me their time, shared their thoughts, and trusted me with their experiences. While this work could not have been done without them, the exchanges and political activities I shared with them have meant, to me, still much more, both professionally and personally.

In the more scholarly journeys, I have been lucky to have the best of guides and companions. Risto Alapuro has been a devoted teacher and great friend, whose thinking and experience, as well as moral support and help, and quiet humor, have always been available to me. The Helsinki Research Group for Political Sociology (HEPO) that has grown from his students has been my principle academic home for years. All its members, and students that have participated in our seminars have contributed to the accomplishing of this work. I want to thank especially Tuomas Ylä-Anttila, with whom I have shared years of fun and intellectually sparkling writing processes, projects, travels, and morning coffee meetings; Markku Lonkila, whose questions and comments have been of great help, and with whom I have shared many moments of amazement before the trade of comparative research; Laura Lyytikäinen for encouragement, sharp comments, and sharing the ups and downs of everyday (office) life; Samu Lindström for helping out in several big and small things; and Veikko Eranti, a student-become-colleague-and-friend who, on the homestretch of this book project, was an irreplaceable help from sparring me with the last text versions to making sure my shoe laces were tied.

Nina Eliasoph has probably taught me more about sociology than any other one person, and it is in discussions with her that I have seized many of the most crucial insights of this work. Bike rides and long walks in France, Finland, and California with her have been like visits to the small, hard-to-find treasure planet of joint collegiality and friendship that I wish to visit on a regular basis. If it wasn't for her, and Paul Lichterman, as well as Olivia, Leo, Nobody, Who, and Else, the planet Hollywood would have not been as welcoming a place for a stranger of my kind.

The HEPO international affiliations have been a constant source of great intellectual stimulation and meetings full of hard work, friendship, and endless amazement with comparisons, translations, and engagements. The heart of these meetings has been Laurent Thévenot, who is an inspiring, demanding, and heartfelt teacher and discussion partner – and a first-class cooking companion. In addition, he has introduced me to a wonderful crowd of scholars with whom I hope for a long and fruitful cooperation.

Johanna Kantola has the rare talent of being able to challenge and encourage simultaneously. Marja Keränen and Loïc Blondiaux gave sharp, clear, and encouraging critique that helped me to brush-up the manuscript in important ways, and made me hope for future occasions to continue intellectual exchange with both of them. Aino Sinnemäki's clear-sighted and down-to-earth questions and remarks pushed me to think further. Eeva Raevaara, Anne Maria Holli, and Risto Heiskala were encouraging mentors and friends. I am thankful to the great number of people who have patiently commented upon different versions of the chapters in this book, and contributed to making it better (so I hope): Anu-Hanna Anttila, Pia Bäcklund, Marion Carrel, Julien Charles, Peter Holley, Alicia Kitsuse, Meri Kulmala, Sofia Laine, Damien Lecarpentier, Turo-Kimmo Lehtonen, Jonna Louvrier, Laura Lyytikäinen, Lena Näre, Eeva Raevaara, Suvi Salmenniemi, Iddo Tavory, and Juha-Heikki Tihinen. Katherine Greatrex's help in polishing style and language issues was priceless.

I have taken part in many intellectually stimulating arenas of discussion in Helsinki, Lyon, Paris, and Los Angeles. I have been surrounded by inspiring, critical, intriguing, and fun colleagues and friends, whose comments have shaped my thinking and writing, and who have made workplaces – and life in general – in different locations enjoyable.

My academic existence would not be the same without summer trips with the Ageing Beauties Club, Merja Kinnunen, Anu-Hanna Anttila, and Riikka Homanen. I felt at home in Lyon thanks to the friendship of Caroline Martinez and Florence Méry. Rémi Elicabe generously shared information with me. The Writer's Villa crew in Los Angeles threw me a birthday party far away from home, like any good family. With Iddo Tavory, the connection was undisturbed regardless of physical locations. The Sociological Salon – including among others Maija Jäppinen, Sofia Laine, Lena Näre, Emilia Palonen, Riikka Perälä and Suvi Salmenniemi – has combined a way to relax with intellectual stimulation. The collegiality and friendship of Sinikka Aapola-Kari, Anna-Maija Castrén, Karin Creutz-Kämppi, Kirsi Eräranta, Antti Gronow, Lotta Haikkola, Lotta

Hautamäki, Ilpo Helén, Peter Holley, Nahoko Kameo, Anu Katainen, Turo-Kimmo Lehtonen, Kaisa Ketokivi, Mianna Meskus, Lena Näre, Elina Oinas, Antti Pelkonen, Riikka Perälä, Martti Siisiäinen, Karoliina Snell, Harriet Strandell, Teemu Tallberg, Tuula Teräväinen, Anna-Mari Tapaninen, Aaro Tupasela, Sampo Villanen, Keiju Yesilova, and many, many others have made the turbulent academic world a warmer, less lonely, and more joyful a place. A special thanks to Leena Siimes-Erkkilä for a long journey together.

Finally, there are those who constantly saw me off and welcomed me back at the airport, listened to my homesick complaints both while away and when back home, and bore with me when the solitude of this work was at its greatest. I thank my parents Malla and Kale Luhtakallio for their steadfast support, and my friend Tia Teckenberg for being more than a sister. I'm grateful to my dog Toska who was always happy to see me, and to my husband Jussi Hämäläinen for his love, care, and understanding. Where ever I am, they are always with me.

1
A Sociological Travelogue

On a chilly day in May 2007, in a Helsinki city hall meeting room, two groups gathered to ponder issues of local democracy. One group was from Lyon and its surrounding areas in France, while the other was from the hosting city of Helsinki and its surrounding areas in Finland. The visit was initiated by the French group, which consisted of the leader of the Rhône-Alpes regional council, local councilors and leaders of party junctions from Lyon, members of the regional opposition, as well as members of different local associations, who wished to learn from experiences of local democracy abroad. The Finnish group had been chosen in order to respond to the request of the visitors in the best possible way, and included Helsinki city officials, Helsinki Urban Fact Center's researchers (and one sociologist), and representatives of several associations, such as a the umbrella organization of Helsinki neighborhood associations. The introductions, however, showed that the first group consisted of French citizens – citizens and only citizens, one could say, as each participant repeated this status with care and emphasis. The Finnish participants, in contrast, introduced themselves as representatives of various organizations, and specified meticulously each of their affiliations.

The concern, however, was common: how to change local democracy so that it would better include citizens and, in this way, interest them more so that they would participate more, and thus make democracy more legitimate. Several experiences were exchanged and local practices presented during the meeting. Some topics seemed to create mutual understanding more easily than others. What became clear was the shared pain and worry concerning the ossified power structures of local democracy, the struggle and slowness of its transformation, and the troubling gap between most citizens and most decision-makers in the two local polities under consideration. It was harder to find common ground regarding the role of politics and the politicization of issues, or on the methods of 'including citizens'.

Other tensions also arose: it turned out that the French group was not entirely satisfied with the composition of the hosting party. The French group had been brought together initially by a process of participatory democracy organized in the region of Rhône-Alpes, but nevertheless the presence of elected bodies was strong. They wondered why no Municipal Councilors or other elected representatives had been invited to join the Finnish group. The Finnish group, brought together through cooperation between various parties, was surprised by this fact: it had not occurred to anyone that inviting councilors to the meeting would be important, nor that it would enhance the quality of the information the group had set on its agenda. In their understanding, the best expertise available on the issues of local democracy was present. Despite this small discrepancy, both groups claimed to have learned a lot, and toasted to hope and democracy at dinner later that evening.

This encounter captures several key features of the story this book tells. First of all, it is a small anecdote in the worldwide tale of the crisis of democracy. In all parts of the globe, democracy troubles people – be it citizens, decision-makers, or officials – and they constantly search for better solutions of democratic governance on different levels of the public sphere. This search is underway in the midst of globalized and corporatized powers nullifying the decisions of democratic governments, governance reforms depoliticizing and disempowering democratic processes by rendering them mere technicalities, and growing civic dissatisfaction, distrust, and suspicion – expressed in terms of decreasing voter turnouts, vivid collective action, social movements and networks, and even anti-democratic activities – towards the state of this mode of governance. Democracy is sometimes described as the least of evils, or the best option so far, but at the same time, even though at times used as a mere label put on almost any kind of a governing system, it has never been as extensively accepted in the world as it is at present. It is, however, noteworthy that the major crisis diagnostics stem from old representative democracies: namely Western and Northern Europe, and North America. Understanding 'the crisis' requires understanding its foundations, conditions, and consequences in these contexts.

Hence the comparative dimensions of this book, and the second point the story illustrates. The questions the French and Finnish delegates addressed while talking about democracy, citizenship, and politics are not only subjects of transformation in the global turmoil of the crisis of democracy but they also reflect the profound differences in understanding these words and acting according to them, and the different bases for democratic practices in different countries and different local contexts. Even in such a brief encounter, it became clear that the possibilities for politics and politicization, as well as the contents, conditions, and practices of democracy are deeply contextual questions. In this book, contextualized answers to these questions are sought. By analyzing politicization, civic action, and the struggles and dialogues in the local public spheres, this book shows the crucial importance of people's local contextual processes of putting democracy into practice in two cities: Lyon in France and Helsinki in Finland.

The third point the story makes, somewhat discretely, is the question of the storyteller. How this story wound up in the introduction of this book is part of the narrative of the delicate position of a comparative researcher engaged in producing contextualized knowledge. I participated in the encounter, and I had participated in its organization, offering my contacts and local knowledge from both sides to help achieve a successful fruition to the visit. In fact, the reason the Lyonnais chose Helsinki as their main visiting point in the Nordic countries was in great part due to the group leader's meeting with me, a Finnish sociologist, during my fieldwork for this study in Lyon. During the visit, I ended up translating part of the discussions, from French to Finnish, Finnish to French. Thus, the encounter crystallized something of the entire process of this study: I found myself physically in between two cultures, observing the two groups that were trying to understand each other, while also having my say in how the understanding was or was not made possible. In addition to linguistic interpreting, I had to provide a lot of semantic explanations too: what does the same thing mean in each context, what is similar, and what is really different? In so doing, I certainly affected the impressions the two groups took home. Also, the details of the encounter that stuck in my mind were definitely not the only significant things that happened during those days, but were the ones intelligible to me, based on my previous encounters within these two contexts, these ways of representing and doing politics, these ways of arguing and justifying chosen solutions, and so on.

Comparative research involves a lot of travelling and translating back and forth, both physically and in more abstract terms. Each journey is unique: on the one hand, incidences and coincidences direct its course, and on the other, the traveler is responsible for the path she takes. An important part of this responsibility is to accept the task of making the road by walking it, and being prepared to check and alter one's own presuppositions. And so it was: the problems that seemed the most crucial to me in the beginning of the journey altered quite a bit along the way. The more the destinations of this round trip gradually became familiar to me, the more my original theoretical, methodological, and hypothetical starting points required further clarification, new directions, and tailor-made approaches. Treading this path led me to conceive of politicization – the process of opening an arena for political action, or raising an issue to political debate – as the central organizing metaphor and key question of this study.

How do the processes of politicization diverge in different local contexts, and what kinds of consequences do these processes (and differences in them) have on the local civic practices, the definitions and redefinitions of democracy and citizenship, the dynamics of power and resistance, and the ways of solving controversies on the public sphere?

This book, while being an empirical study of two cities, is also a travelogue of the conceptual, contextual, and empirical journey between cultural contexts, and an attempt to render transparent a research process that was required to produce sensitive, yet non-trivial and multi-level comparative knowledge.

In the next sections, I overview the key theoretical, conceptual, and methodological issues that map the journey, with an emphasis on insights to comparisons and comparativity. Furthermore, I introduce the destinations – the empirical contexts – of the study: influential features of the French and Finnish polities regarding politicization and democracy, and of the politico-administrative systems of Lyon and Helsinki, as well as some central characteristics of the respective local civil societies. In the last section I briefly introduce the empirical materials I use, as well as the structure of the book.

1.1 The itinerary: constructing problems, traveling with concepts, and comparing politicizations

Constructing problems cross-culturally

The traveling metaphors I deploy in this chapter stem from the nowadays rather common currency that different levels of context specificity need to be considered in comparative research, and that a substantial part of this consideration has to do with the theoretical concepts the research operates with (see e.g. Lamont & Thévenot 2000; Lammert & Sarkowsky 2010, 14–15). 'Comparative research', however, is a broad field of studies ranging from statistical analyses of social capital in multinational surveys to micro-level ethnographic studies. On this spectrum, this study locates somewhere slightly past the middle grounds and closer to the latter end with its triangulation of different qualitative data and methods and concentration on two local societies combined, however, with historical and secondary data introducing comparative perspectives also on the national level. In terms of another famous categorization of comparative research, the number of compared societies is small, they are quite distant, and quite different from one another, but troubled by similar problems (cf. Marsh 1967, 6–11). Rather than just fitting in categorizations of the long tradition of comparative sociology, the particular journey of conducting this study made a contribution to the pressing question of how to carry out comparative research in a complex, globalizing world.

As I wanted to overcome some of the pitfalls of both the macro-level, and the most micro-level comparisons, I found useful Marja Keränen's (2001; cf. Hantrais 2009, 39–42) emphasis of the epistemological differences between comparatiste and cross-cultural research: the former refers to comparisons that parallel the compared contexts in regard to questions set 'from the outside,' and the latter to comparisons that build the questions 'from within' the contexts to be studied. Keränen notes that the former position is often combined with the concrete ways of conducting research she calls the 'safari method', in which the researcher does not quite stay in her armchair, but goes to the 'other' place with a ready-made question and presumption pack, collects data to answer the questions, and returns home to compare the findings. This method becomes problematic when it turns out that the 'problem' compared is understood in different terms in different contexts – or not understood as a problem at all in one context, and emphasized as a serious concern in another (Keränen 2001, 85–7). Indeed, as Carol Bacchi (1999, 2–4, 7) has noted, the definition of a problem has significant consequences for the cultural means available for solving it, and these definition struggles are at the core of structuring a society. In a comparative setting, tracing what is and what is not 'the problem' in different cultural contexts also requires tracing the fundamental conceptual differences concerning the recognition, presentation, and solving of societal problems, and, *mutatis mutandis*, constructing the research problem concerning them.

Empirical comparisons are always theoretical comparisons as well: empirical material, cases and results are contextually bound, and so are theories and concepts, and the culturally intelligible understandings of them – academic cultures included. This notion is organically intertwined with the project of this book. Empirical objects like activist groups, local political bodies, public conflicts, or gender order, as well as concepts such as democracy, citizenship, and the public sphere, do not mean the same thing, and are not acted on or used similarly in France and in Finland. Taking this self-evidence literally has consequences to all of the different phases and parts that compose a research project (cf. Hantrais 2009, 72). In order to render the key concepts of this work 'transportable,' and even more so translatable, I needed to build a compromise between abstract universalism and its relativist denial that abandons abstraction altogether. I have combined a conceptual comparativity that sets to open and modify the concepts in order to meet the requirements of cultural specificity with the comparison of a small number of contexts I have been able to acquire substantial amounts of local knowledge from and familiarity with (Landman 2000, 42–3; see also Hantrais 2009, 90–1). But this was not the whole story.

In this study, I did not go on a safari, by a necessity that I only vaguely understood at the beginning of the journey. Instead, the comparative approach I have followed could be called the 'traveler method,' referring to the fashionable back-packer mode of exploring the world. The traveler method engages in the idea of comparative research as a holistic endeavor (cf. Ragin 1987), in which every element of the on-going study is subjected to the comparative situation: the research problem, the empirical materials, the interlocutors, the theoretical concepts, the methodological ideas and methodic tools, and so on. In other words, apart from the researcher's occasional trips, the research questions, the theories, and the methodologies travel as well, and do not return home unchanged. The questions, concepts, and methodology of this study altered and varied, and were finally sharpened little by little, during my trips back and forth between France and Finland and finally also during a few trips across the Atlantic. They did so concretely when I sat in planes and trains, packed and carried bags, settled in and left again, and brought endless sets of souvenirs and gastronomic specialties both ways, and all this already way before I really began this study.[1] My recurrent travels between France and Finland got yet another perspective of my sojourns in the US during the writing process of this book: looking at the themes of comparison from a third angle, and looking at both contexts of the study from a distance at the same time, shaped my way of understanding them substantially.

In addition, the questions and definitions of problems altered, varied, and sharpened by means of traveling with the Finnish, French, and Anglo-American theoretical and methodological corpus, and by means of discussing it with both interlocutors and colleagues in different destinations. My understanding of the corpus was significantly influenced by the journey and the encounters during it. But most importantly, all of the above was influenced by the local actors' ways of talking and writing about, and filming and performing the topics they considered relevant in the local society, that is, their ways of practicing democracy, politicizing, publicizing, conducting 'civic activities', and representing the latter in various ways. These words, deeds, images, and events stemmed from fundamentally different grounds of organizational styles, cultural understandings of politics, and principals of negotiating the common good, and despite many apparent similarities, followed dissimilar logics and had diverging consequences in France and in Finland.

Thus, the solution I propose in this book to the problem of the 'transportability' of concepts, and moreover to the challenge of treating comparative contexts subtly without getting stuck at the level of anecdotal particularities, consists of the following two dimensions of constructing and defining the questions, and deconstructing and reconstructing the concepts. The work is carried out, first, in a cooperative manner, and secondly, as an enduring process. The former has meant direct and mediated discussions both with different academic contexts and with different actors in the field, in which the conceptual framework of the study was treated more like a series of adverbs than nouns with stable definitions. My interpreter's role resembled, in sum, perhaps the position of an improvisation theater director, who watches the play 'happen' much like the audience, but who at the same time has an idea of where the characters and plot developments come from, and who guesses more and more at every show where the actors are headed – and who still always gets surprised by the outcome. The latter, an emphasis on the processual nature of concepts, resulted in an approach to comparison that combines the careful 'how's' of ethnographic research with the localization of patterns of differences between contexts. This approach comes close to what Paul Ricoeur (e.g. 1991) has referred to as the processes of sedimentation, in sociological terms the idea of social structure as a set of continually moving processes that appear to people as stable and (almost) invariable. In other words, it means 'to see the river flow while simultaneously seeing how it sediments into patterns that participants [in these historical processes] experience as solid, real, and nearly incontrovertible' (see Luhtakallio & Eliasoph 2012). In the following, I overview some of the landmarks that have been influential in regard to the conceptual work this book engages in.

Politicization and its preconditions

Politicization is the key example of an empirically 'grounded' and processual concept, in the sense that it is, gradually, the findings of the empirical research that have made me understand that the processes of politicization are at the core of this research, and that they hold the key to solving the riddles the empirical contexts in question produce (cf. Keränen 2001, 88–9). Politicization has thus come to be simultaneously both a theoretical concept that directs the discussion of my empirical findings, and an empirically informed understanding of what is at stake. To prepare the journey, I have drawn the silhouette of the theoretical concept from multiple sources in multiple academic debates and contexts.

In determining what the conceptual process of politicization can mean in different contexts, I have followed, first, political philosopher Kari Palonen (2003) who has defined politicization as a process that opens something 'as political, as "playable",' and creates new, previously unidentified spaces for performing politics. Politicization marks something as political, and names it as such. Politicization requires effort: Any issue can be politicized but only through deliberate efforts that are more than mere declarations, and that envisage in some way the new political forms thus made possible. In Palonen's account, politicization can be either inventive or disruptive: the construction of entirely new chances, or the detection of political potential (ibid. 171, 182).

Secondly, political scientist and ethnographer Camille Hamidi (2006) has called for an 'enlarged definition of politicization' that enables taking into account politics (*le politique*) taking place outside the sphere of institutional politics (*la politique*), but also one that does not depend on our knowledge of whether or not the actors 'actually think' they are engaged in a process of politicization. The second point is particularly important when analyzing politicization in contexts in which political modalities – objectively verifiable or subjectively labeled as such by the studied actors – are not available, or not observable. This is the case whenever the consequences or results of politicization are difficult to assess definitively, and whenever the subjective accounts of the actors involved in the process cannot be fixed and revealed with certainty (ibid. 9–10). Taken literally, this is always the case in sociological studies: processes such as politicization are typically so complex that their thorough causes or consequences are definitively out of our reach. Furthermore, being certain of the subjective accounts of actors would require reading their minds. In Hamidi's account, two elements allow us to recognize politicization in everyday practices and discourses. The first one is an understanding of politicization as a rise in the level of generality (*montée en généralité*). This means making a reference to the general principles of common good in a society, and 'moving' from the individual level towards them and the public (Hamidi 2006, 10; see also Boltanski & Thévenot 1999; Thévenot 2010). In other words, politicization is publicization, rendering something public (see Eliasoph 1996, 1998). The second element is the recognition of the conflict dimension to the positions taken in a particular situation. This recognition refers to acknowledging confrontation, not necessarily in the sense of an explicitly contentious register of talk or repertoire of action, but in the sense of an opening, a possibility, an existence of confronting ideas (Hamidi 2006, 10–11).

In sum, politicization is a process of articulation that takes place in public, is enabled and triggered by citizens of a polity, and generally requires a governing system that recognizes the participation of citizens as a general rule, a system that in the context of this study is broadly labeled as 'democratic.'[2] These three – public, citizens, and democracy – form the heaviest contents of the conceptual baggage this work travels with, and simultaneously, portray as the three main aspects of analyzing the processes of politicization. In the following, I briefly overview the key starting points for the conceptual 'sedimentation processes', and shared reconstruction work this book proposes regarding them.

First, as John Dewey (1927, 146) once said, the public is a process in itself: it needs to recognize itself as one in order to become a democratic public sphere on which problems concerning the common good can be negotiated and re-negotiated. The public, in other words, is a process of recognition, and multiple processes of negotiations and re-negotiations of its own being. The public sphere, hence, becomes an empirical question, or, more exactly, a series of empirical questions about the publics[3] recognizing themselves as publics, and thus coming into terms with treating controversies (Dewey 1927; Fraser 1992, 126–7). If the public sphere is in itself something multiple, and, following Nina Eliasoph (1998, 10), created by people acting as citizens, then studying the public sphere means studying where this creation happens, and how. Eliasoph (2004) points out further that the locations of public conversation differ according to the society in question. In some situations, the important political talk in a democratic point of view can only be heard in kitchens and backyards, as was the case, for example, in many Soviet-ruled countries in the early 1980s. Thus, the minimal definition of the public sphere would be that where there is civic-minded talk, there is a public sphere (ibid. 299–300). This 'where' can be a newspaper, a website, or a public place, but it can also be a 'private' place.[4] It may indeed be more and more the latter in current urban realities, where the public places are increasingly taken over by the market – and yet again, there is no reason why political conversation cannot also happen in an entirely commercial shopping mall environment, for example. The public is whatever and where ever it recognizes itself, whence the importance of not predetermining the public sphere in narrow terms, or contenting to the 'commonly accepted' locations of the public in a study that approaches the actors' understandings of public processes. This said, there is no reason to deny or diminish the importance of the commonly accepted dimensions of the public sphere – newspapers, the Internet, and the like – but rather complement this picture with a more flexible conceptual apparatus.

Second, as the title of this book indicates, practicing democracy is at the center of the empirical realities met in the French and Finnish contexts. Democratic practices form the field of activity in which politicizations emerge. Hence, the theoretical perspective of process-oriented or deliberative democracy,[5] and the *zeitdiagnostical* perspective of the 'crisis of democracy' are the principle angles from which I consider democracy in this book. The two are intertwined: the academic debates about what should be done with the legitimacy of this governing system, and the mundane diagnostics and concern of decreasing voter turnout are in constant dialogue with each other.[6] One of the most paramount and influential voices in this dialogue has been the work of Pierre Rosanvallon (1998, 2006, 2008). In Rosanvallon's (2006) account, the established conception of democracy, consisting of a representative political system, based on suffrage, and practiced through institutions such as the parliament and the government, has been hit by the crisis of the principle of representation throughout the world, at least in part as a result of the decline and degeneration of the system's political dimension and content (ibid. 10, 16, 257–60). In consequence, the concrete democratic experiences of today's citizens are often marked by disappointment and frustration, which, in turn, discloses the political forms of 'counter-democracy,' and renders them pivotal. These political forms are not 'against democracy' but are, and have always been, an inherent part of it, even if in different forms and intensities in different moments in history. In other words, the crisis of representative democracy brings grass roots politics, social movements, citizen groups, and the like to the center of attention – it is with these kinds of actors that the hope for a 'remedy' of the crisis resides (ibid. 15–24). Politics, increasingly practiced elsewhere than within instances of representative democracy, is the source of a 'common world,' and it is through political activity that society is represented to itself. Hence democracy cannot be reduced to a mere system, but rather it means the form a society takes in the process of being a society (Rosanvallon 2006; see also Palonen 2002; Luhtakallio & Alapuro 2008).[7]

Finally, the third notion 'in process' in this book is citizenship.[8] In the process of a society 'representing itself' described by Rosanvallon, citizens have always had an active role as the practitioners of counter-democracy. A lot of talk about passive citizens, political apathy, and individualism, or sometimes, declining social capital 'killing' politics, coincides with the crisis-of-democracy-talk (e.g. Putnam 2000; Braconnier & Dormagen 2007). In the process-oriented understanding of democracy in general and within the counter-democratic problematic in particular, citizenship is an active, public status, marked by an ethic of participation. In this sense, there is no such thing as a passive citizen, as 'citizen' is an active position as such. Rosanvallon (2006, 24–6) has as far as claimed that the idea of a passive citizen is but a myth created by political agents who either innocently or willingly fail to understand the modes of being active and 'doing citizen' other than voting for representative governments and organs. This does not indicate that politically passive people are 'not citizens.' Instead, by treating citizenship not as a status but as something that actualizes in the situations and moments of activity, it is possible to avoid labeling people as passive or active, and to recognize that nobody is either completely passive or entirely active, nor are these qualifications lasting and invariable. To be a citizen is to 'do citizen,' to act as a citizen in the framework of rules and practices of a given context (e.g. Lister 2003, 7, 37).[9] In regard to this concept, ready-made definitions remain abstract promulgations unless taken somewhere and expressed in relation to people's lives, their understandings of citizenship, and the ways of actualizing these understandings. This is what will be done with citizenship in this study: instead of giving other predefinitions except for the idea of a citizen as a societal and political actor, I listen to what these actors in France and Finland have to say about citizenship, and about the practices connected to it.

In sum, comparing politicizations means studying practices and processes connected to democracy, citizen activities, and the public sphere. Where to look for these processes and how to analyze them – the question of methodology – will be briefly overviewed in the next section, before turning to the contextual sediments and sources of the empirical material this book builds on.

Traveling methodology

The methodological design of this book is a triangulation of several distinct methods that share the same foundation. This foundation can be defined as cultural sociology, but it can just as well be labeled as pragmatist sociology (see Silber 2003). The basic idea of this methodological package is the observation that both in habitual course of actions, and in situations in which it descends into crisis because of a disruption of some kind, people use collectively shared repertoires and reflexive accounts in order to make their actions both in routine and in deviation intelligible to others, and in order to keep the life going. These repertoires, or symbolic reserves, provide people with skills and habits, a cultural 'tool kit', in Ann Swidler's words (Swidler 1986, 273–7).

These kits should, however, not be understood as essential collections of what this or that culture 'is,' even if the metaphor offers a tempting simplification of a comparative approach, and even if it certainly also is so that, for example, there may be a hammer in both French and Finnish kits, although not an identical one, and there most probably are tools in one kit a user of the other would hardly recognize, let alone know how to use them. But more important is how the actors in the two contexts use these tools at their disposal in order to construct meaningful strategies of action to pursue their goals, and whether these strategies of action result in politicization of the issues pursued (ibid. 278, 284). I try to answer this question in several different ways, making use of the different empirical material I have produced and collected: participant observation, thematic and in-depth interviews, visual representations, and newspaper articles.

Nina Eliasoph and Paul Lichterman (2003) have developed Swidler's concept of culture further to better fit micro-level situations in their theory of *group styles*, or the ways in which people use and understand collective representations: how people understand the boundaries, the bonds, and the speech norms of the group they take part in (ibid. 739). Group styles are based on Eliasoph's and Lichterman's empirical ethnographic and theoretical work combining insights of the Durkheimian approach to culture as collective representations, the pragmatist–cognitive approach to interaction, and the use of collective representations in making meanings. Through this combination, at the center of analysis are actors making meaning with collective representations in ways that complement a shared ground of interaction (ibid. 736–7). The importance of the group styles theory in this book is based on the unpronounced, yet in my view, apparent move it makes towards a deeper intertwinement of cultural and pragmatist sociology. This move is based on the idea of the concept of habit as something essentially, and perhaps even primarily, collectively negotiated, interaction-based, and processual (see also Kilpinen 2000; Gronow 2011).

The connecting factor of the methods I use in working with my empirical material is Erving Goffman's (1974) notion of framing: the habitual processes of structuring experiences, in which meanings are produced in communication with a given situation. In combining different perspectives to framing, I analyze and treat frames both as meaningful structures necessary for 'navigating' in the world, and as active processes of producing and reproducing social reality. I use framing as the basis for analyzing my empirical material in three principle ways. First, I apply frame analysis to interpreting interview talk. I analyze the talk on democracy and citizenship in interviews of local political actors by looking at how they frame the things they say – and the things they 'do not say.' I also look at what kinds of cracks and fractures shake the frames of talking about things people have strong opinions on – or, contrarily, do not really know what to say about (Raevaara 2005; see Chapters 3 and 5 in this book, in particular). Secondly, I apply frame analysis to visual representations. Asking what frames stem from a set of images, and what kinds of relations these frames have with each other and with the wider 'sources' of cultural representations, renders the analysis of even significantly large bodies of visual representations feasible (Luhtakallio 2003, 2005; see also Chapter 4 and Methods Appendix in this book). Thirdly, frame analysis also partly provides the basis for the Public Justifications Analysis (PJA), a method built on the theory of justification by Luc Boltanski and Laurent Thévenot (1991; 1999) that I use in analyzing local media disputes (Luhtakallio & Ylä-Anttila 2011; see Chapter 6 in this book).

With these means of orientation, the following section sets out towards the destinations of the journey. It approaches them first from afar, as nation-state constructions called France and Finland, and then gradually moves towards the local scenes of practicing democracy.

1.2 The destinations: studying politicizations in France and Finland

European polity models in comparison

France and Finland represent different groups in several common divides of European societies. Finland is a relatively small and young nation in the Protestant Nordic block, and France an old, central state marked by Catholic culture and usually placed among the southern or the western block, depending on the emphasis (cf. Salamon & Anheier 1998). Regarding this book, two axes of dissimilarity are particularly important: the relationship of the state to its citizens on the one hand,

and the ideas of association between the citizens, and thus more generally the question of representation, on the other (cf. Alapuro 2005a; Raevaara 2005). Ronald L. Jepperson (2002) has proposed a model of forms of political modernity, based on, notably, institutional differentiation, and the above types of relations within societies. Following his account, France forms the core of the state–nation model, while Finland belongs to the social–corporate model, 'the Nordic Block' (ibid. 72–5).

The state–nation model is marked by 'a canonical statism conjoined with an anticorporate reconstruction of society' (Jepperson 2002, 72). It is suspicious of interest groups, and has historically banned group identities in the constitution of the public sphere. However, groups – in particular, social classes – have strongly marked the French society in different phases of its history. The republican ideal of universalism has strived to reject namely organized mediation between the state and its citizens (ibid.; Rosanvallon 1998; Alapuro 2005a, 379). In the French imaginery, people indeed are associated with the state as citizens first and foremost (Wieviorka 1996, cit. Jepperson 2002, 72). The defense of particular interests through associations within the public sphere was rejected, as the universalistic principle (and, historically, the fear of chaos after the continuous unrest of the revolutionary period) created an imaginary of a society in which solidarity directly bound all individuals to each other. In this societal climate, associational culture grew very close to the state, and the coercive nature of this link created an enduring tension within associational life between integration and contention (Alapuro 2005a, 380). Hence, state–nation model societies lack consensual basis, and are instead marked by strong oppositional currents and protests.

In contrast, the social–corporate model countries are marked by a strong interdependence and integration of state and civil society. The state is not weak – in the sense of a withdrawn state at the extreme liberal end of the spectrum – but it is envisioned 'as a natural extension of a governing societal community – and as intermediating the organized interest of society' (Jepperson 73–4). The intertwinement of state and society in social–corporate polities results in a low salience of the public–private distinction. In analyses of the Finnish case, in particular, the state and civil society have often been described even as completely merged into one another, resulting in a multiply intertwined private and public, and official and voluntary spheres (ibid. 74; see also Alapuro & Stenius 1987; Kettunen 2008, 91). Associations were, in many respects, the crucial pillars in building the state and forming the political culture. This led to a state–civil society relationship characterized by a broad inclusion of citizens and their organizations in decision-making

(Alapuro 2005a, 379). Rather than a hierarchical order, a functionalist–rationalist polity is produced in which 'people enter the public sphere not as independent actors carrying private "interests", but as functionally specific role players carrying delimited competencies, intensively mobilized into a multitude of formal organizations' (Jepperson 2002, 73–4). The emphasis on rationality and functionality has a wide range of repercussions in the politicization processes in Finnish society, as this book will show several times (see also Kettunen 2008, e.g. 126–7). One of the most important consequences is the by and large hegemonic status of consensual decision-making: inclusive, but not pluralist. Even though the explicit goal of the expanded organizational participation is meant to enhance democracy, it does not enhance a democracy based on ideological discussions or politicizations in an open public sphere (Alapuro 1997; Jepperson 2002, 74; Kettunen 2008). Jepperson's formulations are also illustrative with regards to principles of collective action in the two contexts. In France, the emphasis is on non-contractual, 'natural' joint action between individuals, whereas in Finland, the representative function of associations dictates the general atmosphere of collective action (Alapuro 2005b, 20–1).

In more general terms, the conception of representation in the respective societies is differently based. Making use of Pierre Rosanvallon's (1998, 308) analytical division of representation functioning as the 'political figuration of the social' in two ways, descriptively and constructively, Risto Alapuro (2005a, 2007) has suggested that the Finnish idea of representation is a descriptive one: an image of the society 'as it is,' transparently composed of groups with fixed interests. The French idea, on the contrary, forms a constructive interpretation of the society: an image of a society, the composition of which remains opaque and can only take form through constant construction (Alapuro 2007, 7–10). These characterizations are especially related to the historical role of associations in the two political cultures: in Finland, associations were integrated early on into the political culture as the mediating structure between the state and the people, whereas in France the republican ideal of universalism rejected all organized mediation between the state and its citizens (Alapuro 2005a, 379).

Étienne Balibar (2001, 213) has described this difference as one between cultures of struggle (*lutte*), characteristic of France and Italy, and the cultures of mediation (*médiation*), characteristic of Northern European countries. These labels also reflect the common consequences of the differences on the repertoires of collective action. The struggle culture emphasizes the use of contentious, direct action-oriented repertoires whereas the mediation culture tends to favor less disruptive, consensual ones. This description captures the general trend of action repertoires in France and in Finland: the Finns are less experienced in various repertoires of direct action, and far more reluctant to take part in any activities on the fringes of lawfulness than the French (see World Value Survey 2004; Alapuro 2005a). Stereotypically, while the French rage on the streets to get their voices heard, the Finns sit at committee tables hoping for the same thing.

Simultaneously with being illustrative, typologies and models such as the ones referred to above are also frustratingly reductionist. They capture trends and generalities, but lack sensitivity and touch on the (endless) variation within each 'model.' Historical analyses, in contrast, are more sensitive, but at times tend to trivialize recent change, or current conditions, while being illustrative of long-term developments. There are French civic actors sitting on committee tables, and Finnish activists roaming the streets, and everything in between the two extremes. There are, certainly, general trends to be found, but even more so, there are contextual processes to be explored and followed. State–citizen relations, politicization, developments of democracy, and other generally commented features are, indeed, ever-moving processes in constant alteration. They are affected by innumerous historical and current factors: in the context of this study, the most prominent current factors are connected to the neo-liberal wave that has swept over French and Finnish polities during the past three decades. It has installed new dimensions of distrust, changed, and often complicated, the conditions of politicization, and affected both the everyday lives of the citizens, and the imaginaries as well as statuses of the states in unforeseen ways (Eräsaari 2002; Jepperson 2002, 77–8; Koebel 2006; Rosanvallon 2006; Holli *et al.* 2007; Sennett 2007).

Institutional contexts of local democracy

The scenes of this study are two similar-sized cities, Lyon and Helsinki, one of which is a regional capital, the other a national one.[10] French and Finnish local governance systems diverge in regards to different legal standings, historical roots, and relations to superior levels of governance, and yet, they face similar contemporary challenges.[11] I do not pretend to analyze the entirety of local governance, not even in the two cities explored. Instead, I concentrate on the civic practices of local citizen groups, and the interactions between the citizens and the politico-administrative institutions in Lyon and Helsinki. I approach the two cities as local societies, to paraphrase Max Weber (1992[1921], 23–34,

69–71), in two ways: first, as public spheres in which conflicts and interests are interplayed and politicization either takes place or is tamed and, secondly, as arenas of urban governance, with a strong emphasis on the former. During my field research, the municipal council of Lyon had a Socialist, Communist and Green majority alliance, and an opposition of a Right-wing coalition (UMP and Unir pour Lyon). The city was led by a Socialist Mayor elected by popular vote. The council in Helsinki was led by the National Coalition (Right Wing), accompanied by the Social Democratic Party and the Green League in an altering order, but as the executive board in Finnish municipalities includes all council groups, there is no official division between the majority and the opposition, even if the number of council seats naturally defines power positions.[12] The two Mayors in office in Helsinki during the research period were elected from the Right.[13]

Studying contexts of local governance today requires taking into account the 'trend' of participatory democracy: the increasing interest of both policy-makers and researchers in processes of citizen participation aimed at the strengthening of democracy and provoking a change in the downward trend of voting turnouts. Wider citizen participation portrays, through a plethora of practices in different political cultures, as the remedy for the legitimacy crisis of representative democracy in different parts of the world (Blondiaux 1999, 367, 2008, 5–6, 49–62; Bacqué *et al.* 2005, 10–44; Baiocchi 2005; Rosanvallon 2006, 300). In France and Finland as well, the legal basis for direct participation has been strongly enhanced in recent years (Bäcklund *et al.* 2006, 8; Robbe 2007, 12–13). In France, attempts to decentralize governance since the 1980s have resulted in a growing importance in local level administration and politics, and increasing citizen participation has been the central theme of major legislation and policy reforms.[14] In Finland, several legislation reforms of the past three decades have reinforced citizen participation at the municipal level, in particular in issues concerning urban planning politics.[15] The implementation of the participatory practices is rather precisely enacted in the French legislation, and less leeway is thus left for local decision-makers, whereas in Finland the implementation details have been, to a large extent, left to the municipalities' decision (Delbo 2005; Bäcklund 2007).

Consequently, the ways in which the official information channels of Lyon and Helsinki presented local democratic practices and citizen participation were diverse. Also, the actual structures and practices concerning citizen participation differed. In Lyon, the center-stage was occupied by the promotion of a participatory 'spirit' and enhancement of democracy. On the city's website, a solemn presentation of the issue signed by the Mayor welcomed the visitor:

> Democracy is never self-evident: it ranks rather as an exception in the global scale. In a time where we talk of strengthened individualism and crisis of public engagement, thousands of Lyonnais invest in different instances of dialogue and cooperation offered by the Town Hall; they express their concerns, their expectations and their wishes. I intend to render Lyon a city that listens to its citizens: share your ideas with us by participating in neighborhood councils, youngsters' municipal council, the Lyonnais council of respecting rights, the council of foreign inhabitants or the integration initiative groups... There are so many workshops in which the citizenship of today is prepared, and democracy of tomorrow is constructed. To participate in the life of the *Cité* is to make oneself heard, to improve the collective projects, and to promote the 'will to live together.'[16] Mayor Gérard Collomb (Lyon 2008)

Regarding participatory practices, the city website in Lyon listed eight different municipal structures of 'democracy of proximity.' The (statutory) neighborhood councils were open to all adults, both in the neighborhood of residence and (with certain restrictions) of professional or voluntary activity.[17] The Municipal Council of the Young offered minors the chance to influence decision-making, and the Council for Foreign Residents of Lyon (CREL) offered similar opportunities to those not entitled to vote because of their nationality. In addition, the website presented several extra-municipal commissions, and different instances of participation in Grand Lyon.[18] These structures were mainly commissions, councils and boards destined to debate either issues concerning a specific group of people, or a general theme, such as 'the life of a neighborhood.' In addition, there were web-forms that one could use to express opinions on the work of the listed structures.

In Helsinki, by contrast, the emphasis was on knowledge, information and formal procedures concerning participation. The Helsinki City General Strategy, cited on the city website, stated:

> The municipality's inhabitants' knowledge of the city administration, as well as the administration's knowledge of inhabitants' opinions, will be developed through channels of information technology. (Helsinki 2008)

Furthermore, a site entitled 'Participate and influence' primed:

> An inhabitant of Helsinki can influence the city decision-makers in addition to voting in the election, also by taking initiative, sending questions and propositions to elected representatives and officials, and by participating in the debate concerning the city and occasions organized for inhabitants. (Helsinki 2008)

Helsinki indeed seemed to put a lot of faith in 'e-participation.' A citizen could find information and channels to ask questions, discuss, complain or make initiatives in the activities of most of the municipal services through the city websites. The website also introduced the municipal initiative, as well as how to contrive a municipal referendum. Both procedures are statutory. In addition, the Town Planning Office staff included two 'interaction planners', assigned to create and facilitate interaction between citizens and the city administration. In the Youth Department, a project called 'The Voice of the Young of Helsinki' had been on-going since 1998, involving the majority of schoolchildren in Helsinki in a participatory budgeting process (Hesan Nuorten Ääni 2008). The Department of Environment had realized several participatory projects on a very concrete level, such as planning a shopping center together with the inhabitants.[19] There were, however, no permanent municipal structures for exchanging views between citizens and city politicians; instead, the above practices all mainly depended on the administration and were operated by civil servants.[20]

In sum, while Lyon promoted participation as an extension of democracy and public debate, Helsinki emphasized information, knowledge and legal procedures. The differences in the ways Lyon and Helsinki promoted the characteristics of local democracy and citizenship seemed to crystallize in the names of the information magazines of the two cities, distributed to all inhabitants: *Lyon Citoyen* (Lyon Citizen) and *Helsinki-info* (Helsinki Information) (see Chapter 4 for further analysis on these magazines).

Exploring civic practices in Lyon and Helsinki

Lyon and Helsinki are both lively centers of activism, social movements, associations, and other type of civic practices, the processes 'by which citizens create contexts for political conversation in the potential public sphere' (Eliasoph 1996, 263). In the following, I do not attempt to draw a general, extensive overview of the two local civil societies, but rather to introduce some elements of the empirical contexts I encountered.

In Lyon, the alter-globalist, squatter, and peace movements are the active backbone of progressive collective action. Furthermore, an anti-authoritarian youth movement is particularly characteristic of the city, alongside a lively alternative public sphere with the independent *Radio Canut*, the *Pot Pourri* newsletter, and the *Rebellyon* web portal (Radio Canut 2010; Rebellyon 2010). The Lyonnais public sphere has also been marked by joint contention of the anti-authoritarians and movements and groups defending the position of undocumented immigrants, and victims of human trafficking. Lyon has constantly been the scene of hunger strike demonstrations of the '*sans-papiers*,' un-documented immigrants claiming their rights, and their supporters (see e.g. Franguiadakis 1997 2001; Overney *et al.* 2008). Also local associations working in the social and health sector have often been closely connected to these movements: *Cabiria*, an association working with (mainly immigrant) prostitutes, held literacy and French language courses, and APUS (*Association Praticiens Urgence Sociale*, an association of the 'practitioners of social emergency') worked with health, integration, and habitation problems of substance abusers, prostitutes, and convicts (APUS 2010; Cabiria 2010). In addition, a lively student movement has taken part in especially the numerous national struggles, such as the contention against the CPE[21] bill on first employment in 2006, and a profusion of informal neighborhood groups, as well as people taking part in processes of participatory democracy, had their hand on the alternative picture of the local public sphere. In addition to the extremely lively scene of activism today, strong traditions of collective action stretch far back in Lyon's history. The '*Canuts*,' the silk-weaving industry laborers, began a strong labor movement in Lyon in the early years of the 19th century. Their famous 1831 revolt has often been considered one of the first workers' revolts in history. The local understanding is that during the Second World War, the French Resistance movement started in Lyon, and the importance of the movement still today is manifest for instance in the museum of *La Résistance* located in the city (Marsura 2004; *Centre d'histoire de la Résistance et de la déportation* 2010). The Lyonnais activists I met in the field often referred to these historical accounts.

The local history was less present in the activist contexts in Helsinki, even though the city has been a central scene in most milestones of the history of Finnish civil society ever since the general strike of 1905.[22] Helsinki was also the principal scene of the 1960s and 1970s student movement in Finland, with the event of the taking over the University of Helsinki 'Old Student House' in November 1968 that has marked an entire generation of activists (cf. von Bonsdorff 1986; Purhonen *et al.* 2008).

Typically, international waves of social movements have come ashore first in Helsinki, and spread thence to the rest of the country, as was the case of the environmental movements in the 1980s, and the global justice movement in the early 2000s, for instance. Still today Helsinki is, due to its status as the national capital, the base location of the majority of Finnish nation-wide social movements and associations, from the labor unions to the animal rights movement.

During recent years, Helsinki has been a central scene for Finnish alter-globalization, squatting, anti-nuclear power, pro public services, animal rights, peace and anti-war, and many other movements. Innumerous associations, citizen networks, and on-the-spot organized groups have taken part in these movements by organizing debates, publishing statements, lobbying officials, updating websites, marching on the streets, and putting up other events and actions. For instance, a youth movement squatting empty real estate to establish social centers and organizing 'Reclaim the Streets' parties, and the alter-globalists, led by ATTAC Finland, organizing national and local social forums in Helsinki, have marked the local public sphere (see Hoikkala & Salasuo 2006; Stranius & Salasuo 2008; Lindström 2009). Also, an increasing number of thematic groups have emerged to defend public services, such as particular libraries or schools threatened with closure, and to resist certain zoning plans. A nation-wide alternative magazine, *Voima,* was established in 1999 in Helsinki, and has consolidated itself as the voice of the Finnish progressive movements, a voluntary-based radio station, *Lähiradio,* is on the air, and nearly a hundred neighborhood associations engage in a multiplicity of activities in the city (HELKA 2010; Lähiradio 2010; Voima 2010; for a historical analysis, see e.g. Anttila 2004).

Observing activism and politics in Lyon and Helsinki was, for me, obviously a somewhat different experience. In Lyon I was a visitor, even if both a long-term and a frequent one. Helsinki is my hometown in which I have also been an activist myself for years. Despite the different grounds of the fieldwork, my own activism was in many ways the key to it in both cities. In Lyon, it meant that, in spite of the cultural distance, I had an idea of what to look for, and a facility to find interlocutors that wanted to help me out because of my activist background. In Helsinki, it meant that I already knew the field quite well, and had an idea of different groups and their place on the local activist 'stratosphere.' Participant observation, as well as interviewing and other means of data collection were thus facilitated by my own prior experiences that helped me access tacit knowledge on practices and habits within the activist groups.

1.3 The tour guide: what this book is made of and how

A backpack of data[23]

Traveling is, of course, partly about experiencing places, spaces, climates, and other dimensions of more or less material environments. Nevertheless, I assume most travelers would agree that the most important thing about every trip is the people you meet (or the ones you travel with). So is this one: it is about the local actors I have met, with whom I have shared ideas and participated in various activities. In the following chapters, we will be meeting with local politicians and officials, but first and foremost, with a number of local activists, engaged in different struggles on different arenas. This book is above all about their actions in the two local public spheres: their stories, the images they have published, and media reports about their doings. In short, it is about the different accounts of the practices in which (counter-)democracy was in the making in the two local contexts.

These accounts stem from four different bodies of empirical material. The first consists of ethnographic notes taken during a fieldwork that consisted of following the activities of several local activist groups. In Lyon, I attended meetings, squat parties, preparations of demonstrations, demonstrations, and all sorts of other activities of activist groups mainly attached to the Libertarian–non-authoritarian scene during a seven-month period in 2005–2006, followed by several shorter trips back to the field afterwards. In Helsinki, I participated in various activities of local groups of the alter-globalization movement, helped in organizing local social forums, sat in squat events, and attended demonstrations and meetings of different local groups during 2003–2004, and 2006–2008. The fieldwork conducted in the two cities differs by intensity, as my time resources in Lyon were more limited. Also, my role as a participant observer was somewhat different in the two contexts: in Helsinki, I was a long-term activist known as such in some, though not in all, of the milieus of this study, whereas in Lyon the activists did not have strong presumptions about me. I have proceeded with the analysis of my data keeping these conditions in mind.

The second set of material consists of 47 thematic and in-depth transcribed interviews conducted in the two cities in 2003–2008. I interviewed activists from the groups I followed, and from other locally salient ones, as well as local politicians from both the majority and the opposition.[24] The activist groups were chosen so that the selection would include a maximum of different local groups, and they thus vary from service-providing associations to alter-globalists, and from popular education movements to squatters.

I collected the third corpus of material, visual representations of the local societies, from activist websites, and city information magazines. The first set of images (*N*=506) was collected on several occasions in 2005–2007 mainly through two activist portals, *Rebellyon* and *Megafoni*, as well as the sites of all the groups involved in the study. The second set of images came from volumes 2004–2005 (*N*=565) of *Lyon Citoyen* and *Helsinki-info*, the city information magazines, consisting of all cover images and a sample of the inner spreads.

Finally, the fourth corpus is composed of newspaper articles concerning local issues of dispute and controversy, and more generally, reporting on the encounters between local citizens and representatives of the cities. I collected the articles within a time period of six months (January–June in 2005) in *Le Progrès* (N=102) and *Helsingin Sanomat* (*N*=96).[25]

The road map: structure of the book

In the following chapters, I put the concepts and backgrounds presented in the previous sections to work on two levels. First, they guide my thinking and interpretations of the empirical findings. They do so in different combinations and arrangements in different chapters – some being more central in some cases, others in other cases – and intertwine with each other in different ways. Secondly, these concepts are not static products of an academic ivory tower, but they exist, and are renegotiated, in people's actions, talks, and ideas. A third level of conceptual work emerges on the course of the two described above: in serving both as theoretical guidelines, and as empirical frameworks, the concepts may not go unaltered, like every trip changes the traveler.

The order of the upcoming chapters has a particular logic to it: the structure of the book follows a gradual movement from the most micro-local setting towards a more macro-local environment. Parallel to this movement, the empirical treatment of the question of politicization becomes gradually more 'dialogic,' in the sense that, in the beginning, the activist voices dominate the scene, and towards the end of the book, they are increasingly joined by actors of the local politico-administrative instances. In Chapter 2, I ask, what kind of group bonds, boundaries, and speech and action norms emerge from local contentious practices, and what are their consequences for politicization? I describe local collective action and its contexts in Lyon and Helsinki with an ethnographic eye, making use of the theory of organizational styles. In

Chapter 3, I analyze the framings of citizenship and gender, and the gendered dimensions of local collective action. In Chapter 4, the visual dimension of the local public sphere is in focus. The chapter answers the question what kinds of representations of the local society two juxtaposed imageries produce, and how visual representations portray mechanisms of power and resistance – in particular, counter-democratic mechanisms – operating at the local public spheres. In Chapter 5, I ask what does democracy mean to different actors? I compare the local activists' and politicians' conceptions of democracy, and their ways to solve the tension between representation and participation. In Chapter 6, the analysis answers the question of how the actors in each context justify their claims in a conflict situation, as reported in the local news media. Finally, in Chapter 7 I draw conclusions from the answers to questions asked in the previous chapters, and reflect upon the comparison of the conditions, possibilities, and realizations of politicization in the two contexts of the study. In addition, the conceptual results and 'souvenirs' of the journey will be summed up, as well as challenges bequeathed to future research.

2
Local Scenes of Global Action: Group Styles of Local Collective Action and the Place of Politics

French and Finnish grass roots politics represent two opposite ends of a spectrum of common stereotypes: the expressive, emotional, and conflict-driven French rage on the streets of their cities for whatever reason, while the reserved and consensual Finns quietly lobby in their thousands of associations, rarely acting any more spectacularly. Yet the globalization of collective action, the intensification of global social movements, and the international diffusion of action repertoires have resulted in more and more uniform images of collective action. In order to understand how these differences and convergences are articulated and what the articulations mean to the people involved in these actions, a closer look is necessary.

In this chapter, I describe some of the local social movement scenes and activist groups in Lyon and Helsinki at the time of my fieldwork and analyze their activities. How are different meanings of 'we' built in the two contexts, what kinds of allies are imaginable, and how are internal conflicts dealt with? How do the activists define and pursue their goals and what are the groups' 'norms' concerning possible and desirable sayings and doings like? In comparison, what kind of places, conditions, and possibilities of political action and politicization emerge in the two contexts? In sum, what kind of civic practices, 'the fundamentally sociable processes by which citizens create contexts for political conversation in the potential public sphere – [and] develop meaning-making powers together' (Eliasoph 1996, 263) do these two cultural contexts foster?

The empirical cases I chose for this analysis stem from the heterogeneous variety of local collective action I encountered in Lyon and Helsinki. The idea is not to portray a general picture, nor to pretend to cover the whole range of collective action in the two cities, but to discuss, through six examples, the similarities and differences of political activities in these contexts.

The compared cases have certain common denominators. They are part of, or in some way connected to, the global justice movement, by the very broad definition of Donatella della Porta and Mario Diani (2006), and therefore marked by Left – Green, liberal, and progressive thinking rather than conservative or Right-wing. According to della Porta and Diani, the global justice movement encompasses all social movements opposing the neoliberal economic globalization, be it anti-authoritarian demonstrator blocks, groups in the ATTAC[1] organization, current peace movements, or, like on my field sites, squatters, activists against the privatization of public services, and opponents of video surveillance and the commercialization of the urban space (ibid. 2–5). As globalization is one of the key issues debated in public opinion forums, and as it is so closely intertwined with local processes, it is not surprising that the majority of actors I met on local activist scenes were, in a way or another, linked to this label – although many of them were also quite critical of it.

Explaining participation in movements and political processes at large often concentrates on individual micro-level, institutional and organizational meso-level, or structural macro-level analysis, although most of the recent literature acknowledges the need to incorporate the dynamics between different 'levels' (see Morales 2009, 17). Indeed, in order to understand the way the democratic public is made and molded by civic practices, we should be able to go beyond 'inner' and 'outer' explanations, that is, concentrate neither on the utterly subjective feelings and meanings, nor on the 'objective', structural explanations. Instead, analysis should focus on interactional, inter-subjective patterns and the different ways these patterns tie people together and make them engage in joint efforts (Eliasoph 1996; Thévenot 2006, 2007).

Therefore, in comparing the local global justice movement groups in France and in Finland, I wanted to grasp what the local groups' activities meant to the activists, and how the groups came to do what they did in the ways they did. This focus required following different processes: I traced the patterns of interaction within a few different groups, as well as between them and their political environment, and looked at how these interactions directed their activities. Making sense of the activist practices became feasible particularly with the help of Nina Eliasoph's and Paul Lichterman's (2003) theory of *group styles* that I use in this chapter as an organizing conceptual grid. The group styles, 'recurrent patterns of interaction that arise from a group's shared assumptions about what constitutes good or adequate participation in the group setting', enable us to grasp the interactional elements of culture (Eliasoph & Lichterman 2003, 737).[2] These assumptions can be divided into three dimensions: group bonds, boundaries, and speech and action norms.

Group bonds relate to the constitutive principles of the group. Different groups have different definitions of the ties between members. These definitions help in examining the considerations the group members have of the group: what they share, what keeps them together and how strongly, and how does the nature of these ties influence the actions of the group (Eliasoph & Lichterman 2003, 785–6). On a more general level, even if bonds are group specific, the predominant understandings of engagement and ties between people in a given cultural context may direct the formation of the bonds (Swidler 1986; Koveneva 2010). Group boundaries, secondly, concern the group's relationship with the world, with 'the others,' and the members' assumptions about what this relationship should be like: what kind of positions the group members take *vis-à-vis* other institutions and organizations, what are the channels they use to publicize their message and how, and what is the relationship between the group and the wider public (ibid. 785).[3] As Andrew Abbott (1995) has convincingly argued, boundaries pre-exist entities: we know a group is a group by its boundaries. In the case of activist groups, the efforts of defining, maintaining or altering group boundaries were ever ongoing, and resulted in diverging relationships with the surroundings. In section 2.2, I show how the processes of defining boundaries happen both towards the world outside, and by creating new entities grounded on differences within the groups (Abbott 1995, 860, 862–4). The third dimension of group styles reflects the understanding of 'what appropriate speech is in the group context' and the members' defination of the goals of interaction in the group: what, in the group context, would be a mistake, or a wrong approach, and how are things usually said and done (Eliasoph & Lichterman 2003, 739, 786). I suggest that this dimension can and should be extended to cover interactional doings other than just speech, such as non-verbal communication, and group members' collectively worked out understanding of not only what is possible to say but also what is feasible, and what constitutes good and appropriate *action* in the group setting. Therefore, I call the third dimension of group styles speech and action norms, and connect it to the notion of action repertoires. Used in this manner, speech and action norms express the dynamics between the observable action repertoires a group uses, and the group's subjective understandings of them.

The activist practices have also made me reflect on Laurent Thévenot's (2006, 2007, 2010) ideas of the multiple levels of engagement people have with each other and with the world, from the most generalized and publicized means to solve conflicts and justify arguments to individual interests and plans that people work out together, and finally to the most intimate level of familiarity and closeness that may not even be possible to verbalize, but has to be shared by other means. These three levels and especially the processes of generalizing a topic from more individual scale to an increasingly public level are important specifications of what actually happens in situations that lead, or fail to lead, to politicization. As the objective of this chapter is in producing comparative knowledge rather than theory building, I will not go into systematic detail of sociology of engagements, but be content to point out that despite its rather high level of abstraction, the idea of multiple levels of engagements is promising in defining certain comparative differences that other conceptual tools would be in considerable trouble with.

In the following, I look at three pairs of empirical cases of emerging civic practices in Lyon and Helsinki. In the first case, I compare local activists' group bonds, and engagements especially on the level of familiarity: their ideas of belonging to groups, and the prerequisites of politicization that these ideas carry. In the second case, I analyze group boundaries by looking at squatter movements in Lyon and Helsinki, especially from the point of view of the possible and impossible allies outside but also within the group, and efforts of solving external and internal conflicts: who can be in the group and how, and what kinds of differences within the group can be dealt with. With the third pair of cases, I look at speech and action norms through analysis of action repertoires and the imaginaries of politics expressed through them. This scrutiny highlights the articulations of the groups' public goals and claims as well as the members' less public understandings of the influence of their efforts. The six 'groups' that these cases portray both seemed to capture well the different sides of local organizational styles, and provided for a rather wide overview of civic practices that I encountered in Lyon and Helsinki. This way, they also pave way for the upcoming chapters by introducing many of the main characters of this story.

2.1 Living activist life in Lyon and Helsinki

Strong bonds of familiarity in La Croix-Rousse

La Croix-Rousse is a district in the heart of Lyon historically famous for the *Canuts*, the silk industry and its laborers. In the 18th and 19th century, it was the largest skilled workers' district in this old bourgeois town. It has hosted the Lyonnais social movements since the beginning of the 20th century, and is today still an important center of the city's lively activist scene.

Nowadays, the district is touched by rapid gentrification, becoming *bobo,* as the expression goes. *Bobo* stands for bohemian bourgeois and it indicates the changes in inhabitants when an old, 'romantically' bohemian district becomes fashionable and the prices of real estate start to rise. Yet, La Croix-Rousse continues to be the location of many key institutions of the Lyonnais activist scene, such as the alternative station *Radio Canut,* a bar named *La Fourmi Rouge* (and many others, of course), and a Leftist bookstore *A plus d'un titre.*[4] The district has also been the site of many famous squats during the 1980s and 1990s. It still hosts many activist collectives, although, for the past ten years, most squats have been evicted and have moved to other districts. The inhabitants of La Croix-Rousse remain a rather heterogeneous mass, ranging from *HLM* (*habitation à loyer modéré,* a form of subsidized housing) dwellers with a strong representation of immigrant and immigrant-originated population to upper middle class inhabitants living further up the hill.

In many ways, La Croix-Rousse had an atmosphere of a village, although it could not be much more urban: the Lyon City Hall is a block away from the district's borders, and the city center is a short walk away (for a rich sociological description of the neighborhood, see de Certeau *et al.* 1994). Getting to know life in La Croix-Rousse, it quickly began to occur to me that presence on the spot was important, and that the neighborhood was indeed a strong identification point for certain people – even for some who had previously lived there, but did not anymore. People made an effort to be present. They sat in cafés, hung out on the streets, in bookstores, and in bars, and spent lots of time out and about in the neighborhood. La Croix-Rousse had a tradition of regular 'neighborhood meals' that gathered strangers and neighbors out to share food and conversation and that Julien,[5] an activist in the early thirties, used as an example to describe the lively, independent, and convivial spirit of the neighborhood:

> 'So there's the Croix-Rousse market on Sunday mornings and what we do is that everybody buys their stuff and buys something extra too, and then we meet at Colbert square, we might set up a small table that people can use to share the things they wish, it can be a piece of bread, a piece of cheese they've bought at the market, and then we discuss. ... And the thing is that it used to be every week, and it had become, we didn't even have to specifically spread

> information .... There were "Market Agoras" with ... seventy-eighty people, and so really people from a lot of directions, I mean, it was not only activists .... And so it was like, we discuss, and it could well have been a problem in the neighborhood like sometimes it was a little bit more general things, about consumption, finally about politics and all that. ... I mean, you see, ... when I say "spirit of the neighborhood," ... it's more like well, I'm part of this neighborhood, and in this neighborhood there are these people, and if we have to make this neighborhood better, it's together, it's not with the town hall that we have to do it.'

People like Julien, who felt they were 'part of the neighborhood', shared the idea of promoting the neighborhood spirit, but at the same time one could say that the neighborhood spirit was in itself a *commonplace* (Thévenot 2010, 2011) these people shared and fostered,[6] and that constituted their group in many ways. The notion of a 'neighborhood' is, of course, a vague definition for a group, and it should not be taken as reference to the entire population of La Croix-Rousse. Instead, the neighborhood stood for a general term in describing rather specific group bonds and referring to a familiarity that consisted of an array of material, immaterial, nonverbal, spatial, and emotional points of engagement.

Walking on the streets of La Croix-Rousse after participating in activist circles for a few months, one did meet a familiar face at every other corner, and could observe similar encounters happening all the time. People living in the neighborhood who recognized each other as sharing some basic political values – generally Leftist–Greenish, anti-authoritarian, anti-*gauche caviar* – formed a group whose members claimed belonging and ownership of the neighborhood in various ways. Thus *'c'est mon quartier,'* 'it's my neighborhood,' was due to aspects other than mere residence. Being a *'Croix-Roussien'* was, in the activist circles, an identity category that meant something beyond the fact of just living somewhere, and at the same time, it was a source of group bonds that were about living somewhere. Many activists I met did not live there anymore, as the rents had gone up considerably in the past years, but they always stressed that they used to live in the district, and made sure to point out on which streets they had lived. Also, they kept coming back. They hung out in the cafés and collective apartments, not only to meet someone in particular on a set hour but also just to do the thing to do: be present and meet people by coincidence. Nevertheless, there also were a significant number of local activists still living in La Croix-Rousse, and thus friends to visit for those who had moved elsewhere. These features also had a multitude of implications, for example, concerning local commerce, as the following episode illustrates.

One afternoon, while walking towards a café together with Cloé,[7] she said that she wished to buy cigarettes on the way. I remembered having seen a *Tabac* (a French tobacco stand) around the corner and signaled it to her. To my surprise, this banal event turned into a small lecture on Lyonnais political culture: Cloé told me she would rather walk a few more blocks in order to find another one, as she 'preferred to avoid' the manager–owner of this shop. I tried to figure out why, by asking what he had done, and got a winding, rather indirect explanation of the manager's unpleasant previous behavior, suspicious suggestions he had made towards her, as well as insinuations directed at his political views. Based on the local 'political dialect' I had began to understand somewhat by then, I gathered that in sum, the reason why cigarettes were to be bought elsewhere was that the manager was suspected to be a racist and sexist extreme-Right voter.

This little incident was not unique, but rather an illustrative example of what formed the backbone of everyday practices of the activists living in the neighborhood. It also partly explains why it was so easy to meet people on a simple afternoon walk: they only frequented certain cafés, bought books from the one bookstore owned by the man with converging political views, and hung out and had meetings in a few bars run by people sympathetic with their world views. The meticulous choice of consumption was a way of strengthening group bonds – not only because this way people met each other more but also because they talked about it a lot, and constantly exchanged information on reasons to use or not to use these or those services. Immigrant-owned and run businesses were often recommended: in addition to refraining from supporting unacceptable world-views, there was also a pro-active side to their choices. Of course, I was doomed to make mistakes, as I was unaware of the detailed rules concerning the local commerce. I bumped into these rules of everyday political practices constantly. For example, when I had made a purchase in the wrong place my activist friends looked at each other knowingly and told me I should not shop there, but should use another place.

The intertwinement of group bonds with different concrete and abstract aspects of the neighborhood also arose in an issue that had previously to my arrival been a major conflict between the Croix-Roussien activist groups and the city. I kept hearing about the issue of free bill-posting (*affichage libre*) as the ultimate example of the current anti-activist atmosphere among the city leaders. The city had banned the pasting of posters and communications on walls, sanctioning it with a very elevated fine. Instead, it offered panels placed here and there onto which posters and information were to be pasted. A mobilization against the new edict followed, and was met with extremely heavy-handed police response: a demonstration in La Croix-Rousse resulted in police violence, several arrests and injuries.

In addition to causing outrage among the activists as one more oppressive rule by the City Hall, the restriction of bill-posting seemed to have hit the heart of the bonds and attachments that the activists shared in La Croix-Rousse. Solange, an activist in her late twenties, for example, explained when we were sorting out her collection of old tracts and posters she had showed me that, before, she would get all the information she needed on her way home, as the walls were covered with activist notes, tracts and posters. These would contain, for instance, 'minutes' of the City Council meeting (one activist was specialized in sitting in the council meetings and reporting the relevant topics to the activist groups), announcements of upcoming events, demonstrations, and parties, but also a lot of last-minute information concerning changes in the evening's program, a new place for the meeting, and the like. Now, the City's panels were situated so that she would not pass by them on her way home, and the relevant information didn't appear on them, so she had to go to much more trouble to learn what was going on. In an interview with me, Solange explained the mobilization against the city:

> 'And especially, you know, thinking that the first free bill-postings took place during the Résistance, and these people ventured to paste small papers on the walls saying "Nazis out." I mean, that does kind of show ... . So, we all took our old posters that we had kept at home, some of them dated ten years back or more, and then we had a demonstration in which we all went pasting them on the streets. We were blasted by the cops, it ended really badly and there were several arrests. ... After it we put up the collective "Free bill-posting," and the slogan was "White walls, mute people," and we tried to do things around this issue, but well, the group didn't last very long time. But the thing is that ever since that moment, I've been a whole lot less informed about what's going on in the activist milieu in Lyon.'

Wall information was part of the practices of being present in the neighborhood, and of communicating, in addition to the factual information, the shared engagements and affinities among the activists: in addition to keeping people informed, it gave them a sense of recognition as a group, and linked them to the roots of activism in the neighborhood that they took great pride in. The information was there for all to see – but not for all to understand. From the group's perspective, losing the wall information meant losing a part of their 'ownership' of the neighborhood. The eviction of one of the last functioning squats in La Croix-Rousse provoked similar kind of reactions as the banning of wall information. The squat, too, was a material proof of the group's belonging to the neighborhood – and of its members belonging together.

In this manner, the means of building trust between people, and thus constantly building grounds for mobilization, were very concretely embedded in the local environment: on the walls, the cafés, the daily routes. In addition, they were being built on a continuum of temporal trajectories and of collective memory concerning the key events of the local social imaginary, like the silk-weavers' union activity, the *Résistance* movement, and the 1960s Left movement. These shared historical points of reference helped bear the threats all the activists talked about: the increase of police violence towards activists, and the city's neoliberal politics narrowing the latitude of alternative groups. Facing these threats, they could still hang on to something unchanged, or at least a little less changed than the rest of their environment. However, the activists' group bonds were also vulnerable to changes in the physical environment, although their weakening, as in the case of bill-posting, was only temporary. Although embedded, the bonds were not ossified, as 'broken' ones were soon replaced by something else – a new series of neighborhood meals, new issues of a neighborhood activist leaflet, or the like – in the ever-moving process of binding people together, and creating shared notions of familiarity and comfort, the *loci* that Thévenot calls commonplaces.[8]

Networked bonds without a place in Helsinki

There are nearly a hundred functioning neighborhood associations in Helsinki that base their activities primarily on the neighborhood, on living in a place, and on sharing common matters in an environment (cf. Helka 2010). However, in the case of the global justice movement activists in Helsinki, contrary to their Lyonnais colleagues, places and neighborhoods were not the key to understanding their group bonds, and the primary ways they shared engagements with each other. Trust, necessary for overtly political activism, was built on recognition of a series of memberships, and on intimate friendships, rather than on the material environment.

The cluster of districts of *Sörnäinen-Kallio-Hakaniemi*[9] in Helsinki could, in many ways, be seen as a counterpart for La Croix-Rousse as the 'activist district' in Helsinki. It similarly hosts many 'key institutions' of local activism, such as *Voima* magazine, a nation-wide alternative publication, and the office of the Left Youth of Finland (the youth organization of the Left Alliance party, very embedded in local activist networks in Helsinki). There are several ecological and vegan stores, and numerous popular bars, of which, for example, the *Rytmi*-bar is known for being frequented by activists, young Left-wing and Green politicians, actors and journalists. In addition, the *Hakaniemi* market square is the location for the majority of the headquarters of Finnish labor unions, and in the vicinity the castle-like building of the Helsinki labor association, dating from 1908 and currently hosting the *Juttutupa* bar[10] where union activists and staff members roam. These institutions do not form the core of the contemporary local-level activist scene, but give the location a traditional label of dense civic activity. In the social imaginary of an inhabitant of today's Helsinki, however, these districts would not be seen primarily as activist neighborhoods.[11] These eastern downtown districts are more and more gentrified, but also carry the reputation of both lively student districts and somewhat rough neighborhoods of dwellers with drinking and substance abuse problems.

The *Tabac*-incident from Lyon is a revealing one when compared to Helsinki. I have lived all my life in Helsinki, mainly in four parts of town, and have never had a clue about the voting habits of a neighborhood salesperson, or for that matter, nearly anyone else. My interlocutors in Helsinki did not make this point either, and seemed instead to detach their political activities somewhat more from their personal lives than activists did in Lyon. Many of the activists boycotted McDonald's – as would their Lyonnais counterparts – and other chains of commerce considered unethical, but they did not choose an *Alepa* (a Finnish chain of grocery stores) or an *R-kioski* (a Finnish chain of newspaper and general kiosks) over another because of its owner, and they did not regularly avoid a particular store or café because of the political views of a cashier.

This had to do with the organization of many things in the city, and perhaps even on the national level. In Lyon, and probably quite generally in France, the culture of 'my baker/butcher/pharmacist' is still a pivotal part of people's everyday lives and the organization of daily activities. In Finland, large chains have long replaced small businesses in most areas, especially in the capital region.[12] The question is, however, not only about commerce, it is about the relationship between public and private spheres of life, and the role of politics in this relationship. Even though consuming is considered a political act among the Finnish activists just as among the French, the politics of consumption is mainly actualized on a more general level: The level of a 'faceless', often multi-national chain more than a personalized, one-on-one level of interaction.

This is one of the aspects creating difference in the 'materiality' of local group bonds and engagements in the two contexts. In Helsinki, bonds were not primarily embedded in walls, streets, shops, and other physical places. Instead, activists shared something else that constituted the meaning of who 'we' were: they were all members of associations, mostly of several ones. Associations, and memberships in them, were the key to understanding local group bonds. The clusters of associations and the activists' memberships as bonds were, however, different in the sense of engagement from the commonplace the neighborhood constituted in the Lyonnais case (Thévenot 2010, 2011). The association networks created rather a platform of carrying out projects and generalizing topics towards the public than spaces of intimacy, even if they also made people feel comfortable and confident in their groups.

An illustrative example of this feature was one neighborhood branch of ATTAC Helsinki, the *Sörkka*[13] ATTAC, founded in the Sörnäinen district. Shortly after the foundation of ATTAC Finland, the activists of the national association organized events in Helsinki in order to establish neighborhood branches following the example of ATTAC France. This turned out to be a tricky task: the neighborhood structure was problematic to put in place, and even more so to keep functioning. Disputes concerning the local organization frustrated many of the activists. They wanted the organization to be non-hierarchical, yet there had to be a decision-making organ of some kind in order to distribute money fairly. There was a lot of trouble concerning other associations co-opting the neighborhood ATTAC groups, and in endless meetings the activists tried to work out a model of democracy that would both guarantee everybody an equal position, and prevent the 'hijacking' of the groups, especially by small parties of the radical Left. In the end, most of the neighborhood-based ATTAC groups were neither long-lived nor very active.

However, the Sörkka branch was an exception. Over the years, it became the nerve center of ATTAC activities in the city, and occasionally even nation-wide. For several years, it organized most of the public activities of ATTAC in the capital area. These activities included, for example, an ambitiously displayed 'Tax haven' performance in the Helsinki multicultural summer festival. The activists had built a pontoon island they set loose on the *Töölönlahti* bay (located at the Western part of downtown), and on the shore they dressed up as businessmen, kept booths 'selling' false diplomas and giving mock advice on laundering money. They also organized a panel discussion with the President of Finland as a panelist at the Helsinki University New Student House (located in central downtown), and numerous other events in various parts of the city. Irina, a long-term member of the group, explained the group's exceptional zeal and energy with the members' shared experiences from the national ATTAC association, and their good personal relationships. In her mind, these features made the activities of the group so attractive that it kept attracting new members and being active. The neighborhood had, in the end, very little to do with it:

> 'In many other neighborhoods, ... there were too few people willing to really put their time into this, and then there was this 'personal chemistry' thing: [In Sörkka] there happened to be sufficiently many people who were happy to meet each other anyway. ... But it wasn't for the [neighborhood], you know, we all moved many a time, and I think that in the end none of us lived in Sörkka anymore. ... I think it just turned so that people in the associations of the other districts, the ones who really wanted to do something ... were absorbed into Sörkka [activities].'

Irina, like many other members in the group, also acted as a member of the board of ATTAC Finland for several mandates, but preferred to organize activities with the Sörkka group. It was easier and less bureaucratic, and people had fun together: they 'escaped' the disputes and bureaucracies of the national level association, and formed a well-functioning team that got more things done than any other subgroup (and often more than the national organization). The neighborhood that gave the group its name proved to be a practical 'camouflage' for a group whose bonds were based on something else.

Associations have a very special role in Finland both locally and nationally, historically and in the present. In many ways, they have formed the backbone of Finnish democracy, and the country has been called 'the promised land of associations,' sometimes even accused of suffering from 'an organization syndrome' (Alapuro & Stenius 1987; Siisiäinen 1992; 2002). The organization syndrome refers to the common practice of all kinds of citizen groups from squatters to squash clubs to register as formal associations.[14] At the local level, then, it is no surprise that associations afforded 'material' for building group bonds. This was true for many groups I encountered and observed in Helsinki. Roughly said, all activists were members in several associations that performed local actions, and brought people together.

In previous studies, associations have mainly been treated and analyzed as networks. These were certainly formed in the case of the Helsinki activists as well. At the same time, they were 'more' than networks: In Helsinki, in comparison with the Lyonnais case, associations were a significant element in the creation of the local activists' group bonds. The web of associations and people's multiple memberships in them formed the comfortable, shared networks of trust and a sense of 'we-ness.'

In sum, this section has portrayed two active groups of activists, both of whose force of mobilization lay in their strong group bonds, trusting personal relationships, and shared understandings about what and who, and where, 'we' were. The ways in which they defined these ties and their origins differed, and this difference had impacts in their actions. In order to understand these impacts better, I next look more closely at understandings about 'the others,' and the resulting logics of action, among groups of squatters in the two cities. Things did not always go smoothly inside the groups any more than with outsiders. Hence, the mutual trust and comfort described in this section were, by far, not the only characteristics of local activist groups, but tensions within the 'we' were equally present. The following comparison of squatters thus portrays local group styles especially from the point of view of drawing boundaries with 'the world outside' and solving conflicts within the groups.

2.2 Squatting the city

Standardizing movements for free urban space

Squatting stemmed from rather different historical backgrounds in the two contexts. Nevertheless, current squatter movements in Lyon and Helsinki took similar forms, due to the effective and dense international network of squatters through which both ideas and action repertoires were diffused from one country to another (e.g. Mikkelsen & Karpantscho 2001; Uitermark 2004). In both contexts, however, activists paid quite a lot of attention to the 'genealogy' of local squatting. Therefore, in the following, I tell two parallel stories with a focus on both the currently active groups and the roots of the activity.

In Lyon, like elsewhere in Western and Southern Europe, the squatting movement emerged in the early 1970s, largely inspired by the Italian neo-Marxist *centro sociali* movement. In 1980's France,[15] the squatters had close connections to first punk, and later on, to rap subcultures. Open confrontation with the rest of the society, in particular with the police forces, was characteristic of the movement (Crettiez & Sommier 2002, 492). The ways in which present-day Lyonnais activists perceived squatting was in terms of this history: they constantly referred to stories of the old, legendary squats there used to be. Squatting seemed to stretch and diffuse across generations of activists. Many activists mentioned squats when I asked about the triggering events to how they became activists in the first place, like Miriam in the following:

> 'I started questioning what happened in my city and I went about to see ... a bit here and there, and I tried to find ... associations or something, some place where I'd feel like doing something. ... And actually, it was then when I started to hear talks about squats that existed in Lyon ... and then I started going to concerts ... that were organized in squats. And those were the first times that I stepped into a squat. ... I still remember it very well, there was one on Bourdeau street, ... and I started asking ... who lived in it and stuff, really by curiosity. ... So there it was. It really fascinated me, because I learned that these people had decided to live together and do things, and that a lot of things were organized in that place. It was not only concerts, there was also a small vegetarian restaurant, a small bar, and every week there was something organized for the kids of the neighborhood. ... It was really, really impressive.'

Miriam described something that came up repeatedly both in interviews and in talks and gatherings with activists in Lyon: the squats used to be, and still were, the connecting nodes of different groups of the local alternative Leftist movement. A lot of things happened in them, and a great deal of local activism was in one way or another connected to them. The squats were often entire apartment buildings, or stories of one, or abandoned small industry real estate. These spaces made it possible to organize big parties and concerts, and host different kinds of groups and activities at the same time. For the activists, the squats were the heartbeat of a neighborhood, and thus important places in terms of group bonds (see previous section): They were often true nerve centers of local contention, as well as, indeed, important places for initiation to local activism.

In Finland, collective action related house squatting was nearly unknown before the late 1980s, when it began in Helsinki (cf. Mikola 2008; Tuominen 2008). The housing shortage of the time, and a number of empty buildings that a group of young people had detected, triggered the first talks about squatting. Mika, a pioneering squatter activist, described the events in the following way:

> 'At that time there were these three empty wooden houses in Kumpula, and so, well, we were young, and this housing shortage

united us, and the will to do something. That's how it started. – In the beginning, there was actually no thought of continuing or enlarging the activity, or that we'd do any more than that, and the gang was rather small, too. But then right at the first squatting we noticed that it arouse a lot of interest especially among young people. After the news started spreading about the first squatting, dozens of people showed up at the house.'

The squatters' political views concerning environmentally friendly living and the cost of housing were quite radical and new to the Finnish context of the time. Their main objective, nevertheless, was to make inhabitable and inhabited squats, and less so to build a political community around them, and they certainly did make choices in favor of the former rather than the latter. The squatters quite rapidly organized their group into a registered association, *Oranssi ry* (The Orange Association). The rationale was to facilitate cooperation with the local authorities, unwilling to negotiate with a group of youngsters, but more welcoming to an association with a bank account and a board with a legally responsible status. After the registration, Oranssi gradually gained legitimacy, and finally became a contractual partner of the Helsinki city in youth housing matters. As the organization grew, the functions were divided between the original association and the Oranssi Accommodation Inc. (*Oranssi Asunnot Oy*), a firm in charge of financial and maintenance issues of the housing it rented out. In 2009, Oranssi owned 10 houses and altogether 66 apartments in five different neighborhoods in Helsinki (Oranssi ry 2009). Oranssi is a good example of a common trajectory of Finnish collective action: the movement attained its goals, i.e. created collective, affordable housing for young people, by transforming from a movement into an institutionalized actor.

In contrast, the current squatter movement in Helsinki, mobilized since the early 2000s, was much closer to its European counterparts. The theoretical inspirations and political arguments of the squatters I met in Helsinki stemmed for a great deal from the same sources as the ones in Lyon. In Helsinki, too, buildings were now squatted to found social centers and to create non-consumerist and anti-capitalist spaces in which to organize concerts and parties. Henna, a squatter activist in her twenties, explained why her group squatted houses in today's Helsinki:

'We want a place where we can hang around and do the stuff we want to do. Like organizing workshops, theater, live-music, without

> having to pay for it, and without sponsoring anything, any capitalist activity. It's about being able to do uncompelled things. And if there's an empty building, why couldn't it be put to use?'

The change in the rationale of squatting compared to the 1980s and 1990s seemed remarkable. The squatter groups in Helsinki were now in tight contact with squatters in other cities, both in Finland and elsewhere in Europe. The squatters traveled a lot, visited squats in other cities, and received guests from foreign squats. They constantly exchanged news with other squatters through websites and email lists, provoking solidarity actions: when a squat in Helsinki got evicted, squatters in Copenhagen color-bombed the Finnish embassy. Squatters in Helsinki were part of a globalized, or at least a Europeanized, movement (see also Mikola 2008).

Thus, squatting in present-day Lyon and Helsinki seemed like very similar activities. Even the quite recent novelties of Lyonnais squatters' repertoires, such as squats founded to host the *sans-papiers* and *sans-abri*, mainly immigrants without identity documents and/or domicile, were soon after also practiced in Helsinki, although to a lesser degree, since the scale undocumented immigration was radically larger in Lyon.

Furthermore, the policing of squats had also become increasingly similar. Violent evictions and repeated confrontations with the police forces had been an integral part of the squatting culture in Lyon for many decades. Similarly to many other European countries, the French police had become still more heavy-handed towards local activists, including squatters, since the beginning of the 'war on terrorism' in the early 2000s.

Large-scale police operations in squat evictions were, however, rather a gradual change than a novelty in the squatters' eyes. In the following, Miriam, who had been in the squatter movement for over a decade, talked about the events that engaged the entire Croix-Roussien neighborhood, and eventually led to the eviction of one of the frequently mentioned, 'legendary' squats, *Le Rapthou*, in Lyon in the early 1990s:

> 'First there was a demonstration in the whole of La Croix-Rousse, it was a cross- squat [event], and so there were folks coming from everywhere, ... several cities in France and Europe and Italy, [it was] like a movement. There was a kind of festive demonstration that got started in La Croix-Rousse. So a concert was organized on the *Chat noir* -square, and ... some folks were caught at the end of that, they were [just] juggling, and ... here you go, they were caught by ... the

> BAC [*Brigade anti-criminelle*, Anti-Criminal Brigade]. ... And then, what happened is that ... we all went down towards the Police station. And there it went all wrong. Everything began to degenerate, in the whole La Croix-Rousse, and there were fights between the police and the demonstrators and so on. And I guess about a week after, ... Le Rapthou was evicted.'

In Lyonnais squats, even back in the 1990s, police raids were expected from the start. Squat evictions occurred often alongside other police operations directed at activists, who often interpreted them as police's 'revenge' of some other episode in the 'cat and mouse' game constantly played between the activists and the local police.

Around the same time in Helsinki, where Oranssi was squatting houses, police operations and evictions were very different. Mika described the squatters' encounters with the local police forces as quite peaceful, even pleasant:

> 'In the beginning of the nineties, when we squatted houses and the police came, it was more like, the police van drove to the spot and the old boys came around and sneered, like "what are the boys up to here again." Then we'd chatter away. We had this non-violence and passive resistance thing right from the beginning, we had settled these principles for ourselves, and we told the policemen about them, and agreed with them that "you'll come carry us out of here then." In a way it all happened in a kind of a cheerful atmosphere. ... It was like we did our job and the police did theirs. The police was not the adversary against whom we were rebelling ... that party was elsewhere.'

This nearly pastoral idyll draws a rather contrasting picture to the police encounters habitually going on in the French squats, but also to what had became the mode of operation in Helsinki in the 2000s. Spectacular police operations unforeseen in Finland took place, for example, during the *Smash Asem* demonstration in 2006, and at the eviction of *Ruoholahti* squat in 2007, resulting in several arrests of activists, and complaints against the police (cf. Salasuo 2006; Stranius & Salasuo 2008). Policing has begun to resemble much more the police practices in France than the previous generation squatters' experiences in Finland: riot gear, helicopters, several arrests, and heavy-handed handling of the activists. These confrontational raids marked a change in the Finnish activist culture, both regarding activist repertoires, and the attitudes of the surrounding society towards them (on the changing media representations of activism in Finland, see Lindström 2009).

Nevertheless, when I talked about the evictions and about policing in general with the squatters, they still had a different take on the issue compared to their Lyonnais friends. Criticizing the police, and telling 'horror stories' of their actions was common pass-time among the activists in Helsinki, too, but the antagonism seemed thinner than in Lyon. I sometimes felt that the 'official' discourse held in group settings was more critical than the activists' opinions given in 'private', as Henna's:

> 'I think that the police, it's a good thing, they do a good job, but sometimes their actions have been too provocative. And when we've been in touch with cops and talked about things, even they have said that, and some have even regretted it, that it has gone a bit provocative. And these situations have come to head so that now it's enough that a police van approaches the squat, well, part of the people think right away that now it's an eviction. And some refuse to talk with the cops altogether. But some cops from certain precincts have become a little familiar already, and sometimes we chat with them and they sort of regret it a little and even write down some of our demands, such as during eviction, when we're about to be locked up, there should be a female cop to check the women. And so on.'

Henna was sorry that things had turned sour between the squatters and the police, and made efforts to look at the situation from both sides. The police had been too provoking, and now some squatters were too provoked, but all in all she thought that negotiation was still possible. She also wanted give the police some credit, and clearly the relationship she portrayed between the squatters and the police forces was marked with a sense of confidence that was unimaginable in Lyon.[16]

These first observations on the squatter groups show that despite the recent, rather isomorphic developments in both contexts, the differences in understanding and drawing boundaries with the 'outside', above mainly the police, were significant. Why was this? These kinds of differences are often linked to action repertoires characteristic to the prevailing political culture. But in order to avoid explaining political culture by political culture, we need to scratch the surface and trace these differences on the group level: In the interaction that makes the groups what they are, that is, in the collective efforts of drawing boundaries, and of engaging in an activity (Abbott 1995; Eliasoph & Lichterman

2003; Thévenot 2010). In the following, I trace these features by looking at how some squats that existed during my fieldwork managed encounters with the 'outside', and how they dealt with conflicts and tensions within the groups, combining the analysis with material emerging from the interviews I made with squatters from different periods.

The permeability of boundaries: managing conflicts in and out

Indeed, the most drastic differences between squatters in Lyon and Helsinki emerged when looking at their relationships to the surrounding society, but also in their ways of handling differences and conflicts within the groups. These two aspects result in, first, different articulations of the 'permeability' of group boundaries, and second, different articulations of internal conflicts. I look at these differences particularly through stories from *La Scièrie* squat and *Elimäenkatu* social center.

La Scierie was founded in Lyon in fall 2005 in an old abandoned small industrial estate, and it had both accommodation and party, event, and concert functions.[17] The squatters consisted mostly of libertarian activists, many of whom already had robust experience with squatting. Visiting the squat, for instance, to attend a concert, required preparations: there were careful instructions on how to arrive, and the door was always locked. The squatters verified new entries from a small window on the door. In order to get in, one had to have a familiar face or be in the right company. The atmosphere at the entrance was excited, especially at party nights with plenty of people arriving, and the walls inside were covered with instructions on what to do in order to avoid the police, and what to do when it could not be avoided. In addition, there were unspoken instructions that I learned about by asking stupid questions: it was absolutely forbidden to mention the squat to members of the media, and bringing new people in had to be done with a lot of circumspection, which in practice meant that the newcomers had to get accepted, or 'recommended' by a trusted member of the group, or two. The concerts and parties were well organized: a number of local artists, but at times also some true underground celebrities performed. An impressive amount of sound engineering had been installed and mounted in the midst of the old factory hall for the concerts. The crowds were often big, but predictable – many of the young people were familiar to me from the activist circles, and all shared a certain recognizable habitus: dreadlocks, ragged style of clothing, and the like. There was normally vegan food and sangria in huge buckets, priced with a request for a voluntary donation, and other alcohols for sale at low rates. Police roundups were frequent and often led to arrests.

The Lyonnais squatters drew rigid and inflexible boundaries between their group and its adversaries: the city, the police, and even the media. There was no question of negotiating with the city, and even the idea of reasoning with the police made the squatters laugh. Media was not treated with much less suspicion: it would have been impossible for a journalist of the 'regular' media (i.e. not considered alternative) to cover a story in a squat. The squatters took pride in their independence, and 'outlaw' position. In some cases, negotiations with the city officials actually took place, and sometimes they even succeeded, as for a squat remotely located almost off-city-limits that became a semi-official alternative rock club. But these cases were rare and the squatters never emphasized them (in fact, it took a lot of discretion and circumlocutory work to find out about the aforementioned case).

The only institutional form of alliance the squatters in Lyon had was a group of lawyers specialized in defending activists in various situations. The lawyers were well known in the local activist scene. Their role was important both concerning squatting and in cases of arrest and police violence during demonstrations. Due to their efforts, squats often managed to keep electricity and running water, as well as to gain prolongation to their activities. The lawyers successively, and often successfully, applied for injunctions of the eviction orders' enforcement. *La Scierie* was a typical example of a confrontation between the police forces accompanied by the real estate owner, and the squatters with lawyers at their defense. These battles were bitter, and there were rarely signs of compromise from either side. Also, during the 2000s, the city of Lyon hardened its policies towards the squatters, and both the local and the national police became increasingly rapid and effective in evicting squats. This resulted in further radicalization among some of the squatters, and increased tensions between them.

La Scierie was evicted in late spring 2006, after which the group squatted in a series of houses, sharing some of them with asylum seekers. Police practices leaning on the war on terrorism legislation had turned squatting into an extremely risky business. In addition, the relations within the squatter network had become severely inflamed. In 2009, being a squatter outlaw in Lyon had become so tough and dangerous that the groups had reinforced their external boundaries in an unforeseen way. Evictions occurred more and more quickly, and during my last visit to the field in spring 2009, the situation was so tense the squats could no longer be visited at all – even by many of the former squatters. Romain, an activist who had renounced living in a squat, told me the still existing squats and squatter groups were nearly at war even against each other, and let no strangers in. In sum, the squatters' ways of drawing boundaries grew increasingly firm and impermeable, and the conflicts within and between the groups began to have a nearly paralyzing effect to the activity.

The *Elimäenkatu* Social Center in the *Vallila* district, near Eastern downtown of Helsinki, was squatted in early fall 2007. The building was challenging, since it had no electricity, and water supply was cut off soon after the squatting. Therefore, it served mainly as a temporary sleep-over, party, and debate spot. Similarly to Lyon, the squatters organized parties, concerts, small workshops on cloth printing and bike repair, and the Pirate cinema club, showing illegal copies of movies. The latter activity provoked a police roundup and a few arrests, but otherwise the police were not a frequent visitor at the squat. Going to Elimäenkatu was different from La Sciérie: there was no control at the entrance, and one could walk in without notice. In front of the house, people were often sitting in garden chairs, chatting and smoking, going in and out. On an occasion of a debate, I asked a woman I met in the still empty hall about the evening's course. She turned out to be a journalist from *Suomen Kuvalehti* (a conservative, weekly news magazine), who was at the squat with her photographer covering a story on the Helsinki activist scene. Her presence did not seem to bother anyone. Among the people who came to the particular debate there were, for example, university researchers, the leader of the Left Alliance party youth organization, and a crowd of people that did not all seem to have many acquaintances, but spent the evening making notes with their laptop Macs.

In Helsinki, in contrast to Lyon, the group boundaries – ideas about what the group's relationship with the wider world should be like – included the possibility of alliance with officials, and were thus vertically permeable. In the early years of squatting, Oranssi's was a remarkable success story of negotiating with the city officials. Mika explained the shift from squatting to rebuilding and inhabiting as follows:

> 'We started to get fed up with the squatting quite soon, because for the people who participated it didn't really lead to anything ... finally we didn't get the houses for residential use anyway, or if we did, the houses were naturally deteriorated and of course no one would plunge into renovating them for us. So we started to talk about that what if we'd start patch them up ourselves. ... So we made a businesslike suggestion to the city of Helsinki that it would rent them to Oranssi as youth housing to be refitted. And I've heard afterwards

> that the paper went up to the desk of the mayor of the time, and he himself made the decision to give out this positive signal. Say, "OK, let the boys show [what they can], since they're so full of it." And maybe it was also a bit like "let's put them to work, so they won't squat houses." ... We were really surprised that the city rented the house to us. Next we went to the bank to take a loan, and then we went to the hardware store to buy tools. And then we went to rebuild those houses.'

The way Mika talked about the Mayor had almost an affectionate echo to it: he had taken a fatherly stand in favor of the squatters, and was credited for it – in the same way that Henna credited the policemen for listening and taking into account the squatters' viewpoints. In this sense, the Finnish squatter 'generations' were perhaps not that far from each other after all.[18] Foreign imports concerning the form and the political motivations of squatting had been included in the local activity, and its forms and repertoires had changed visibly, but boundaries had remained quite similar.

Unlike in Lyon, representatives of various 'outsider' institutions visited the squats in Helsinki regularly, and quite freely. City councilors from Left and Green council groups were not a rare sight in Elimäenkatu, and understandably so, as some of them used to be squatters themselves when they were young. Journalists went in and out and did their work without meeting significant resistance, as did social scientists. The squat was a subject of heated public debate in Helsinki, including the City Council and especially the Youth Board. The city youth policy officials opened negotiations with the squatters, and for a while it seemed that the group could keep the social center, and receive financial aid for the rent from the Youth Department. Finally, this plan was not realized, because the city health authorities stated after an inspection that the building was too dangerous: the inspection report said it was damp-damaged, and there were significant amounts of mold in its structures, and thus it would harm the squatters' health if they stayed. The Youth Board decided the squatters would have to leave, and the squat was evicted in December 2007. However, the negotiations between the squatters and the city continued, and thus even the *centro sociali*-inspired new generation directed their claims to the city officials and finally accepted a place 'squatted' for them by the city Youth Department: in 2009 the Youth Department officials offered the squatters a house, and engaged in taking care of the rent and some other expenses. The *Satama* Social Center,[19] founded in an old warehouse located on a wasteland near the limits of Eastern downtown, was thus created in a rather peculiar way.

The squatters in both Lyon and Helsinki did not, however, work out conflicts only with the external institutions. Especially in Lyon, internal conflicts and constant articulations of new group boundaries influenced the squatting scene. In a comparative perspective, I found the treatment of gender differences within the groups particularly interesting. In Lyon, the local radical feminist movement was closely involved in many squats, and influenced the squatting movement especially by raising questions about gender inequality within the local social movements. Gendered tensions were an integral part of the squatting movement quite early on, resulting in debates about discrimination, speech rights, and gendered practices of the movement. In the 1990s, some 'non-mixed.' i.e. women-only, squats also appeared, creating space for experiences in radical separatist feminism, and along with them, huge tensions and conflicts within the squatter movement. (cf. Martinez 2003). In the 2000s, notably in La Scièrie, many of the male squatters had an outstandingly gender-sensitive way of talking. In addition to regular festivities, the squat hosted a study circle on 'body and politics' organized by Romain and Fabrice, who were doctoral students in social sciences. These sessions were usually held in the squat's kitchen, where we drank tea from old, cracked cups, and sat on a miscellaneous collection of seats, old footstools and packing cases. It was a cold place in the wintertime – no heating – and quite small, so it was by far not the most comfortable place one could imagine having a study circle meeting in. It was evident that holding the meetings in the squat carried political meaning, and the sessions had a manifesting spirit to them. Addressing this kind of a theme was somewhat a surprise to me, as activist men speaking so overtly and willingly about the political implications of male and female bodies concerning, for example, the living-together practices of a squat, was something I had not expected to witness. The study circle discussed theorizing of sex and gender by authors like Judith Butler, which in my previous study circle experiences had been treated in almost always all-women and/or all-gay study groups within gender studies departments – not in squats, and not organized by (heterosexual) men. In the meetings, uneasiness was not absent: for example, Fabrice, who was by far the most radical and 'hot-headed' of the group, claimed that bodies were marked more by capitalism than gender, which made feminist participants, such as Cloé, protest. However, this example demonstrated that in Lyon, the queer-theory-reading crowd had indeed expanded from the women-only squats to other settings within a decade. This did not mean there were no longer clashes around the issues of *non-mixité*, or other gender-related issues, but the clashes did not prevent gender from being continuously on the agenda of the squatters. The constant clashes had had, and kept having, an apparent impact on the gender-consciousness of the group members (see also Chapter 3 in this book).

Among the Finnish squatters, there was a lot of talk about 'boys'. When I interviewed the 'Oranssi-generation' squatter, Mika, he described both the police and the squatters as 'boys' every time he referred to them as groups. Squatting was a boys' business, and, in addition, that of the (male) cops and of the (male) city leaders. Indeed, the first squatter groups in Helsinki had probably been rather male-dominated – as one of the initiators described, 'first there was a bunch of friends that could hold hammers in their hands.' The group soon grew more heterogeneous and, for example, recent web reportages of Oranssi building projects portrayed a noticeable share of female construction workers (see Chapter 5 in this book). Also, the current squatter movement was neither observably, nor according to the interlocutors, particularly male-dominated. But the boy-thing did not end there. At the Elimäenkatu social center, the 'boys' organized wrestling rehearsals, chaired debate events, and took care of maintenance, setting up concert spaces, and so on. The traditional division of labor peaked with women taking care of cooking and shopping. Henna's way of putting it was illustrative: as she was 'a kind of a feminist,' she felt that these kinds of arrangements should perhaps have been resisted. It was not, however, an issue worth while taking up, because everybody was equal in the squatter group. Compared to the continuous clashes in the daily life of the Lyonnais squats, Henna's description of the regular house assemblies[20] in Elimäenkatu sounded peaceful: a facilitator always made sure that everyone got their say, and there were no gender or other differences influencing the decisions:

> 'When we have a house assembly, and someone is pro and someone is con, we don't vote or anything, we just make the compromise. ... It's like so that at some point both the supporters and the opponents would be just like well okay, this is *fine*.'[21]

So, nothing from the 'inside' disturbed the peace of the squat, and the division of labor was seamless? The non-conflicting treatment of the gender issue in the Finnish context was by no means a specialty of the squatters. A pattern of downright avoidance of the topic has come up in several previous studies of civic and political practices (Korvajärvi 1998; Holli *et al.* 2003; Holli, Luhtakallio & Raevaara 2006; 2007; see Chapter 3 in this book). However, the apparent absence of the gender conflict in Helsinki, and its seemingly routine presence in Lyon was, in my view, not only a sign of a different take on gender. It illustrated also something more general about the groups' ways of handling internal conflicts and differences. On the one hand, in Lyon, the squatter groups treated and talked about gender-related and other internal conflicts rather openly, and preferred to dissolve groups and form new ones instead of keeping the group definitions tight. In Helsinki, on the other hand, the squatters seemed to worry more about keeping the group's inner differences minimal and avoiding conflicts rather than dealing with the risk of dissolution of the group. Their ways of working out new entities within the group were neither particularly developed nor flexible.[22]

These two perspectives of conflict, external and internal, and the differences in the organizational styles they bring forth, enable a deeper understanding of the differences in local engagements that in the previous section were portrayed in terms of bonds and shared commonplaces, but also led towards the questions of speech and action norms and repertoires of the local groups. The Lyonnais squatters' way of drawing boundaries and dealing with conflicts carried a close connection to the personal, even intimate level of engagement, to the point of being constantly politicized, but also sometimes unbearable (cf. Breviglieri 2009). They were engaged in a political struggle in which they vigorously denounced the actions of the police and the city administration, as well as the entire capitalist system. At the same time, they constantly dealt with the difficult conflicts concerning very intimate-level aspects of togetherness, gender-related issues being one example that sometimes led to dissolutions, but sometimes functioned as openings of new political space. Did the rather concrete understandings of a commonplace and the materiality of group bonds influence also the squatter groups in making these conflicts less dangerous, at least to a point of not concealing them? As for the squatters in Helsinki, group boundaries and the tendency to avoid conflicts point towards a different level of engagement. Even though in declarations and *communiqués* the political aspect – claim for anti-capitalist space – was exactly as explicit in Helsinki as in Lyon, looking at the processes of drawing group boundaries gives the impression that the squat was also a project that was being carried out. The squatters' engagement in a joint *plan*, the project of a social center (or, in earlier years, the project of youth housing[23]), directed them to negotiate more than rebel, and make deals instead of making war (see Thévenot 2010, 2011). This logic of engagement also influenced the internal group relations: conflicts would have been disruptive to the project, and the shared understanding of this rendered the internal relationships, if not completely peaceful, at least less overtly contentious.

These findings relate closely to the activist groups' efforts of politicizing their causes. In order to understand the link between group styles and politicization better, I wanted to analyze the local groups' understanding of their activities, successes and failures, and their ideas of what was the sensible thing to do. In the final pair of comparison, I focus on the third aspect of group styles, speech and action norms, and the resulting perceptions of 'success', of two local groups.

2.3 Reasoning and resisting before local politics

Proving expertise, performing opposition

The previous section showed that the squatters' demands for free and anti-consumerist urban space were marked by very differently drawn boundaries, but also that the different institutional actors in Lyon and Helsinki responded to their demands quite differently. In Lyon, they seemed to give mostly rather curt answers, whereas in Helsinki, they apparently showed some understanding to the young people's needs, and tried to work out deals acceptable for all parties. But what happens when an activist group directs action against the decision-making of local political organs, calling for change in a particular political issue? In this section, I explore cases of contention directed at city politics, and examine how two groups in particular pursued their causes, and at the same time constituted their understandings of possible, effective, and desirable ways of acting as contentious groups. In sum, in the following, I trace the speech and action norms of the groups, and the ways in which these 'norms' influenced the politicization processes the groups involved with, and their engagements in public conflicts (Eliasoph & Lichterman 2003; Thévenot 2007).

During the time period of my study, a number of citizen groups in Helsinki seemed to have achieved their goals concerning several issues. An active citizen group lobbied vigorously against a traffic tunnel planned through the centre of Helsinki, and the plan was finally abandoned by the City Council. Another group pressured the city officials to cover part of social and health care deficits with the profits of the Helsinki power company. Eventually, the partly city-owned power company was forced to enter its balance sheet into the city accounts and share out part of their gain. These two were not the only examples of social movement success in Helsinki. I do not suggest there is a direct causal chain of the social movement claims to altered city policy. It would be impossible to come up with a thorough understanding of the various elements that led to these political decisions, and to measure exactly the impact the movements had in the processes. However, put in a comparative perspective, these examples certainly create an interesting puzzle.

In contrast to the successes of some citizen groups in Helsinki, there seemed to be no reason to cheer in Lyon. The activist groups I studied there, as well as those I came across more briefly during the fieldwork, did not seem to get many of their demands through, and did not seem particularly shocked by it. Instead, there was a plethora of groups expressing strong opposition to various city policies, with no mentionable echoes from the part of the municipality, but firm conviction about their cause nevertheless.

How should this contradiction be understood? Should we conclude Helsinki thus to be an open and inclusive democratic community, in which citizens deliberating with sensible arguments got their points across, whereas Lyon excluded citizen voices in a tyrant's manner? In Chapter 5, I analyze the understandings of the functioning of democracy by different actors, showing that this was definitely not the picture either activists or politicians had. Was it, then, a mere coincidence? How had 'the success' come to be in Helsinki, and not in Lyon, and how did the activists perceive their actions? In the following, I look at two groups, Pro Municipal Services Network (*Pro Kuntapalvelut -verkosto*), an expertise-stressing activist group in Helsinki, and No to Big Brother (*Non à Big Brother*), a contentious, performance-organizing group in Lyon, in order to understand what kind of means the activists deployed to achieve their goals, and what seemed to be the right things to say and to do in their opinion – and the consequences of these dynamics.

Pro Municipal Services (ProMS) was a citizen network of some eighty people, launched in Helsinki in 2002. It criticized the neo-liberalization of municipal services and their gradual fall in quality. The ProMS activists stressed the fallaciousness of the city decisions they opposed, and claimed that they had (better) expertise on public services and finances than the decision-makers. The network was a new kind of lobbying group in the context of Helsinki: it tried to enter in a deliberation process directly with the city management and officials, and did not have one clear interest group, but rather gathered several interest groups to work together. The network had a website and a mailing list, and besides the core group – Jarmo, Pirjo, Irma, Pertti, Marita, and Lassi, who sent out invitations to the meetings and took care of most of the needed organizing work – most of the members participated primarily through these two communication channels.

ProMS activists presented themselves as 'concerned citizens' or 'worried grandmothers,' underlining the network's political neutrality (see Eliasoph 1998). Many of them were, however, employees of the city of Helsinki, or of organizations that cooperated closely with the city, such as the Lutheran church where Marita worked, and of many service-providing associations, typically from the social and health sector. Some of the activists, like Pertti, were also members or vice-members of the Left-wing party groups in the City Council. Some activists participated in the network with a more or less official mandate from their associations of origin, such as the local branch of the National Rheumatism League, a mental health patients' organization, and a local tenants' association.

The network had not been registered as an association (which is a deviant choice within the Finnish activist culture, as we saw in the squatter case in section 2.2), and did not have a nominated leader, a secretary, or official rules. The activists were eager to emphasize the informal nature of the network, the facility to join in, and voluntariness of participation. Many of the members had a long experience with acting in associations, and this form of participation was for them clearly something quite new and exciting. However, participating in the network's activities made me soon realize that there indeed was leadership and structure, even if it were unofficial, and the habitual practices of an association directed the activities in many ways.

The network's objectives were wide. The target of the mobilization was the entire city management and the issues ranged from the deficit of the welfare budget to the considerable profits of the public utilities and the municipally owned enterprises. On their website, they presented their claims as follows:

> 'Municipal services must be under democratic control; Basic services must not be subjected to profit seeking; Services are to be developed in a customer-oriented manner and with quality consciousness and cost awareness; Basic security and justness must be ensured through services; Marginalization and inequality in society must be prevented by municipal services (Pro Kuntapalvelut 2009).

In 2004, ProMS claimed that the social services budget of the city of Helsinki had been subject to a conscious and deliberate under-budgeting, making use of the prevailing political rhetoric of scarcity of resources. Pertti explained the events that led to the founding of the network:

> 'The city administration gave really hard edicts that ... three-four percent cost cuts had to be made in the basic services ..., and the next year five more, and the next year again five more ... in other words, a really hard shutdown pace. ... And there were the citizens who got scared of the destruction of health services, but also city employees who saw that, hey, we're heading towards a horribly tough foreclosure of jobs and a possible way towards privatization. So I think this is it, the point where the municipality's employees ... and also citizen, patient, and client associations necessarily had to combine their forces, in order to stop this madness.'

The group had discovered that the city planned to implement yet again important cuts to the social service budget, while in the same year, the profit figures of Helsingin Energia, the city-owned power company,[24] were sky-rocketing. This was a real discovery, since the power company's gains did not figure in the city's balance sheet. An accountant, consulting local finances for the Finnish Delegation of Industry and Commerce (EVA), assisted the discovery by pointing out this abnormality of the Helsinki City economy in his report. After the publication of the report, Irma, who was a retired accountant herself, took further interest in the issue and went through the power company's result reports as well as the city budget proposition. She concluded that at least 100 million Euros more could be accounted from the power company without endangering its business activities. Furthermore, the network activists calculated that even with the cuts of the social and health services budget, which they claimed were going to be impossible to carry out without breaking the law,[25] the city budget was still underestimated by some 100 million Euros (cf. Forssell 2005).

The network launched a campaign in order to prevent the social service cuts by transferring the needed funds from the power company profits. They published a leaflet on the issue, held meetings, and invited local politicians to debates. A few public demonstrations were also organized, although on a rather small scale. One of the network's most successful events was a session of 'citizens' budget proceedings,' in which they presented their own budget proposal to the City Council. Some 200 people participated in the event, but only a handful of councilors were present, to the ProMS activists' disappointment.

The reactions of the leading political parties, namely National Coalition[26] and Social Democrat groups of the City Council were unenthusiastic, to say the least: they treated the network's demands as outright hogwash. Only part of the small Left Alliance council group backed up the network's demands. Finally, however, the issue did make its way to the public agenda. The network members wrote to newspapers: Irma and the consultant, who in the first place had put out the information, cooperated closely and got several readers' letters through *Helsingin Sanomat*, the biggest daily newspaper. Subsequently, journalists started to show interest in the case, and Irma was interviewed several times on the radio. The network organized a number of public debates in which Irma in particular starred, defending the case on the grounds of her expertise in accounting and business management.

Eventually, the city leaders had to take a stand on the issue. The chair of the executive board (a National Coalition representative) declared in a Council assembly that the demands of the network were impossible to fulfill, because they would violate the competition legislation. The ProMS activists responded by taking the case to the National Competition Office that decided in favor of the network's claim, stating that the city could indeed transfer money from the power company it owned to, for example, the social service budget, without violating competition laws. From then on, the profits of the city-owned companies have figured on the city balance sheet, and the sums that the city has accounted this way have in some cases nearly doubled.

After this successful campaign, the network continued to lobby against the under-budgeting of health and social services, increasingly relying on legal measures, such as municipal motions and appeals to the Helsinki Administrative Court.

No to Big Brother (NBB) was a group of some 15–20 activists resisting the increasing video surveillance in Lyon. It was loosely part of a nationwide network that linked together small local associations with a similar cause, but remained rather independent and locally bound with only sporadic contacts to the wider network. Lyon was at the time the most 'monitored' city in Europe. The Mayor in office took special pride in his city as a forerunner in surveillance technology through installing a dense network of cameras in the city, and in developing new strategies of surveillance in order to increase street security. The NBB activists opposed the Mayor's views strongly, as they summed up on their website:

> The city is ours, social segregation and video policing must not pass!!

> Video surveillance is a violation of individual and public liberties;
> It constitutes an additional technological instrument for social control;
> It is a dangerous tool that adds up to the 'securitarian' logic
> It allows disregarding associations, politics, unions;
> Dangerous today, it can be the absolute arm of a totalitarian power tomorrow;
> It attacks the consequences, not the causes of misery;
> It serves to reject the 'unwanted' from this city;
> This measure means deploying a logic of urban planning that aims at sanitizing the city;
> It is an electioneering and demagogic measure;
> The hundreds of millions of Euros spent in it surely deserve to be used in a better way.
> (Non à Big Brother 2010)

The website provided location maps of the surveillance cameras, and various materials from comics to research report links criticizing the city policies on the issue. In an interview, Chazz, one of the key members of the group, explained the motivations and actions of the group rather bluntly:

> 'So I'm part of the Big Brother in order to tell people that it costs like hell these cameras, because it's a huge market ... And besides, I'm not at all persuaded [that video surveillance reduces criminality], and still besides, it's an individuality problem you know. So ... we try to sensitize [people to the issue] by making maps ... of the city of Lyon, or maps by neighborhood, where we put precisely the placement of the cameras. ... But then we've also done a few demonstrations ... to forewarn people. People are not in the know. ... And so with a big fuss and bustle we masked the cameras and all, you see ... having fun all the way. And besides, we also try to shove the public powers a bit.'

The worry over the neoliberal public government handling public money badly – either by spending or by saving it – was something the NBB and ProMS activists shared, but their ways of reacting to the worry were quite different. The NBB emerged originally within the libertarian milieu of Lyon as a reaction to installation of new cameras around 2000. In 2005, they campaigned vigorously against the new wave of installations in view. They distributed flyers, 'revealed' the cameras, and the new spots where cameras were to be installed, with tags and stickers carrying the NBB logo, and circulated the 'global plan of video surveillance' of the city with new cameras marked on the city map.

Their bravura, however, were public performances. They marched the streets with banderols stating 'Video Surveillance: Totalitarianism within a Zoom's Range,' and hung posters stating, for example, 'Monitored liberty' on walls near the cameras. Once they hid their heads in cardboard-crafted movie cameras with the NBB logo on them and occupied a square in their neighborhood (La Croix-Rousse, naturally) for an afternoon and an evening, turning the square into a street party with music and dancing.

Another time, they put up a series of carnivalesque shows of blanketing the cameras' views. One of these shows was organized in *St Jean,* a neighborhood in the oldest part of Lyon. A dozen activists with gas masks or white theater masks on their heads and clothed in black togas, followed by a growing group of audience and bystanders, went from camera to camera and 'bagged' them. This was a rather complicated operation in which a bouquet of multi-colored helium balloons was tied on three sides of the mouth of a rubbish sack. Long strings were attached to each balloon bouquet, so that the device could be flown and directed like a kite. It was then released in the air and guided with the strings to a video camera, placed approximately seven meters high on the wall, and adjusted to sink the camera in the sack. The balloons would then keep the sack in its place. The scene was colorful, and it did get some coverage in the local media (see examples and analysis of the visual representations of the events in Chapter 5 in this book).

One of the biggest moments of publicity for the network was the awarding of the Mayor of Lyon with the Orwell Prize, which was the national network's ironic award for advancing video surveillance. The network activists had found out that the Mayor was to appear in the opening of a fair, so they made their way to the exhibition area, waited for the Mayor to arrive, and 'attacked' him as a 'committee' to hand over the prize. They made the Mayor sign a document guaranteeing that he would take good care of the prize, which was a piece of recycled artwork representing an old-style camera. The Mayor added on the paper: 'And I engage in working with this organization in order the civil liberties to be totally guaranteed in Lyon. Had I been in your place, in Lyon, in 1968, I would have with no doubt done the same thing. Let us work together during my mandate as the Mayor of Lyon,' and signed it. This message was a subject of jokes and mockery among the activists for a long time afterwards – they were absolutely convinced that the Mayor's message was nothing but lack of sincerity and dishonest sweet talk. The award action made it to the news: the local newspaper reported that a bunch of unruly kids had messed up the mayor's press conference, and even the national TV news showed some images of the event, although giving the voice to the Mayor alone.

However, there was no sign of an effect on the city's surveillance policy that continued on its track despite the network's efforts to change the course. The Mayor's written statement never led to anything. The councilors I interviewed – the few who recognized the group's existence – called the network's claims into question and seemed reluctant to talk about the group. Even a councilor who was very critical of video surveillance himself was uneasy when I mentioned the group – he rather abruptly concluded that the NBB did not want to negotiate and it was thus not possible to deliberate with these activists.

Another example of a similar use of action repertoires – by more or less the same group of people that were the key actors of NBB – was the campaign against Nicolas Sarkozy, the then Minister of internal affairs. The campaign was launched in the thick of the suburban riots in 2005, after Mr Sarkozy, on a visit to a suburb, had called the rioters '*des racailles*' – the 'dregs' or the 'trash' of the French society. The rioters being mainly youth with a North-African background, the overt racism of the Minister's statement was shocking to a lot of people, the Leftist activists in particular.

Among the Croix-Roussean activists, a badge campaign against Sarkozy was planned. The campaign started one evening in Cloé's apartment, where people came and went as usual, and discussed the recent news. Solange said she knew somebody who had a machine for compressing badges, and she promised to borrow it. Théo, who worked in a school, said he could bring over some colored paper and other accessories. Cloé promised to buy the badge soles on her way home the next day. There was indefinite talk about the repartition of the costs. The badge 'bees' were set for the next evening, as easily and in a business-as-usual manner as this type of things always took place.

The next evening, a handful of people – Cloé, Théo, Julien, Chazz, Casper and me sat on couches and floors, babbling away, and exchanging ideas for badge texts. '*Nous sommes tous des racailles*'; 'We are all dregs/trash,' was one of the slogans that ended up on the badges – many others provoked laughter and chains of funny modifications. Someone had brought beer, and the evening turned into a party. When Solange arrived with the machine, people were tipsy and hysterical. The badges were finally written, drawn and compressed by Cloé, Solange, and me, as the guys headed to a bar. The following week, we carried and distributed the badges at the university, in cafés, and among acquaintances. But finally, the whole thing came and went rather unnoticed, and the attention of the activists was soon drawn to something else.

Succeeding as a social movement in Lyon and Helsinki

Success of social movements has been a topic of a great number of studies, and several different concepts and methods have been proposed to measure it (e.g. Giugni 1998). Political opportunity structures and strategic framing by the movements have been popular conceptual tools in analyzing the success or failure of a contention. My key question here, however, is not to find out why or even if the movements succeeded or failed, but, instead, what did the movements themselves make of the consequences of their actions, and what would this tell about their means of politicization.

The ProMS network publicly stated that its decision-making followed ideals of communicative democracy, so that all decisions would be based on open conversations between the members. In the network meetings, however, a kind of political pragmatism was the prevailing strategy. There was no discussion concerning the network's practices, and decisions were mostly taken on a suggestion-followed-by-supportive-nods basis. In my presence, no open conflicts occurred, but underlying tensions seemed to exist, especially between the communist party representatives and the non–partisan members of the network. The communist members had a tendency to make public statements as representatives of the network, which irritated the other members. It was not good publicity to be 'labeled' as communist within the Helsinki public sphere, and this created uneasiness on some occasions, although the subject seemed to be too sensitive to be treated openly. Instead, people would look embarrassed and change the subject. Sometimes, after the meeting, activists would refer to the issue in smaller groups showing signs of frustration and fatigue. These reactions were quite similar to how they reacted to 'politicking' in general: as something possibly hindering their cause.

Thus, politics as such was a somewhat difficult issue to treat. Instead, the activists concentrated on strategizing and struggling to be acknowledged and recognized for their *expertise* in municipal finances and service production. They were pretty good at this, as the previous section showed, but they were rarely content with their achievements. In the network meetings, a sense of frustration often burst out in terms of discussing the network's action repertoires. Despite the events that could be regarded as great successes, the network members felt they were 'shouting at walls' and getting little response. They felt it was hard to get people to come along, and harder still to get any message through to the city. In one meeting, Jarmo exclaimed:

> 'So do we have to roll two hundred hospital beds down *Aleksanterinkatu* [the main shopping street in downtown Helsinki] to make them listen?!'

However, they never rolled the hospital beds onto the streets. The few demonstrations they organized were small and quiet. There was sometimes even an awkward atmosphere of shame and embarrassment – embarrassment over the small number of people who showed up, and about the somewhat shabby appearance of the event. This was certainly not their genre, but they seemed to think it should have been. From an observer's point of view, the results of their work were quite remarkable. While sometimes expressing their pride over the expertise they had and the 'righteousness' of their claims, the members, however, felt they would have done better if they were 'more like a social movement'. Their way of engaging in public struggles emphasized expertise and law-abiding, but they clearly would have wanted to lean more explicitly on solidarity, human rights, and democracy in their public actions (cf. Chapter 6 in this book). The logic of politicization they followed was that of building a case with factual arguments, but at least as important was their project of becoming recognized as experts.

In contrast, the NBB network members, as well as the campaigners against Sarkozy, proudly 'banged their heads against the wall' with no signs of shame or even strong frustration. There was a zeal in their activities, most of the actions had a strong 'fun factor,' and despite the lack of response and the negative publicity, the groups went on and invented yet new ways of expressing opposition. The activists of these groups were genuinely worried about the things they opposed to, but in their activities, the tone was joyful. The activists were mostly in their late twenties and early thirties, and they belonged to the relatively large group of 'lifestyle activists' dwelling in Lyon. Thus, the energy and joyfulness of their contention was undoubtedly in part due to their ages and life situations. However, these mobilizations were a serial expression of politics, very overtly displayed as such. The ease and habitual hold on politics and politicizing, and the public performances of political views, were obviously the essentials of the group style concerning the choice of repertoires. These activists did not talk about unsuccessful campaigns as failures, but remembered them cheerfully and with pride. Opposing and expressing opposition was good in itself, regardless of the results, as part of a chain of politicizations they engaged in that was in itself more important than a particular project or issue. Thus, definitions of what could, or should, be said or done, did not depend on the outward consequences of the words or deeds, but were set following a more self-contained logic. For them, arguing for civic values and rights was a self-evidence, and all other lines of argument merely spiced and gave back-up to the fundamental claim of democratic freedom. Their engagement in political struggles was performative: the individual topics of contention were less important than engaging in processes of politicization as such.

2.4 Group styles and the place of politics

This chapter set out to explore the civic practices, and consequent processes of politicization, among social movement activists in Lyon and Helsinki. In the first set of cases, I considered the aspect of *group bonds* in particular: who were 'we,' and how did 'we' come to be. I showed that the French activists built their group bonds in close relationship to their living environment, and things concretely 'close' to them. The neighborhood – more and less concretely – was the commonplace the group shared, and the potential grounds for building politicization on. For the Finnish activists, associations and chains of membership in them were the source of trust and of building bonds also between people previously unknown to each other. Thus, associations were the grounds for raising the level of generality of a topic, and politicizing it.

In the second case pair, the emphasis was especially on *group boundaries* of the squatters, and the ways in which they managed external and internal conflicts. The Lyonnais squatters could hardly imagine making deals with the city officials, and it was important for them to be seen as strictly oppositional *vis-à-vis* 'official' institutions (with the exception of the few lawyers they trusted). As for conflicts within the groups, there was no attempt to conceal or tame them, and conflicts concerning for example gender discrimination sometimes provided grounds for politicizations, and sometimes proved to be dissolving, 'unbearable' things that paralyzed the groups, at least temporarily. In Helsinki, the squatters' strongest allies were the officials from the city Youth Department, who played intermediary between the squatters and the police and eventually granted the squatters a site on which they could 'squat' with permission. The Helsinki squatters' boundaries were more permeable towards institutional others, rendering possible both mainstream media reportages of squats, and the negotiations between the squatters and the city. However, protecting the group from conflicts and the threat of dissolution meant that the differences within the group were more difficult to recognize.

In the third case, the emphasis was on the *speech and action norms* of two very different activist groups. The cases of reasoning and resisting the municipality echoed many previous findings in the Finnish-French differences of contentious action. The Finns put their effort in becoming experts, a feature that Eeva Raevaara (2005) in her comparative analysis has showed to be at the very core of claiming political credibility in the Finnish context.[27] The Lyonnais activists preferred to express their resistance and outrage, as well as keep on with the persistent joyfulness of their mobilization, rather than strategize about the best ways to influence city policies.

The Lyonnais activists were prone to generalize issues touching them on a very personal level to public, politicized matters – be it the man who sells you cigarettes bombarding you with sexist remarks, the violent police officer evicting you from a squat, or the street you live on being monitored by video cameras day and night. Their efforts of politicization arose often from the least public level of engagement: the commonplace they shared and fostered, but that they also managed to communicate in terms of public claims and resistance. This did not necessarily help in getting their point across, but in their eyes, successful politicization did not depend on influencing city policies on a concrete level. Instead, politicization was a process in which the immediate environment, symbolic attachment to it, collective memories and trajectories of local (and sometimes national, or international) civic practices, and even national stereotypes of how to represent resistance, were all intertwined, and resulted in, nevertheless, public processes of conflicting views. The activists in Helsinki, in contrast, were leaning on association networks, consensual negotiations, and expertise, and their acts of politicization were often based on engagement in a plan. They were projects to be carried out rather than something immediately close to be communicated like the shared commonplace of the Lyonnais. Furthermore, the activists in Helsinki protected their groups from inner conflict, and made efforts to avoid conflict with outsiders, too. They also made significant achievements, if we take achievements to mean concrete policy change or, like in the squatters' case, a quasi-permanent arrangement for the social center. These comparative results can be discussed in the light of previous studies that also use the approach of sociology of engagements to compare political action. On the one hand, Olga Koveneva (2010) found, in comparing French and Russian environmental activists, that the French were, contrarily to my suggestion, prone to distance themselves from the immediate environment and instead, generalized their political claims eagerly. Her descriptions and analyses have made me think that more than an opposite finding, the differing interpretations were due to a continuum. In Koveneva's study, the Russian activists were even more attached to their immediate surroundings than the French. Comparing the French to the Finns in the above cases, then, brought up features that were perhaps overlooked in Koveneva's study. On the other hand, Markku Lonkila's (2011) study on neighborhood activism in Finland and Russia has shown along the same lines with my interpretations that the Finnish activists leaned heavily on public level generalizations in their claims. However, it should be bore in mind that these characteristics cannot and should not be taken as national traits, but interpretations bound to certain situations – that perhaps can be found more repeatedly in some contexts than in others (Thévenot 2010; 2011).

The group styles approach has enabled the analysis to go beyond the already publicized, first-degree representations and discourses concerning local civic practices. In the following chapters, I examine the elements of local civic practices introduced above from different angles, partly following the theoretical frame set in this chapter, partly introducing new conceptual tools as needed. Next, I turn to the styles of acting as citizens, and the prevailing conceptions and conditions of citizenship the activists in Lyon and Helsinki put forward.

3
Citizenship and Gender in Local Activism

> 'The notion of citizenship, actually, I don't really know what it means in fact. ... That's why I don't manage using that word anymore. Is one a citizen of one's country? A citizen of one's city? Is one a citizen? I have ... the impression that it's a judicial term, slightly technical maybe. ... I'm sure there are folks that are able to adopt the word and make of it what they want, but it's pretty vague to me. I don't know whether I'm a French citizen, a Lyonnais citizen [laughs], a citizen of the yard right next door, so yeah, I see myself more like an individual in a society, active maybe, but not necessarily citizen.' (Julien)

> 'It [citizenship] is really a part of my identity. ... And as a citizen, in my opinion, I also have rights and responsibilities. ... It [citizenship] is maybe easy to define ... through society. .... Or I can think that I'm a citizen of the Helsinki city.
> Q: So what does citizenship of Helsinki mean?
> A: Well, it also means a great deal. ... I have like a number of roles in my life, but it all happens here in this town. ... So my responsibility is, for example, to keep this place tidy and safe and so. And then about rights, I think I also have the right to enjoy it.' (Henna)

The excerpts above illustrate the salience and power of expression of the notion of citizenship in understanding local civic practices. Talking about citizenship with local activists in Lyon and Helsinki quickly gave the impression that they framed both the notion, and the variety of features they connected to it, very differently and defined the entire question from differing standpoints. Julien's confusion and reluctance before the notion literally summed up the predominant line of thinking among the French activists. Similarly, the rather optimistic and self-assured tone Henna used to talk about citizenship was typical of the Finnish activists. Where did this difference stem from?

In the previous chapter, exploring the local activist groups in Lyon and Helsinki shed light on the different conditions of politicization prevalent in the two contexts, but also left questions open concerning, in particular, the activists' take on their own place and actions. In this chapter, I continue the analysis by comparing French and Finnish activists' conceptions of citizenship, and their ideas of what it was to act 'as a citizen' in Lyon and Helsinki.

Key concepts of social and political thinking are always closely tied to the contexts of their use, as well as their users' intentions. By framing the meanings of citizenship and the kinds of identity processes – gender dynamics in particular – included in the activists' experience, the French and Finnish activists illustrated local civic practices, but also the configurations of state, local and national political institutions, and different levels of political culture that portrayed their ideas of their own role and activity as citizens. In these illustrations, gender provided a lens that made the links between the framings of citizenship and the possibilities and obstacles of politicization in the local contexts visible (similar observations in Salmenniemi 2005).

Citizenship has been an exhaustively debated issue by both policy-makers and social and political scientists during the past couple of decades. The concept of citizenship, in addition to the traditional rights and duties debate, has been stretched in many directions: from a social and human rights perspective to globalization, feminist, social movements, and intersectional perspectives of citizenship. The levels and viewpoints of analyzing citizenship have multiplied: from nation-states to the European Union and a 'global society' for instance in virtual networks, to people's attachment to localities, especially urban citizenship as a consequence of the rapid growth of cities and the number of urban dwellers worldwide, to the massive increase of immigration flows and the growth of the 'fourth world' within the industrial and post-industrial societies, and to the challenges these transformations create for defining citizenship. At the same time, understanding citizenship not as a monolithic status, but as a set of multiple practices intersecting gender, ethnicity, ability and disability, lifestyle choices, age, and political views, just to mention a few, has introduced new challenges to the field of study (Marshall 1950; Brubaker 1992; Soysal 1994; Yuval-Davies 1999; Beasley & Bacchi 2000; Faulks 2000; Balibar 2001; Lister 2003; Neveu C. 2003; Giugni & Passy 2006; Rosanvallon 2006).

In the introduction to this book, I proposed a conception of citizenship anchored in action and practices: to be a citizen, thus, means to 'do citizen', and it is impossible to talk about citizenship in terms detached from action (Rosanvallon 2006, 24–6). Treating citizenship as a notion directed to 'doing' renders both possible and necessary to try to do justice to the self-appellations the activists in both contexts felt comfortable with. I make use of citizenship as a contextual concept that offers a basis for comparisons because of the widely shared view of its importance in understanding political culture, acts of politicization, and the role of the people in democracies, both as groups and as individuals. Even if the Lyonnais activists did not want to call themselves 'citizens,' they were deeply concerned with making me understand why: citizenship was not in any way an irrelevant notion. They emphasized, much more than the Finns, the crucial feature of the current citizenship debates: the relation between citizens and non-citizens, and the consequences of these positions for individuals and groups.

The contextual nature of citizenship appears in the French and Finnish notions of citizenship – *citoyenneté* and *kansalaisuus* – that have very different political and conceptual roots historically, and currently, both differing and common challenges. In the interviews I conducted with the local activists, two particularly central comparative themes emerged: first, the ways the activists framed citizenship when they talked about the definitions of the term and the activities they linked directly to it and, secondly, the ways in which gender dynamics figured in these framings. In the following, I first briefly discuss the comparative historical aspects of French and Finnish citizenship, and then analyze the activists' framings concerning citizenship in Lyon and Helsinki. In the second empirical section, I look at the intertwinement of gender and citizenship in the two contexts.

3.1 Citoyen-ne-s – Kansalaiset

Historical contexts of French and Finnish citizenship

Citizenship and practices, gender relations, exclusion mechanisms, and other intertwined dynamics, such as voting, are illustrative of the social relations that constitute the state (Offerlé 1998, 51; Lister 2003).

Comparing the historical features of the concept provides a basis for an analysis of current perceptions of citizenship in France and Finland.[1]

The French conception of citizenship was first and foremost defined as a political status – a citizen was a judicially universal subject who actively took part in the life of the polity. However, as Michel Offerlé (1998) has shown, the project of 'becoming citizens' was not an overnight result of the Revolution. Instead, Offerlé suggests that 'civic citizenship' involved a lengthy learning process, illustrated by the difficulties, for example, in developing a system of voting. The post-revolutionary movement of 'civic citizenization' required a rupture of old communal ties, and their replacement with the universal category of citizen. This development involved the creation of three figures within the people: the citizens 'on paper' that constituted the electorate, the actual voting citizens, and the aggregated electorates who organized around segments of opinions, and thus enabled the prevision of election results (ibid. 1998, 37–9).

In addition to the importance of the political contents of citizenship, the French case was marked by the salience of territory in drawing the boundaries between citizens and non-citizens. Rogers Brubaker has emphasized the division of the *jus solis* and *jus sanguinis* principles that, in his view, summarize the fundamentals of the French and German citizenship debates. In the former, the base of citizenship is the territory: residing on the French soil, ideally, made the French citizens. In the latter, in contrast, ethnicity and kin relations were the defining features, which was certainly more the case in Finland as well (Brubaker 1992, 91, 39). The recent decades' developments of immigration policies reflect this difference, but also challenge the idea of these two exclusive principles as much more than influential background ideals. According to Numa Murard and Étienne Tassin (2007), for instance, the conception of French citizenship has been divided into 'two politics of citizenship.' The policy-makers' project of making social cohesion through civilization processes, civic education, and all in all the assumption that the republic is one and undivided, increasingly meets the 'citizenship of no' of social movements and groups unable and unwilling to accept the foundations of the processes of integration targeted at them. This is so in particular because of the official handling (or mishandling) of the increasing problem of 'first and second class citizens' provoked by the pretended integration of 'second and third generation immigrants.' Ironically, the label already reveals that this integration has not 'made' those people French in the way people with an ethnically 'French,' or 'European' origins, are French. This phenomenon is difficult to avoid in any context of the current French society, and it was a fact that the Lyonnais activists emphasized repeatedly when discussing citizenship (ibid. 23). In the Finnish context as well, recent developments of immigration influence the citizenship debate, if to a lesser degree – immigration to Finland has been hitherto so limited that there has not been grounds for a weighty societal debate on the topic, and even the recent increase in both the numbers and in the debate is still on a rather different level than in France (cf. Lepola 2000; Keskinen *et al.* 2009; Krause & Pietikäinen 2009).[2] In the empirical analysis of this chapter, the activists' ways of framing citizenship in Lyon and Helsinki were very different from one another, and the question of immigration formed more or less the core among the former, while hardly figuring as a topic at all among the latter.

In his analysis of the conceptual history of Finnish citizenship, Henrik Stenius (2002) has emphasized that in its original use, citizenship was defined through judicial rights and responsibilities, not through political participation. In the Finnish discussions of the 1800s, a citizen was, in contrast to the French, as well as in contrast to most other European discussions, a withdrawing, background figure, and a target of educational projects rather than an active political figure (ibid. 309, 337–8, 340). According to Stenius, the thinkers and political actors who participated in the creation of the Finnish political culture knowingly parted from the European discourses concerning citizenship: they neither tied the concept to the history of European city-states, nor to the history of judicial thought. The Finnish word for citizen, *kansalainen* is derived from *kansa*, the people.[3] Furthermore, the model of governance was that of the local autonomy of (rural) communes, the predecessors of municipalities. Civic virtues and citizen rights were rooted in the society of yeomen, not in that of the city bourgeoisie (ibid. 310, 321–2).

The early definitions of citizenship have had a significant effect on the formation of Finnish political culture. Factually, both rights and responsibilities were extremely limited in terms of political citizenship. The citizen had 'no political existence, and no means to participate in political decision making,' but instead, he (at the time the debate only concerned men) had the possibility to 'participate in the "nation project" – from a voluntary basis' (Stenius 2002, 338). These definitions made citizens apolitical subjects, and the commonly built, collective *nation* became the political subject (ibid. 340).

From the 1880s onwards, voluntary associations played an important role in changing Finnish society. Similarly to other Nordic countries, in spite of varying oppositional takes on the state and its officials, voluntary associations engaged in multiple forms of co-operation with the state and the church, and, in particular, with municipalities, and built a corporatist system in which the former four parties together sought solutions to societal questions. These developments are in stark contrast with the French post-revolution political culture in which the idea of mediating structures between the state and the individual citizens were regarded as the worst of evils. The history of voluntary associations in France is illustrative of the consequences of the 'universalistic' conception of citizenship. Associations were legalized as late as in 1901, and even if a vivid associational culture existed prior to the final legalization, its societal status and importance *vis-à-vis* the state were different, and significantly less influential than in Finland (e.g. Rosanvallon 1998; Alapuro 2005a).

In Finland, the apolitical concept of citizenship merged with a collectivistic political culture in the making. The 'citizen' thus formulated was two-sided: the figure of a debating, law-reforming, political citizen was weak, but instead, an engaged, culturally active citizen who took part in the civilization project intertwined with the nation building efforts, was valorized, if not idealized. Politicization and politicizing citizens' activities were, however, met with great suspicion. A good citizen was, thus, one who participated in the national project of civilization, but not in political decision-making, and hence, 'participation' came to mean consensual acts and agreement (Stenius 2002, 359, 347).

In the historical accounts of citizenship I discussed above, two themes were absent that figure as crucially important in understanding citizenship in France and Finland both historically and today, in analyzing the local activists' ideas of it in Lyon and Helsinki. First, in both contexts, the early histories of citizenship I referred to have mainly been written as histories of male citizenship, even if claiming gender neutrality (see Juntti 1998; Gordon 2006). Hence, the basis of 'universal' citizenship and civic rights they portray is, in fact, fundamentally different, and the implications of these developments still today would not be univocal to all citizens, even if we disregarded the topic of the 'non-, or almost-but-not-quite-citizens' I referred to above. This is problematic, to the least, as the transformation of gender relations and the historical development of political citizenship are largely interdependent processes. The roots and development of French and Finnish women's political citizenship has, however, been extensively examined, and also compared to one another (Heinen & del Re 1996; Holli 2003; Heinen *et al.* 2004; Raevaara 2005; Sineau 2005; Tremblay *et al.* 2007). In these studies, the principal axes of comparison are women's political representation, and the cultural and discursive place of gender.[4]

The first axis portrays, at first sight, a comparison of extremes. In France, approximately 150 years separated universal suffrage and the first woman MP in the French Parliament. In the first Finnish Diet in 1907, after the radical suffrage reform, universal in a factual sense,[5] women represented a tenth of the MPs (Holli 2003, 11–12). Nevertheless, while the difference in proportion of MPs remains important even today, the figures of women's representation in local politics are currently very similar: 33% in France, 37% in Finland (Tilastokeskus 2010; Heinen *et al.* 2004, 41). More interesting are, however, the very different takes on promoting equal substantive representation in political debates. In Finland, equal political representation has been rationalized through women's qualities and expertise that should be used for the good of the nation, whereas in France, the predominant argument has stressed women's representation 'for the sake of democracy' that would be better democracy if its political organs consisted of the 'people' more equally (Raevaara 2005).

In the second axis, that of the cultural gender order, the main division lies in the tension of equality and difference. A few everyday observations, also reported in a number of studies, are enlightening in this respect. Whereas the French are in general rather willing to admit that the country is 'macho,' and that problems regarding gender equality exist, the Finns tend to believe gender equality is 'achieved,' and that despite some minor problems, the country is very advanced in this sense (too). The French stress gender difference, often in terms of almost caricature (and romanticized) hetero-centrism, but recognize the possible conflicts concerning the issue. The Finns, on the contrary, trivialize both difference and gender-based discrimination, and have a strong tendency to project inequalities elsewhere – either temporally or geographically – and thus deliberately avoid the recognition of a possible gender conflict. In Finland, gender equality is an issue of national pride, and questioning it is threatening in many ways (Holli 2003, 18; Holli *et al.* 2006; 2007).

Citizenship is usually treated as a 'national affair,' in particular in historical accounts. However, the ideas of active citizenship, and citizenship as 'doing,' refer to practices and situations that happen in environments in which people act as citizens. These environments are not abstract 'nations' or 'states,' but mostly, local communities of some kind. Many studies have argued that the local-level practices and public culture are, in fact, the only concrete ways to consider the state as such (e.g. Gupta 2006, 212). In both France and Finland, the 'locality' of citizenship and urban citizenship in particular, has attracted increasing attention and enthusiasm during the past decade, and functioned as a powering force of debates concerning participation and democracy (e.g. Harinen 2000; Rättilä 2001; Perrineau & Ray 2002; Bäcklund *et al.* 2002; Neveu C. 2004; Gordon 2005; Carrel 2006, 2007b; Bäcklund 2007). In the following, the 'place' of citizenship between different levels of governance, and different levels of abstraction, emerges in local activists' framings of citizenship.

The engagements of the 'citizens of no' in Lyon

The opening citation from Lyon in this chapter was Julien's, who was an alternative radio activist (and member of several other local activist groups) in his early thirties:

> 'The notion of citizenship, actually, I don't really know what it means in fact. ... That's why I don't manage using that word anymore. Is one a citizen of one's country? A citizen of one's city? Is one a citizen? I have ... the impression that it's a judicial term, slightly technical maybe ... . I'm sure there are folks that are able to adopt the word and make of it what they want, but it's pretty vague to me. I don't know whether I'm a French citizen, a Lyonnais citizen [laughs], a citizen of the yard right next door, so yeah, I see myself more like an individual in a society, active maybe, but not necessarily a citizen.'

Contrarily to what Julien expected, my other Lyonnais interlocutors did not find ways to 'adopt' the notion of citizenship much more than he did. Their aversion towards it varied somewhat, but they all framed the topic in a way that emphasized its problematic nature, and the unease it provoked in their minds. The French framed citizenship mainly either by refusing it, or by evoking the themes of engagement and the common good, or usually, a little bit of both.

Apart from the confusion prevalent in Julien's talk, more straightforward and firm refusals occurred as well. The 'citizens of no' introduced by Murad and Tassin (2007) were, indeed, present in flesh and blood in Lyon. In the following, Chazz (a libertarian activist in his early thirties, who participated in squatter groups, the alternative radio, and many other contentions in Lyon at the time of the fieldwork) both said 'no' to citizenship, and clear-sightedly presented his reasons, as well as some options:

> 'Citizenship is not a big deal for me. Active struggle is a bit more like it. I'd say that citizenship, I don't know, it's just a big word.

> I absolutely disagree with all this. I don't vote, I'm not inscribed on the lists, I refuse to take part in that electoral masquerade, it's out of the question. But one has to get engaged in associations, I find that a shame that people's only worry is to put that ticket in the urn, and that's the end of it. I think that we've got to engage, we have to be a counter power.'

Pierre Rosanvallon (2006) could have cited Chazz when presenting the fundamentals of counter-democracy: from the crisis created by representative democracy 'gone masquerade' to the counter power used by engaging, active citizens that reveal the society to itself, denounce the status quo, and find new ways an forms of political action and politicization (ibid. 19–20, 67–71). In addition, Chazz's emphasis on associations indicated that he was probably well-informed about the conceptual history of French citizenship – he had a degree in history – and the impertinence of mediating structures, collective movements and associations, to the form of citizenship he objected to.

Furthermore, the exclusive mechanisms inherent to the concept of citizenship were often at the center of criticism. The load *citoyenneté* carried were the echoes of the universalistic, republican 'Frenchness.' Citizenship made the activists think of state institutions, borders, the political system, and national emblems, like the *Marseillaise,* that they often whole-heartedly scoffed at. Citizenship was not 'their' concept, it was 'colonized' by other forces. Equally, in their minds, the republic was responsible for excluding and colonizing practices that still went on today, as Cloé, an activist in her late twenties, described:

> 'So, that big word. Citizenship, I have a bit of a problem with it for several reasons ... because it's a notion which, in order to be formed, it ... meant excluding people right from the beginning, the women, the slaves and so on. ... I think that this load ... is still there, I mean, when they say they're going to take the citizens into account, actually the question is, the citizens but which ones? ... Who is listened to? ... I'm just afraid that the word does it that we forget once again all those people that are excluded. ... And maybe ... it's also because 'citizen' is very much attached to the state, ... and I've been really critical ... of the idea of the state. ... It's not really the level ... that would make a lot of sense to me, you know, it took me a tremendously long time to get a voter's card for instance. ... That word is interesting only if it can be something that opens up rights and also reforms, that is, something that really engages people.'

Cloé's concerns were widely shared among the activists. In the above, she referred to the historical exclusion of women and slaves. Generally, issues surrounding the *sans-papiers*, and the French 'fourth world' – comprising of the non-European (or, rather, non-Western/Northern European) immigrant-origin population – also arose. Cloé, along with many others, thought that citizenship, with its republican echo, was too easily abused as a basis for excluding practices. She was, however, willing to give it a chance if it could 'contain' engaging practices and reformatory mechanisms. But whether citizenship could be 'something that opens up rights and also reforms,' seemed to depend not on the citizens, but on some other quarter's definitions of the concept.

However, not all of the activists were quite as hostile towards the state as Cloé and Chazz. Alongside a more 'statist' attitude, more positive accounts of citizenship also arose. The common characteristic to the French activists' citizenship discussions was, however, that they reflected much on how they *felt* about citizenship. The obligation of being a French citizen, even with the right to refuse using the term, was either an emotional burden for them, or, in case of a more positive 'citizenship attitude', a very personal, emotional tie (cf. Offerlé 1998, 39), as in Christelle's (an activist at the local ATTAC branch in her early thirties) case:

> 'To me, the notion of citizenship consists of, yes, the institutions, I have respect for the institutions of the state, ... and for the public services, among other things. ... And you know, I kind of became a teacher because I told myself ... that it could be part of a citizen engagement, to teach the citizen values, a little bit of the living together, of tolerance, of openness of spirit. Oh well, it's all rather vague in that sense.'

Christelle, with her more positive account of citizenship, tied the concept to the state perhaps even more firmly than the other activists. Indeed, citizenship *was* the state institutions, apart from being an illustration of the Republican values. Finally, something of a middle-ground opinion was Christophe's, who thought the concept of citizenship was not the crucial point of discussion, but rather the practices that the continuous grudge against the state produced. Christophe, a volunteer in a substance abusers' healthcare association in his mid-thirties, recognized, and to a certain extent shared, the general aversion against the concept of citizenship, but stressed the importance of reflecting upon the repercussions it had:

> 'In my mind ... these are really important challenges, to work out something so that individuals would not be alone in their corners

> groaning against the state or withdrawing to their personal lives, but that they would have connections with the others, for the sake of the common good.'

Hence, Christophe seemed to evoke the other side of the coin of criticism towards the state – its possibly depoliticizing effects. This reflection approached Rosanvallon's (2006) idea of a depoliticized, apolitical society, a perversion of counter-democracy in which politics has been emptied of content, and consequently, criticism becomes mere yapping for the sake of yapping. According to Christophe's view, in so doing people would be isolated from one another, and serving the common good required that this development be stopped.

Sophie Duchesne (1997) analyzed the conceptions and ideas of citizenship in a group of French people in the Parisian region, and consequently suggested two major 'models' of French definitions of citizenship: citizens by *heritage* and citizen by *scruples*. In the former position, membership in a natural community – the nation – and the ties between fellow-citizens as a natural succession of generations, rooted in the French soil, were the defining characteristics of citizenship. In the latter, the ties were arbitrary, and each citizen was first and foremost a human being, forced to organize her life within boundaries whose legitimacy she did not recognize. Respect towards others impelled her to make an effort, even a minimal one, to participate in the polity. Age was one of the best explanatory factors to which model dominated each actor's discourse: the youngest informants were more prone to be citizens of scruples, marked by a strong trend of individualization. According to Duchesne, the two models of 'citizenship *à la française*' had, however, a common feature compared to other countries: Citizenship was, in both cases, an inflexible status. There was no possibility of multiple, potentially competing citizen identities, but only one way to treat the questions of identity and belonging: in relation to the national community (ibid. 310, 313–19, 327–9). In Duchesne's words, 'one either belongs to something, and that is to the nation as well as all its echelons, with more or less intensity –; or one belongs to nothing at all' (ibid. 330, my translation).

In order to fully understand or evaluate Duchesne's argument, the sense of belonging she talked about should be clarified. Compared to Duchesne's findings, the Lyonnais activists were certainly closer to 'citizens by scruples', but they did not, however, quite 'fit' in it. In fact, citizenship was for them almost a pejorative word, a word marked by a binary position: one between the citizens and the non-citizens.

Their emphasis on the gravity of immigration regarding the question of French citizenship, and the various manners through which they explained why they did *not* want to call themselves citizens, indicated that they defined citizenship as an extremely inflexible notion that carried such a heavy load of pre-definitions that it was safer to decline using it altogether, rather than to engage in giving it new meanings. Nonetheless, this definitely did not mean that they felt they did not belong anywhere. Julien, among many others, stressed the options of 'belonging' by wondering whether he was a citizen of Lyon, of the neighborhood, or what, but ended up concluding he was an *individual in a society*. This was not an isolated, atomistic position, but instead, Julien like nearly everybody else, stressed the importance of engaging locally, acting collectively, and strengthening immediate ties.

The rights and duties of the 'civic action citizens' in Helsinki

In the beginning of this chapter, I cited Henna, a squatter activist in her early twenties:

> 'It [citizenship] is really a part of my identity. ... And as a citizen, in my opinion, I also have the rights and responsibilities. ... It [citizenship] is maybe easy to define ... through society. ... Or I can think that I'm a citizen of the Helsinki city.
>
> Q: So what does citizenship of Helsinki mean?
> A: Well, it means also a great deal. ... I have like a number of roles in my life, but it all happens here in this town. ... So my responsibility is for example to keep this place tidy and safe and so. And then about rights, I think I also have the right to enjoy it.'

Henna's way of framing citizenship was very typical among my interlocutors in Helsinki. Her approach was a rather personal one: citizenship was part of her identity, it belonged to her, and its consequences were also very closely intertwined with her life. Interestingly, she also evoked the idea of local citizenship that further deepened the connection of the notion to her daily doings. Many activists I interviewed in Helsinki joined her in what she said, and how she said it. In contrast to the reluctant tones of the Lyonnais, in Helsinki they spoke of citizenship and its dimensions with a lot of ease and even self-evidence. For the activists in Helsinki, the principle frames of citizenship seemed to be rights and responsibilities, closely intertwined with the idea of civic activity. Often both were used, and the two frames intertwined or at least coexisted in the activists' talk.

In addition, the idea of a citizenry that very organically constituted the society often emerged. For example Tomi, an activist in his early forties from an urban environmentalists' group, saw the constitution of the society and of the self as parallel processes that joined in the idea of citizenship:

> 'I guess it is about ... how one is in the world as a human and as a city dweller, that's what one is as a citizen, that one takes responsibility [of things], elsewhere than just on one's own lot. ... Then there are, of course, different roles and different people, even though everybody is not so active, they still have this contact and that's how the society holds together, through these loops that go in different directions.'

In the constitution that Tomi sketched, not everybody needed to be citizens the same way. The most active ones created the contact network, or the ensemble of contacting 'loops,' for everybody, for the society not to fall apart. These thoughts evoke the idea of a society project, a collective building challenge, one in which every citizen joined the common effort to the best of one's ability. The old nation building virtues seemed to be not far away at all. Tomi's was not a radically challenging, political description of citizenship. On the contrary, he talked about civic action that helped hold the society together.

Furthermore, the two historical poles of the development of Finnish citizenship – citizens as the target group of a civilization project, and citizens as cultural actors and a kind of cultural attaché of the nation – emerged in the activists' talk as well. In the following, Mira, a city-district association leader in her mid-thirties, described the duality of her relation to the notion of citizenship:

> 'If I think of it from a national angle, it means to me things like language and a cultural background, as it is just a fact that one is born somewhere. Then on the level of a kind of active citizenship, I have grown to this activity, and because of my family, ... hanging out in associations has been sort of familiar to me, it has been easy to go there.'

The national level of citizenship, then, signified a rather passive status in which the linguistic and cultural background was a given fact, and that was about all there was to it. But there was another level: the level of active citizenship that in Mira's, and many others', mind was an activity carried out in associations. In Mira's case, the facility of acting in voluntary associations was a family heritage, but it is probably quite safe to assume that for most Finns, a general cultural 'heritage,' or a widely shared cultural toolkit concerning the form of collective action renders acting in associations a natural choice (see Chapter 2 in this book). The idea of politicization and political citizenship was, however, not central to Mira's way of framing citizenship either, even if associations naturally carry the potential of politicization.

Political citizenship was, however, not completely absent from the Finnish activists' talk. In the following, Irina, a local ATTAC activist in her early thirties, made a clear connection between citizenship and the starting point of a social movement:

> 'Citizenship concretizes and crystallizes pretty well what is the concern. In the time of neo-liberalism, it's like we're only consumers or perhaps judicial subjects to some extent and so, ... all in all, the political sphere was narrowed terribly. ... It [alter-globalist activism] was a defense of the kind of citizenship, or of the existence of political citizenship exactly.'

Irina's definition evoked the possibilities of citizenship as the direct moving power of politicization. Irina was surely not alone in thinking this way, but the activists rarely made this connection when talking about citizenship. In sum, the notion of citizenship mainly made them think of rights and duties in a somewhat 'textbook fashion,' or of their own activities from a viewpoint of building, maintaining, and securing the society.

It is noteworthy, in light of the comparison to the French activists, that my interlocutors in Helsinki were, all in all, conspicuously comfortable with the notion of citizenship. Participating in the polity was for them a recurrent example of citizen rights, and nearly everybody referred to voting as a citizen duty. In addition, they nevertheless seemed to discern citizenship not as coercive and given, but something that was theirs to define, and they brought a great variety of viewpoints to it. It was clearly a positive, even cherished word for them, and the duties of 'serving the nation' – or the city, for that matter – that it implied were agreeable to them. The questions of citizenship and acting as a citizen did not seem to relate directly to immigration issues in the activists' minds. Even though they would otherwise have expressed concern about intolerance and racism against immigrants, this theme did not figure when they talked about citizenship, neither did allusions to nationalistic extremism.[6] Instead, they linked citizenship directly to their own activities – citizenship enjoined them to vote, but in particular to be activists, and they were fulfilling their duty as citizens through participation in the local social movements. In sum, they gave a strong impression that citizenship was a concept they 'owned' and felt comfortable with. Citizenship was no trouble at all for them.

The ways the French and Finnish activists framed the concept of citizenship included elements that help understanding the processes of politicization – for instance, in the sense of creating or not creating space for conflict and questioning. Further clarification of these elements requires turning from the activists' rather state-bound ideas of citizenship back to the local level, and back to the activists' doings. In the following, I examine the local mechanisms of politicization by analyzing the ways in which gender figured in the activists' talk about the local civic practices.

3.2 Gender dynamics of local civic practices

Gender non-trouble in Helsinki

Among the activists in Helsinki, gender was not 'an issue' that would have often arisen in discussions in the activist groups, or would have been taken up by the activists themselves in the interviews. Also, questions concerning gendered practices were difficult ones for me to pose, and seemingly a little awkward for most of the activists to answer (for a similar account, see Holli *et al.* 2007). Their answers were often short – contrarily to the Lyonnais activists, who typically gave lengthy explanations on this topic – and left me with the feeling that gender was not a topic we should have been talking about; it was not really worth discussing. The activists were, however, not hostile towards the topic, but rather, it seemed to me that they answered patiently, as if they had a habit of it, and as if they felt that this was a question I had to ask and they had to answer, but that the whole procedure was actually a mere ritual. The important questions about local activism were elsewhere.

The 'ritualistic' answers the activists gave had converging features with results from my own previous studies in Finnish municipalities, but they also resembled the discourses Suvi Salmenniemi observed among activists in Tver, Russia (Salmenniemi 2005; Luhtakallio 2007). Quite generally, the Finnish activists understood my questions concerning gendered practices within activism as inquiries of the gendered repartition of the activist groups on the one hand, and gendered division of labor on the other. They all seemed to have 'in their toolkits' the idea that it was not good if the gender repartition was unbalanced and uneven. Thus, they either proudly reported their group was in balance, or apologetically looked for reasons why it was not. But to the questions about how gender mattered in their activities, only few could think of anything significant. If they did, they turned from gendered practices and structures to individual people and their gender, and so doing, mostly talked about women. Seeing gender as a structure seemed to be quite unfamiliar to the activists I met in Helsinki.

In Salmenniemi's study, the Russian activists predominantly combined gender essentialism and gender neutrality (2005, 739). These accounts were rather common among the activists in Helsinki as well. In the following, Jarmo, a Pro Municipal Services activist, gave his account of gender after having told me it did not play a role in the practices of his activist group that was equally constituted of women and men:

> 'Well, in general, women are better people than men, they have a more social mind. ... It's perhaps the woman's responsibility over the everyday things in a family ... and the man decides over the big issues, UN membership and the like, and women decide over what we shall eat.'

Jarmo's wisecracking juxtaposition of the gendered division of labor between 'UN membership' and 'what we shall eat' had, in my view, two purposes: first, it was an apologetic way to tell me, a woman of a younger generation, that Jarmo was aware of being 'a little old fashioned' and, secondly, that the question of gender differences was not an important one in the context of activism. After all, he had already told me there were even numbers of women and men in the group, and that he himself was all for making the coffee and thus no gendered division of labor really existed. In sum, Jarmo exaggerated somewhat in order to make me understand that my question was a little stupid, and that I should know the answer anyway: I had participated in the meetings and activities of Jarmo's group, and thus should have seen with my own eyes there was no 'gender trouble' there.

A series of variations of this standpoint dominated the talk about gender in the interviews, and if the degree of essentialism was perhaps somewhat generation-based, seeing gender as insignificant to civic practices was not. Irina's explanation illustrated this in multiple ways. When I asked her about gendered practices she first turned to talking about numbers of actual men and women, but later also reflected on the lack of gender perspective in her group's actions:

> 'I must have often been [the only woman], well, Pinja was sometimes along, but anyway, maybe in the beginning there were more men.

But I don't believe that in our group, it was in anyway, it was more of a coincidence. And then it happened that Tiina and Mari and Leila[7] came along, and it didn't... in that activity of ours, I don't see anything gender-sensitive in it.

Q: Did it affect the activities in some way if there first was a male majority and then a female one, did it change something?
A: No, not in my opinion. The things we talked about and did, in some way, they were not [gender-related]. But then there have been these actions within ATTAC, ... concerning for instance how neoliberalism has affected especially women's status in the world and so, but in those things we did, I don't see it...
Q: It did not come up substantially...
A: No, no, indeed it was so. It's like, when you're acting pretty much in the marginal, and you have to do all that briefing and research work yourself if you wanted to talk about things and find out, well, in my view, the spirit was rather expertise-bound. And in the public discussions, as well as at the festivals, there were men and women alike, so I don't see that there was anything like that.'

In her choice of words, gender sensitivity seemed to mean gendered practices, but she never really got to talk about them, except for saying there was none. The substantial 'gender issues', such as neoliberalism's consequences to women, were taken care of by other groups within the same association. In Irina's group, these issues did not figure. She concluded by saying that in the public appearances, the group included men and women equally.

The projection of problems concerning gender and equality 'elsewhere' is a repeated feature in Finnish gender discourse (see e.g. Holli *et al.* 2003, 2006), but Irina produced another kind of projection: that of 'the gender issue' being taken care of elsewhere. With this move, she showed that her thinking, as well as her group's actions, fulfilled the 'requirements' of Finnish gender equality, and hence were in concordance with the hegemonic discourse of an 'existing gender equality' (Holli 2003, 15–16; Holli *et al.* 2006, 184–5): gender was not ignored, as someone else was 'doing it', and as the group itself had accomplished inherent gender equality (naturally and by itself), and there was not 'anything like that,' meaning gender inequality, discrimination or other sorts of 'trouble.' Gender just did not happen to be part of the substantial business of Irina's group, since it concentrated in building expertise and credibility. The latter two, then, were widely shared tools of success among the Finnish activists, as I suggested in Chapter 2. In Irina's address, the opposition between taking gender-specific substantial issues into account, and doing hard work in an 'expertise-bound' spirit was, in my view, an indication of two things. First, gender issues – and the potential sources of gender conflict they contained – were not part of the things that improved a group's expertise and credibility (see also Holli 2003, 18). And second, expertise was, apart from being the winning ticket on the Finnish public sphere, also almost the antithesis of a conflict, or at least a certain type of conflict, and hence, also to some extent the antithesis of politicization. The activists undoubtedly strove for expertise in order to open contention, but expertise itself often required avoiding conflicts, and thus, at a minimum, also partly avoiding substantial themes that were too volatile.

Nevertheless, it seemed that the gender conflict was especially to be avoided *within* the groups. The rare remarks concerning gender practices within the groups that noted any differences whatsoever, mainly stressed that the differences were harmless, petty things that caused no real trouble, thanks to the existing equality. Henna described the division of labor among the squatters:

> 'Well, it's true that men are often more apt to the repair works, it's that there are actually people that work at construction sites and they have tools and stuff. And then every time we start making the food, or go to the market to buy stuff, well, it's always one of us women, so that these things go a bit like that. So maybe one should oppose those kinds of things as well, but it doesn't really matter now, because anyway, everybody's treated equally, and not in any gendered way.'

Henna was one of the few among my Finnish interlocutors who called herself a feminist – the rarity of this identification was not a surprise, knowing the particularly negative label of feminism in Finland even in comparison to France (Holli 2003, 16–17). She sounded a bit guilty while talking about the somewhat traditionalist division of labor – it was difficult for her to admit that in the progressive, radical group of hers 'things go a bit like this.' She concluded, however, that despite the fact that she felt she should have done something about these practices, it was not pressing, because equality already existed anyway. Equality, then, equaled gender neutrality: to be treated equally was to not to be treated 'in a gendered way.'

There were, however, a few occasions in which the Helsinki activists reflected a little more profoundly on gender in their groups. One of these occasions was with Tomi, who, contrarily to most others, further reflected the gendered practices and the inherent gender structure of his group:

> 'We have some long-term activists ... sometimes we may meet each other, and just the other day we were astonished when we had a meeting at my place, and all of a sudden there were some seven boys around the table only. But then in the next meeting there were more women again. So, maybe it shows in something like that, it's the degree of freaky, that if we really get to the point in something like architecture or philosophy, it's when there are a lot of men present. Such originals! And then in discussions about a bit more moderate topics, there are women. ... But I'm not, ... let's say that I think it's more allowed for men to develop this kind of characteristics to their extremes. ... Somehow women always have a kind of a social sense of things like ... how to be with people and so on, ... and then ... we have this half-autistic genius, who can develop the wildest ideas but ... he takes so much space to himself that it gets a little, it takes a lot of balancing.'

In Tomi's address, the analysis moved from the habitual head counting to reflections of gendered practices of the group meetings. He described how the atmosphere, and even the themes of discussion, changed depending on, mainly, whether there were women present or not. The expressions he used were easy to recognize from Finnish cultural repertoires of gender stereotypes, and also from my own experiences from the atmosphere at different Finnish activist scenes. Listening to him, I felt I knew exactly what he was talking about: the effective, socially aware, moderate, but perhaps a little boring women who knew how to be with people, and wanted to get the meetings going in an organized way, versus the perhaps a bit difficult and even irritating, but creative, crazy, even 'genius' men with such original ideas. In sum, Tomi laid before us the entire landscape of attitudes lurking underneath the neutral, all-equal surface of the civil society. Tomi talked with a humorous note, and his strong expressions, such as the 'degree of freaky' and 'half-autistic genius' were full of irony, even self-irony. He took the analysis of gender practices further than anyone else by explicitly abandoning the essentialist interpretation of gender: In his – very constructivist, if not performativist – opinion, men developed these characteristics to the extremes because it was culturally more acceptable for them than for women. Nevertheless, his description did not point towards a politicization of the gender practices of the group, but rather lamented a partly unsatisfactory state of the art.

In sum, in the ways the Helsinki activists talked about gender and gendered practices, the momentums of politicization were mainly absent. Words like 'discrimination' were unmistakably replaced by ambiguous expressions of treating people in 'gendered ways,' or assuring there was not 'anything like that,' or that, 'but I'm not' (a macho, a sexist, or simply un-egalitarian). Apart from few exceptions, substantial gender issues were regarded, politely, as important, but not part of the key issues of contention of the group in question – any of the groups, for that matter. Naturally, there were feminist groups in Helsinki that concentrated in discussing gender-related topics, and organizing events, such as the annual 'Women's city' forum. But feminist actions were mostly set apart from collective action that had other core substantial issues, and attempts to bring feminist issues into discussions often failed, or to the least faded away with scarce results, a bit similarly to my attempts at discussing the matter with the activists.

Politicized gender conflicts in Lyon

The situation in Lyon was dramatically different. The Lyonnais activists talked about gender practices all the time, and when talking to me, it was one of the topics they elaborated on the most willingly and with lengthy stories, analyses, and reflections. Gender caused a lot of friction among and within the activist groups. The activists, especially women, but also many men, were very conscious of gendered power relations and discriminatory practices within the activist groups. They told me numerous stories of gender discrimination within the groups, and conflicts concerning gender. They also talked about their attempts to introduce new, anti-discriminatory practices, and reflected on the constantly changing gender dynamics of the activist scenes. There was nothing awkward about posing these questions to the activists – their enthusiasm for debating gender was catchy.

Contrarily to the activists in Helsinki, the Lyonnais generously admitted that both within the activist milieu, and in the French society in general, gender equality was anything but achieved, and that several serious problems, in particular in the position of women, needed constant attention. The stories of gender discrimination in the activist groups were 'text book cases': men dominated in meetings, women's speech was interrupted, and the division of labor in squats and events was traditionalist. In the following, Cloé made an overview:

> 'The man–woman inequalities are, I must say, super flagrant in the activist milieu ... . On the conversational level it's the speech time, it's flagrant, we counted once with a friend of mine: so a girl speaks for a minute, for a man it's easily going to be five minutes, it's completely disproportional. And then ... it's also sharing the ... tasks, you know, and who do we have in the kitchen? Who talks to the media?'

Cloé's construction of the problem (Bacchi 1999) was the opposite of Henna's: in her view, the gendered division of labor was an indicator of the 'flagrant' problems in gender equality. She continued with a story that had 'opened her eyes' to the gender inequalities in the activist milieu. In addition, it was also a story of a conflict with consequences:

> 'It was at a meeting ... where we discussed ... the perspectives [of a squat] and so there's a round table, everybody speaks, and I take the floor and I propose a few things, and bang, OK, we pass to the next speaker, and to the next, and then this guy says exactly the same thing I had just said, I mean exactly the same. And ... for me, the reaction [of the others present] was like "yeah ok," whereas for him, it was a generalized "oh yeah, what a super-duper idea" and stuff. So at that moment, I stood up, because ... if we have to wait for a guy to propose something for it to be heard, ... I said to myself, OK, there's really a problem here, finally we are considered differently even though everybody conceives of themselves anti-sexists ... no, there's something that doesn't work.
>
> Q: Right. And the reaction when you stood up?
> A: Well, they were ill at ease, it was like "oh shit" but well ... that didn't change them for that matter. But ... the feminist milieu in Lyon has had a big impact on general activism, because having followed it chronologically, [I can say that] ... there were things that really didn't pass at all that little by little have entered the current language of an average activist. ... I think it has ... had a hell of an ... influence, ... you see, ... there are those who have learned some things, who have reacted, there are nevertheless quite a few of those men, and then there are other men for whom feminists are in all cases just pain in the ass. ... But the youngest ones, I have the impression that they

understand more quickly because it's beginning to be a little bit more achieved. But then, it suffices to lose the vigor just a little bit and BANG, we're going to have to start all over again.'

Even if Cloé was quite critical of the current state of equality in the activist milieu, she acknowledged that the feminists, herself included, had had an influence over the years. It was easy to believe this, as the 'current language of an average activist' in Lyon was indeed quite gender conscious, at least compared to the one I heard in Helsinki. Not only did the activists, men included, voluntarily reflect on the issue, but many of them also applied gender-conscious terminology in analyzing the practices of the 'general activist milieu'. However, particularly noteworthy in Cloé's address, from a comparative perspective, was the ending of her story. She said gender equality, or sensitivity, was 'more achieved' than it used to be, but concluded right after that she in no ways saw this as a stabile state of affairs. Instead, she saw the struggle against gender discrimination as a continuous one – and this was the case with other political struggles as well.

Listening to other activists confirmed that Cloé was not an exception in her thinking. I did not get to meet any really 'flagrant' machos – on the one hand, because most of the men really seemed to have an understanding of a basic level of gender consciousness, and they applied it carefully when talking to me. But on the other hand, it was because the tendency, familiar from the Finnish case, to project problems to at least a small distance from oneself, also emerged in Lyon. Julien was one of the male activists balancing between the gender consciousness he obviously was determined to deploy, and the characteristics of his own milieu that he tried to give a fair account of:

> 'In fact, the problem in Lyon is, ... at least in the circles I'm in, that there are not that many women, I find that the activist movement in Lyon is rather masculine. I mean, at the Radio Canut, ... we are ... about a hundred DJs, there are four women. And similarly, ... in demonstrations, ... it's true that you find quite few women in that milieu. So I don't know if men and women have a different manner of contention or if it's rather just so that it's from the beginning a rather masculine, and almost masculinist movement, ... I think that good many libertarians have this little trait, ... not macho but a little virile I think. ... And the women maybe don't feel comfortable with the side "we make a front against the bosses and we sing songs and then we drink beer." ... But I see for instance at the CNT,

> there is virtually only guys ... and anyway it hasn't been so much as six months or a year since they began to talk about what it means to be a woman or a unionist, and ... how to come down to getting rid of sexist attitudes ... . Because indeed there is, even if it's not sexism, it's these practices anyway, if only giving the floor to girls, that kind of things ... . It's exactly that: how to take into account ... the specificity of the feminist struggle.'

Julien's primary explanation to gender-related problems was the small number of women in the groups he was in. He thus alleged that it was more a question of majorities than anything else, even though he also seemed to have doubts that there was something about the movement that was particularly masculine, and thus unattractive to women. He made efforts, however, not to make it sound 'that bad': the movement was not 'macho' but 'virile,' it was perhaps not sexist, but the practices were unfair. In any case the men did not mean any harm – they just liked doing things women felt uncomfortable with. Julien's description of the latter was a bit surprising knowing the predominant style of women activists in Lyon (and knowing the women Julien knew): they were not exactly the kind to turn down a drink, or turn reluctant to oppose the 'bosses' or to sing revolutionary songs. However, the most striking part of his description, especially with the comparison to Helsinki in mind, was his almost apologetic account of the backward phase of progress in the movement. This virile, 'masculinist' bunch of guys had started to think about how to get rid of sexist attitudes only a while ago. But they were thinking about it, and there was debate on how to take into account the feminist specificities within the movement's contention.

Nina Eliasoph (1998) has noted that the American activists she studied had to struggle to learn to valorize political talk and discussion, but when they did, it was a medium of change and development in the groups: When they let themselves, they learned through discussing (ibid. 166, 170–3). In the Lyonnais case, the activists did not have the burden of 'proving' the importance of talk – it was inherent to their understanding of activism – and the case of gender consciousness illustrated clearly the transforming power of talk. In contrast, the Finns resembled more their American colleagues in this respect.

Things did not, however, always go smoothly, and 'talk' about gendered practices often meant virulent arguments in Lyon. The topic that caused particular friction was the creation of 'non-mixed' spaces that had been part of the repertoire of Lyonnais feminists for quite some time. These for-women-only spaces were common in squats. The organization of 'non-mixity' was always an explosive undertaking, and it caused clashes both between women and men, and among women. In the following, Chazz gave his critical account of the practice:

> 'Well, there have always been radical feminists in Lyon, and on one of those [neighborhood] meals we organized, they wanted to have a non-mixed table. I found that completely idiotic, because why ... create spaces of exclusion, as if there weren't enough of them in Lyon or in France already. ... Why at a moment when we ... said OK, everybody eats together, the small, the big, the people of the neighborhood? ... When you're a feminist, all that, and because needs be, I open my eyes too, I see very well that the position of women even in France, well it's not Iran and all, but ... yeah, I think ... it's a totally legitimate discourse.'

Chazz's words, as well as his appalled tone when he spoke of non-mixity, made it easier to imagine the violent clashes everybody was talking about, than Julien's careful reflections. So what were the clashes like? An example that many activists from both 'sides' referred to as one of the biggest fights between the feminists and 'the rest' in recent years, was the seminar held for the 20th anniversary of *La Gryffe*, a bookstore that had a long history of serving as the information center for the local movements.[8] The three-day event had gathered together all the important branches of the local Leftist movements, and the topic of the final day's panel was the future of the movement. The seminar had also included several feminist debates, and the feminist activists were appalled to realize that the program of the concluding panel was comprised of male speakers only. A feminist group entered the session equipped with banderols saying 'sexist violence,' and sat in silence to oppose to the excluding composition of the panel. This intervention caused an outrage among both the organizers and part of the crowd, and the female activists were 'lynched with insults', as Cloé described. Solange, for her part, was also present and, for her, the incident turned out to be a very significant one:

> 'It was the twenty years of La Gryffe ... where there was this enormous dispute between the feminists and the guys, I mean, between the feminists and the other people ... and it provoked this kind of hyper vitriolic debate, where I heard all sorts of horrors ... and after having witnessed this monstrous bust-up, I wasn't sure whether

I agreed with the feminists or not, but in any case, what shocked me seriously was the violence of the reactions on the other side. That's when I told myself, if people like that react as violently as that, there must be something there, I need go digging into that, have to go and see.'

Solange said this event was the trigger for her own feminism. In her mind, if something caused as much hassle as the feminist action at La Gryffe, it was worth getting acquainted with. Her reasoning produced a simple formula of politicization: a public conflict fractures the habitual state of things and action, opens up a path of transformation, invites in new actors and viewpoints, and sets a context for political processes to work out new articulations of the society, of the 'good life,' or whatever the particular scene of conflict requires to be reconstituted. The example of La Gryffe was not important to Solange alone, nor was it the only one of the sort among the Lyonnais activists. Gender relations were the manifest illustration of the mechanisms of politicization the Lyonnais activists made constant use of. They were, in all their plurality – from the 'basic' conflicts concerning the division of labor to the complicated intersectional struggles for the inclusion of immigrant activists – the driving force of contention. Unlike the activists in Helsinki, the Lyonnais also valorized conflicts within the activist groups, recognizing more or less consciously that the politicization potential had to be 'kept alive' by allowing talk, allowing conflicts, and, indeed, allowing politics.

3.3 Citizenship, politicization, and the state

In this chapter, I have approached citizenship from two perspectives: first, by looking at the ways in which the local activists in Lyon and Helsinki framed the concept of citizenship, and the tools of politicization these framings gave them. Secondly, I examined conflicts concerning gender among the activist groups as illustrations of the mechanisms of politicization in the midst of 'doing citizenship' – in local civic practices.

In both contexts, talk about citizenship was illustrative of the image of the state the activists held. Their ideas of it varied in terms of flexibility. The French activists had an oppositional position to the state; they wanted to stay at arm's length from it. For them, citizenship represented the entire history – and present – of exclusions and injustices by the French republic: it made them think of the *Marseillaise*, the neo-Nazis and the extreme Right, the history of colonization, the mistreatment of immigrants. They did not feel they had the power to 'alter' the meanings of the concept the way they wanted to – citizenship was a concept 'owned' by the state, the political leaders, and 'the republic' that they treated as something completely – or wishfully – separated from them. In the French activists' definitions citizenship was a controversial political concept full of past, present, and potential conflicts.

The Finns, in contrast, were more prone to think they could define the 'level' of citizenship they affiliated with, and they moved comfortably between national-level rights and duties, and local-level activities. They were proud to be citizens. Citizenship was *their* property; it was their rights and duties, and their definitions of what it was to act for the common good. Despite this autonomy, their ways of defining citizenship echoed the historical foundations of the concept. Indeed, these were the dutiful subjects disposed to nation-building efforts and the merging of the state and the society (see Stenius 2002, 2010). While they were not apolitical as actors, their way of conceptualizing citizenship mainly was apolitical.

For the Finnish activists, acting as a citizen, which consisted of, for example, participating in local social movements, was a duty, a service to the nation and of the common good, 'doing one's bit.' For the French activists, being actively engaged in the society was a way of being in the world, a resistance, a necessity, and something they did not want to reduce to the concept of citizenship.

It has been argued that the essence of citizenship is the transcendence from particularity into the general (Dietz 1985, cited in Beasley & Bacchi 2000, 341). This transcendence is the key to the existence of public action, and, in fact, the public in itself (see e.g. Doidy 2005a; Alapuro & Lonkila 2012). The definitions the activists gave of citizenship were, in this sense, constitutive of the public sphere, and the processes of politicization in the two contexts. How did these differences of definition affect politicization in the two contexts?

The ways in which the activists in Helsinki framed gender partly resembled the essentialist and neutralizing discourses Suvi Salmenniemi (2005) observed among Russian activists. Salmenniemi's study was, however, conducted in an environment in which civic activity in general was considered a 'feminine' sphere, whereas institutional politics were more of a 'masculine' affair, and the construction of political agency was thus gendered to begin with (ibid. 738). This was not the case in Finland, or in France, as although political leadership was certainly considered masculine to varying degrees in both countries, and the field of civic activities was, perhaps, divided into different fields of activism that carried more feminine or masculine images, but it was not a predominantly masculine or feminine field of activity (more development on this theme in Chapter 4 in this book). Instead, the majority of actors in both contexts emphasized the importance of equal representation of both genders in the activist groups. Furthermore, something equivalent to the rare constructivist 'gender asymmetry' discourse Salmenniemi detected in Tver was rather common among the Lyonnais activists, but nearly absent from the activists' talk in Helsinki.

These elements strengthened the image of the possibilities of politicization in the two contexts. The gender 'harmony,' produced by an 'achieved state of gender equality' in the Finnish context, and the openness to gender conflicts in the French context, were illustrative of the very organizing principle that defines the different capacities of politicizing and moving between 'particularities' and 'generalities' in the two political cultures. On the one hand, the French orientation towards conflict made it possible to bring out the gender conflict, just as it makes possible other conflicts, and cultivates a political culture oriented towards a continuous struggle and non-finalized construction of the society (Rosanvallon 1998; Balibar 2001; Alapuro 2005a). The Finnish gender consensus, on the other hand, alleged a transparent, static society in which struggle and conflict were an anomaly of the 'normal', predictable status quo (see Alapuro 2005a). This idea makes conflicts dangerous and something to be avoided. The Finnish idea of already existing or already achieved gender equality is indeed one that 'effectively forecloses opportunities for political action' (Holli 2003, 18). Not only are political opportunities concerning 'gendered' topics foreclosed but also this 'non-trouble' and consensus illustrate the mechanisms of de-politicization typical of the Finnish political culture.

Hence, gender conflict is, in a sense, the conflict of conflicts, because it is both a struggle in its own right, also concerning the inherent practices and structures of political activism, and a struggle that is embedded in all substantial political struggles. This is why it is also perhaps the most tangible example of the de-politicizing mechanisms in Finnish political culture, as well as a powerful illustration of the potential for politicization in French political culture. The consequences are, of course, another story, as politicization does not equal automatically to 'good results' in this respect any more than in other topics of conflict (cf. Weber 2009 [1919]).

In the analyses of this and the previous chapter, the activists displayed their ideas concerning their citizen identity and their doings. In order to dig deeper in the mechanisms of politicization, however, we need to know more about the environment it happens in, and the other parties joining these politicizations, ignoring them, or arguing against them. In the following chapters, I open a gradually more dialogical point of view to the public spheres in Lyon and Helsinki, including in the analysis the representatives of the cities. Next, the focus is on the appearance of the tension between the local activists, and the representatives of the cities, as represented in the visual dimension of the local public spheres.

4
Visual Frames of Representing the Local Society

In the previous two chapters, activists I met in Lyon and Helsinki shed light on the principles of belonging, co-operating, and contesting, as well as shared their ideas concerning citizenship, civic practices, and the ways in which gender figured in these practices. Although the activists talked about the surrounding institutions and political establishment, and their activities addressed and were performed on the local public spheres, the emphasis was hitherto on the activists' points of view. In this chapter, I take a step further by including a wider range of actors and focusing on published visual representations. More exactly, this chapter is about the *framings* that visual representations portrayed of local contention on the one hand, and democratic governance and 'the good life' promoted by the city administrations, on the other.

I examine the competing ways of representing the local society visually in Lyon and Helsinki by juxtaposing visual representations collected from activist websites, and city information and promotional magazines.[1] How were the local societies represented? What kinds of political activities and civic practices were promoted in different media in the two contexts, and by whom? The counter-democratic styles portrayed in the activist imageries, and the styles of the representative government, illustrated the on-going definition struggles concerning local society in the French and Finnish contexts. How did visual representations take part in these processes? The 'impact' of images is not easy to detect, if at all possible, as images as such tend to escape fixed meaning. Therefore, specific attention must be paid to how to analyze visual representations sociologically, what to analyze in them, and what questions to pose on a visual research material. In order to meet these methodological challenges, I have proposed an application of Erving Goffman's frame analysis to analyze images in their social context by using *dominant* and *secondary* frames as interpretative tools (Luhtakallio 2003, 2005; see Methods Appendix). In the following, I briefly describe steps of the visual frame analysis, and present the material I use in this chapter. The following sections provide a comparative reading of the two sets of imageries as representations that framed the on-going local definition struggles about 'representing the society.'

4.1 Visual frame analysis revisited: steps of framing and keying

Cultural representations, be it speech, printed words or images, always speak from within a certain world, objectifying something collectively observed or experienced. Representation is a process of both reproduction and production of 'reality', or more accurately, the meaning of reality we form. It both articulates and contributes to social processes (e.g. Cowie 1994; Hall 1997a). Studying representations requires the simultaneous taking into account of the produced and productive nature of these processes. The images I analyze in this chapter are both cultural representations that a viewer needs to *frame* in order to understand what is going on and why, and framings realized by two groups of actors with presumably different motivations, ideologies[2] and goals. The following analysis is based on the idea that visual representations are primarily seen through *master frames* (see Goffman 1974) defined by the respective media: people interpreting the images are assumed to mostly know what they are looking at. The images in city magazines are first framed as 'messages by the city establishment,' whereas the activist imageries are framed as 'messages by the grass roots activists and groups,' and other framings take place more or less firmly within these master frames.

In addition to different master frames, the two sets of images differ in their original *raison d'être*. The activist imageries were produced and published by activists of the local civil society. They form a multifaceted ensemble of media creations, updated and used by the different voluntary associations, pressure groups and social movements acting in the local contexts to achieve a variety of goals. The websites are an important part of the alternative media – characterized by a varying level of radicalism, small-scale publishing, and non-commercial aims (Downing 2001; Atton 2002; cited in Kolářová 2004) – of the two contexts. Regarding recent studies concerning democracy, activism, and the Internet it is reasonable to claim that the web is increasingly becoming the most important alternative media source worldwide (cf. Papacharissi 2002; Bennett 2003; Dahlgren 2005). Also in Lyon and

Helsinki, websites were crucial sources of information concerning civic activities on most fields.[3]

The activist imageries were collected from multiple sources: I surfed several dozens of websites of locally active groups in order to collect a sample of depictions the activists themselves had produced of their activities, and copied all images I found.[4] Two sites formed the most important sources of images, either directly, or through links to events and groups: *Rebellyon* and *Megafoni*.[5] *Rebellyon* was a Lyonnais production, but the site also covered information from near-by cities, especially Grenoble. *Megafoni* was created and is partly updated by activists from Jyväskylä, a middle-sized town in central Finland. However, the majority of activist events in Lyon and Helsinki during my fieldwork period[6] were reported through these two sites and through links they provided, and the majority of images and stories on the sites were attached to events in Lyon and Helsinki. Therefore, a considerable part of images concerning activism, social movements, and collective contention in Lyon and in Helsinki were collected through these two sites. *Rebellyon* and *Megafoni* provided a good illustration of the local activist sites. Both of them functioned as information channels for activists, but also as link centers for a great variety of activist events and groups that had their own sites, too. They both stemmed from a particular tradition of local, as well as international, activism. *Rebellyon* stated openly that it it was a channel for 'the Lyonnais anti-authoritarian movement,' which was naturally only one *niche* of local activism in Lyon, although a rather important one. *Megafoni* refrained from acknowledgements of political color in their presentation. A closer look revealed, however, that the site was ideologically not so distant from its Lyonnais counterpart. In addition to these two examples, I searched through all the sites of local groups that were part of my fieldwork. There was more political variety in the ensemble of the other sites.

The city magazine imageries were the product of a municipal editorial staff. The magazines, *Lyon Citoyen* and *Helsinki-info*,[7] were distributed to all inhabitants of the cities. I collected images published in them from a two-year period.[8] These magazines, alongside different kinds of 'citizen portals' that currently appear on the websites of every other European city, can be seen as manifestations of new 'good governance,' marked by a claim of transparency and an ethic of the market in which the municipalities portray themselves much like firms, promising good service – information, possibilities of participation, and also entertainment – for their (tax payer) customers (aka citizens) (cf. Holli *et al.* 2007). They can be seen as part of the New Public Management approach to public administration that has become a popular model for governance reforms throughout Western polities in recent years, and furthermore, as an example of the fusion of politics and administration that Pierre Rosanvallon describes as one of the causes of the current erosion of democratic principles (Pollit & Bouckaert 2004; Rosanvallon 2006, 265). The two magazines differed somewhat in appearance: *Lyon Citoyen* was printed on glossy paper and imitated a magazine style, whereas *Helsinki-info* looked more like a newspaper.[9] The first observation, however, was that there was a striking resemblance in the contents of the two: most numbers had a mayor's column, feature stories presenting different municipal services, different neighborhoods, future architectural and zoning plans, and a calendar of cultural events. Visually, the covers in particular were extremely analogous in form and content, themes and esthetics. This feature is certainly at least in part due to the globally increasing uniformity in forms of media representations, and in particular the traditionally international esthetics of cover images, including in France and Finland (see Luhtakallio 2003). This said, however, it is not without significance that city information magazines in two countries propose such similar imageries to their readers.

In the activist websites, crowds assembled on streets in massive demonstrations, disguised activists performed and entertained in public, activists held seminars and squatted houses, police forces acted as a hyper-masculine threat of violence, and traces of these events told a tale of a constant, autonomous civic presence. In the city magazines, happy-looking men, women, and children appeared in colorful pictures studying dutifully, performing or attending high-class cultural events, or enjoying themselves in a sunny park. Politicians and city officials appeared assertive and trustworthy, and urban landscapes evoked ideas of fostering a glorious past and constructing a bright future.

These general observations were the grounds for analyzing the frames of these two sets of images, and for defining the *dominant frames* of the material: the common denominators of the 'at the first glance' meanings produced in the process of looking at the sets of images. As a second step, I organized the images thematically, following the denominators detected at the first reading, and made notes about the *secondary framings* that seemed to key – refine or redirect – the meanings the images produced when seen 'at second glance,' including attentive reading of the captions and headlines attached to the images.[10] I then sketched the titles for the frames based on these thematic categories. In the third phase, I went through the images frame by frame, double-checking the dominant frames, and simultaneously enhanced my notes of the secondary frames. Finally, I counted the frequency of the dominant frames in each set of images, and selected illustrative examples from within each dominant frame. Throughout the process of writing the analysis, however, I went back to the images to verify my interpretations (see Methods Appendix for a more detailed account).

The idea of calculating interpretative frames is at a first thought not a particularly 'Goffmanian' one, nor does it stem from the definition of representation I started off with. As Gillian Rose (2001, 66) has noted in her criticism of visual content analysis, frequency does not equal importance, or the 'density' of meaning in analyzing visual representations. Images make meaning and matter both through repetition and through uniqueness. However, as I wanted to keep the sample rather wide, and thus include different aspects – both the repetitive and the unique – of the visualized local public spheres, the basic quantification helped in the necessary moves back and forth in the steps of the analysis, keeping the basic dimensions of the material tangible.[11]

As for the 'comparability' of the two imageries, both sets had strong converging features – so strong that it was possible to operate with one set of dominant frames per imagery, even if the 'contents' of the frames, the keyings, and the secondary frames in them produced variation and difference. In the activist imageries there were framings that were almost or completely absent in one context while of relative importance in the other. Furthermore, some frames appeared less repetitively, less 'densely,' or mainly as secondary frames, in the one imagery, while occupying a more dominant place in the other.

I named the activist imageries' recurrent themes as dominant frames of *marking, demonstrating, violence, performing, working,* and *deliberating*. Their appearance in the imageries collected from Lyon and Helsinki is shown in Table 4.1.

Table 4.1 Dominant frames of activist imageries[12]

	Lyon	*Helsinki*
Marking	124	99
Demonstrating	67	72
Violence	28	22
Performing	7	41
Working	2	22
Deliberating	2	19
Total (*N*)	230	275

Counting the frame appearances revealed that in both contexts, marking was the most common frame in the activist imageries covering more than half of the French, and more than a third of the Finnish representations. It consisted of representations of markings or 'traces' left behind by the activists: banderols, 'tuned' outdoor advertisements, wall tags, broken windows, and the like. Another very common frame in both contexts was demonstrating. It represented crowds marching on city streets, gathered on squares, holding banners, shouting. The frame of violence contained more variation between the two contexts than the two former frames. The shared features of this frame were marked by signs of violence, or by threat of it, in particular on the behalf of the state-legitimized apparatus of violence: the police forces. The frame of performing consisted of representations of a variety of colorful, theatrical 'shows,' music performances, parties, and the like, organized on the streets, in shopping centers, or in squats. The frame of working included images portraying activists engrossed in renovation of old houses, gardening, or patching up second-hand clothing. The frame of deliberating consisted of representations of meetings, debates, and seminars.

As for the city magazine representations, I named their dominant themes as frames of *culture, cityscapes, occupations, representing, caring,* and *engaging*. Their appearances are shown in Table 4.2.

The dominant frame of culture was the most common framing in the city magazines. It consisted of representations of people engaged in various seemingly non-labor-related undertakings: outdoor recreation, hobbies and sports, and a plethora of different 'cultural' events. Cityscapes framed representations of city architecture and nature: images depicting the material environment without the presence of people. The dominant frame of occupations referred to representations of people 'at work,' either concretely at different working places, construction sites, and the like, or occupied by studying in schools, universities, and

Table 4.2 Dominant frames of city magazine imageries

Dominant frames	*Lyon Citoyen*	*Helsinki-info*
Culture	179	77
Cityscapes	53	65
Occupations	36	37
Representing	68	8
Care	14	19
Engaging	7	2
Total (*N*)	357	208

course centers. Representing was the frame of municipal politics and administration. This frame included two 'categories': representations of occasions of municipal services in which the administrative personnel were depicted executing their duty, and representations of municipal leadership – the personages of top politics and administration. These images, often loaded with different symbols of power, were much more repetitive in *Lyon Citoyen* than in *Helsinki-info*. The dominant frame of care consisted of representations of municipal social and health services, an abundance of them being images of children in contexts of 'being cared for.' Finally, the frame of engaging consisted of rare representations of civic practices, voluntary work, and associative activities.

In the following two sections, these dominant frames form the base for a comparative analysis of the counter-democratic visualizations on the one hand, and politico-administrative on the other.

4.2 Activist framings

Marking, demonstrating, violence

The most common frames of the activist imageries were closely interconnected. They were all representations of different aspects of demonstrating by and large – either actual demonstrations, markings and traces left behind once the procession was gone, or acts, threat, or consequences of violence that occurred during or after demonstrations. According to Charles Tilly's classic definition, a demonstration is an event in which 'some group displays its strength and determination in the presence of the public, of the agents of the state, and perhaps of its enemies as well' (Tilly 1978, 177). The demonstrations in this material did not, however, all quite fit in the definition. Most importantly, the place of demonstration in the collective social imaginaries (see Castoriadis 1975; Taylor 2004) was very different in the two contexts.

Indeed, demonstrations have different 'sources' of reference in the French and Finnish contexts. There is no way of accessing social imaginaries as such, but imagining answers to questions like 'what is the first thing emerging from the collective memory as a reference to a hurtling crowd on a city street?' is illustrative. In France, demonstrations belong to a strongly positive reserve of collective memory. Starting from the revolution – tearing down of the Bastille and the power of the tyrants as the great achievement of the people acting collectively – crowds on the streets make reminiscence of positive direct action and democracy. The imaginary of demonstrations stems from a source of great national pride. Furthermore, the labor movement, as well as many other struggles of the 20th century, in particular the spectacular contentions of May 1968, join the heritage of the revolution in the sense of making demonstrations a self-evident and widely accepted part of French political culture. The French mainstream media has a generally approving attitude towards demonstrations, although the tones of reporting and the degree of enthusiasm depend on the political color of the publication. Nevertheless, it is clear that the urban riots of especially the 2000s have altered the imaginary concerning demonstrations. The Right-wing media in particular has passed judgment against both the riots and increasingly also other demonstrations, and it is evident that demonstrations as well as other types of contentious action by citizens with an immigrant background are not as easily seen as part of the proud French tradition of the will of the people on the streets (see Hamidi 2010).

In Finland, on the contrary, the general strike of 1905, and the labor movement demonstration marches during and after it lost their chance of creating a positive signifier, as they were soon followed by an extremely bloody civil war. Even before the civil war broke out, however, the leading elite regarded demonstrations as dangerous. This hostility has to do with the ideological base of nation building in Finland from the 19th century onwards, dominated by a vision of a citizenry educated and united by the elite (see Chapter 3 in this book). In this context of state making, a people with opinions of its own, and will and capacity of displaying them in public was not a positive sign of a nascent democracy, but a dangerous indication of 'dark forces' lurking among the masses, threatening the order and ideals of the society. Following the same logic, Finnish mainstream media has from the days of the general strike to the present preserved its traditional hostility towards demonstrations (Alapuro 1989; Lindström 2009). Nevertheless, the 1960s and 1970s student demonstrations have a somewhat mythical role in the Finnish collective memory. The imagery of the occupation of the Helsinki university student house in 1968 is probably among the most marking visual references for a demonstration. However, the 'heritage' of the 1960s is controversial: It carries the weight of the era of *finlandization,*[13] and the Leftist movement of the time was stained by its cooperation with the Soviet Union, and labeled as heavily erroneous by the Right-wing and Centralist currents that took over political power in the 1980s.

Considering these historical and contextual differences in the imaginaries of demonstration the similarities of the activist frames in Lyon and Helsinki were striking. The dominant frame of marking, first, portrayed representations of different traces the activists and their actions had left behind. Sometimes it intertwined completely with the frame of demonstrating, showing the demonstrators 'in action,' making the markings, but mainly these images did not include people. Instead, they depicted banderols, tagged walls, 'tuned' outdoor advertisements, and broken property, mainly windows. The images documented the symbolic dimension of demonstration: whereas 'the emblematizing of the grand spectacle endures only the flow of the cortège,' traces remain, and continue the 'game of hijacking' city space, or simply leave behind destruction (Collet 1982, 174). Which of the two – occupying space or destructing – it represents also depends on the viewer. The initiated know the meaning of the markings even afterword, whereas for the spectators and outsiders, it may seem to be only a broken window or a dirtied wall. 'We were here,' the eternal message of urban wall writing, was at the core of these representations. Illustrations 1a–d show two ways in which the activists used space as 'a language' (ibid. 176).

Illustration 1 The dominant frame of marking in Lyon (a, c) and in Helsinki (b, d)

As visual representations published on the websites, the markings were, first, proof of a victory. They were evidence that the activists had managed to occupy a space, leave a trace, and not pass unnoticed even after they left the spot. In this sense, the representations framed as marking were an example of purely indexical signs, ones capable of making present the object they were connected to (e.g. Silverman 1983, 19–30). Secondly, this frame represented a vigilant presence: the activists had their hand on the city. Their message was an abiding one: whatever the theme of protest, it would not go away as quickly as the procession passed. Especially Illustrations 1a and b represent 'shouts' that had remained echoing on the walls. In addition, the examples carried a very similar message: the wall writings 'Solidarity with the undocumented [immigrants]' ('*Solidarité avec les sans*-papiers', Illustration 1a, Lyon) and 'Stop the deportations!' ('*Karkotukset seis!,*' Illustration 1b, Helsinki) both took a stand on the treatment of undocumented immigrants.

Illustrations 1c and d could more easily get the interpretation of mere vandalism. Images of this kind were, at first view, surprising to me. I wondered why the activists would want to publish broken windows, and other traces that in my understanding were more 'bad publicity' than anything else. Breaking and destroying is rather univocally condemned in mainstream media, as well as by a great deal of activist groups. Finnish social movements, in addition to their overall peaceful tradition of demonstrations, have also been particularly respectful of private (and public) property (Siisiänen 2002; Alapuro 2005a). The recent deviances of this rule – like the numerous examples in this material – have resulted in furious anti-activist reactions in the public opinion that confirm the virtual sanctity of property in the Finnish context (see Hoikkala & Salasuo 2006; Lindström 2009). Also in France, destruction was widely condemned during the suburban riots of 2005. In particular, attacks against public libraries, and the massive burning of cars received a public denouncement. This degree of destruction was, and still is, unknown of in Finland. In France, breaking a window or two, or filling the yard of the presidential palace with rotten tomatoes, or the like, have been a routine part of the demonstration culture – that the degree of havoc during the suburban riots only pushed further than before. In this sense, despite their visual uniformity, the representations of the frame of marking were far more radical in the Finnish context than in the French one. In the Finnish context, these representations were a sign of change in the repertoires – a change from the traditionally Finnish ones to repertoires of 'international' activism, for example, those in use in France.

Similar trends emerged in the dominant frame of demonstrating. First, the representations within this frame, too, looked very much alike in both contexts. Secondly, especially the representations keyed by a secondary frame of violence had a different cultural 'sounding board' in the Finnish context.

The act of demonstrating is a corporeal one, and the representations of the frame of demonstrating were indeed 'incorporated' in many ways: they depicted masses of human bodies, staged bodies in motion, and also at times represented particular bodily features. Representations of human bodies are always, and often primarily, gendered – whether the signs of gender are clear or blurred, the question of gender is present, inscribed on the body surface (Valenius 2004, 52). Thus, the gender seen 'on' the bodies depends more on cultural meanings of gender than on the factual sex of the body in question. These cultural meanings were intertwined with the meanings of demonstration in the two contexts. Representations of the frame of demonstrating were performances of gender in displays of demonstrating. At the same time, demonstrations were represented as acts of doing gender.

In the examples above, the performed gender was mainly male. This was the case in the majority of representations within the frame. The 'masses of bodies' naturally consisted of both men and women, but the figures that 'stuck out' from the crowd – the ones these representations displayed as occupying the foreground – were male. Occupying the foreground, then, represents leadership, courage, and sometimes aggression. The male vanguard marched together, first, as in Illustration 2a, forming representations of 'activist fraternities,' analogous to the signifiers of

(a) (b)

Illustration 2 Frame of demonstrating in Lyon: demonstration to support the decriminalization of cannabis in Spring 2006 (a) and in Helsinki: Euromayday march 2004 (b)

homoerotic masculinity common to a long tradition of political representations. Secondly, male bodies occupied the foreground alone, like in Illustration 2b, in which both the microphone in the hand of the man, and the perspective in which he was notably bigger than anyone else, emphasized his position as the leader of the massive crowd behind him.

Masculinity is as plural a category as femininity, and it is not the only thing defining male representations: the signs of gender, ethnicity, sexuality, ability and disability, age, and other visible physiological features cannot be isolated from one another, but interplay and affect the process of looking and giving meaning to images.[14] The meanings of these signs also change through new, differing representations (e.g. Nixon 1997, 297–8). Indeed, the male representations of leadership, courage, aggression, and fraternity in the activist imageries were quite different from for example the 'Herculean' males Johanna Valenius (2004) found in visual representations of nationalism. The activist male bodies rarely signified physical strength, but were, rather, skinny and feminine, and young. Hence, in both contexts, representations of male activists blurred and fractured traditions of representing masculinity. Even though activist men were represented as leaders, the signs of masculinity were very different from, for example, the ones in use in mainstream media to represent political leadership (see Luhtakallio 2003).

Representations of 'women in the lead' within the frame of demonstrating were rare. In the Lyonnais imagery there was not a single case in which women occupied the foreground alone. In a few cases, a group of men and women stuck out of the crowd. In the Finnish imagery, Illustration 3 exemplifies the difference between the ways in which male and female bodies occupied the foreground in the frame of demonstrating. First of all, there was no procession in sight behind the two female figures, and it was thus not evident that they were leading anybody. Secondly, even though the text in the banderol below them seriously informed of a 'strike' ('*Lakko*'), the women's slightly clumsy, playful gestures and smiley faces keyed the meaning of the image towards a secondary frame of the clowneries and fun of the frame of performance, and still further towards the widely recognized Western tradition of representing women 'like children' (see Goffman 1979).

As we have seen, representations of the frame of demonstrating were keyed with a number of secondary frames. Apart from the frame of marking and the frame of performance, as referred to above, the frame of violence also keyed them. Themes of demonstrating and violence were, as dominant frames, so closely interconnected that the transition from one to another was often blurred: scenes of demonstrations where trash cans

Illustration 3 The frame of demonstrating in Helsinki: demonstration demanding a raise to the student allowance in 2006

or cars burned, movements were explicit – as in pitching tiles – faces were angry, and the atmosphere aggressive in one way or another. The sign that most commonly transferred the dominant framing to the frame of violence was, however, the presence of the police. Police officers were depicted both with the demonstrators and by themselves, in portraits of police phalanx in riot gear, of troops of police vehicles, and of riot fences. Not all images including the police were framed as violence: There was a series of representations framed as performing, in which the police were an object of mockery. But as iIllustrations 4a and b illustrate, the dominant frame of violence was, in the end, easy to distinguish from the others, whatever the secondary frames.

These rather shocking images were typical of the frame. The 'faceless', robot-like police often outfitted in heavy riot gear and equipped with shields and arms (mis)used their overwhelming supremacy, both in numbers and in mass and strength, on the skinny, helpless and visibly unarmed activists, remorselessly on the losing side. The moral judgment of these representations was clear. The police were 'accused' of repressive practices and unnecessary heavy-handedness against the activists who were weak, unarmed and unequipped for the confrontation, and totally outnumbered in every occasion.

Apart from representations of repression, these were also icons of 'sufferings of the righteous': the activists who, whatever the cause of the particular contention, positioned themselves to be in favor of a

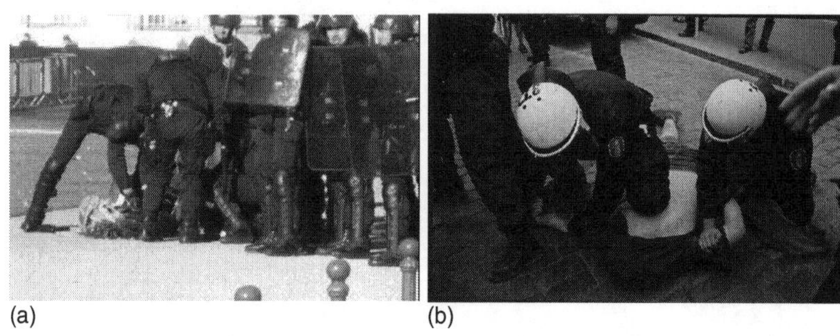
(a) (b)

Illustration 4 The frame of violence in Lyon: anti-CPE demonstration in Spring 2006 (a) and in Helsinki: Omega squat eviction in 2005 (b)

better, more just and equal world, were 'taking the blow' in the name of these values and of all the powerless they defended and stood for. In the course of the events, other kind of images certainly could have been taken of the cat-and-mouse game the activists often played, or had to play, with the police (see Chapter 2 in this book). The tile-pitching, provoking, and 'misbehaving' representations of activists that are often seen in the mainstream media coverage got their counter-representations in these images, showing the other side of the coin of violent demonstrations in the two cities.

Taking into account the secondary frames provided by representations of gender illustrates the ways in which gender is at the core of understanding the visual counter-democratic practices. With no way of verifying the actual sex of the people depicted in these images, these representations were nevertheless primarily representations of masculinity, or masculinity and femininity intertwined so that the former dominated. The military-resembling equipment of the police, as well as their actions towards the activists carried signs of masculine confrontation, a battle over physical strength. Two very different masculinities were, however, at play: a repressive, powerful, physically fit one, and a repressed, helpless, and weak one. The counter-democratic struggle was in these representations condensed as a struggle of two opposite types of masculinity, the masculine male, and its countertype, a fragile, feminine male. Marginal masculinities marked by blurred boundaries with the feminine (as well as the other way round) are 'dangerous' to a fundamentally heterosexual gender order, because they fracture it, if only by existing. These kinds of representations are agents of change: when masculinities and femininities are represented and repeated differently, the entire arsenal of possible gender representations change (de Lauretis 1987, 3–5; Rossi 2003, 111; Luhtakallio 2003, 139–40). In this sense, blurring the boundaries of masculinity is an effective counter-democratic practice that calls into question the legitimacy of the prevailing power structure. Doing this through visual representations is particularly powerful, as the 'argument' of these images is difficult to disprove.

What about blurring the boundaries of femininity then? Despite the strong similarities between the two imageries, within the frame of violence both contexts had secondary frames of their own that had to do with representations of femininity, as Illustrations 5a and b exemplify.

In the French imagery, the keying approached news coverage from war zones rather than photos of local collective action and demonstrations, with images of chaos, running gunmen, havoc, and injured people. The axes of masculinity and femininity were, instead of blurred, firmly 'in their place' in these images: representations of women were few, and they nearly resembled religious portraits of the suffering of woman, often 'as mothers.' In Illustration 5a, a female activist, in tears, was trying to help a wounded man on the ground, with blood running from his head, in the midst of a smoky chaos. Another man was bent down to help her, and three others, apparently civilian police, were running away with shotguns in the background.

In the Finnish imagery, on the contrary, there were examples of very different femininity: aggressive and masculine, as Illustration 5b shows. The group of activists confronting the police in this image consisted of

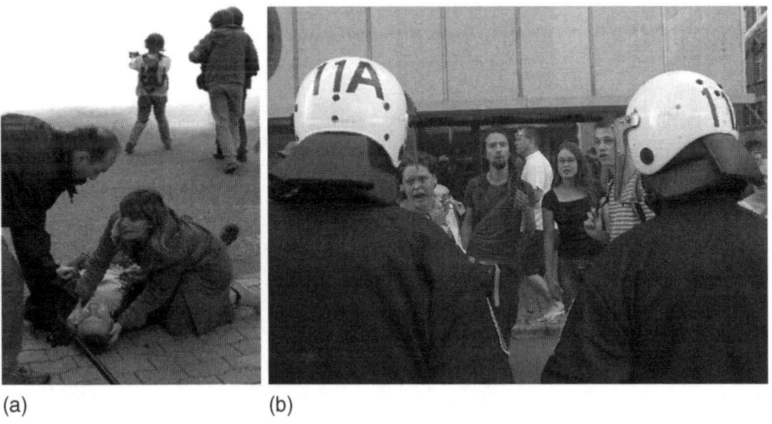

(a) (b)

Illustration 5 Frame of violence in Lyon: anti-CPE demonstration in 2005 (a) and in Helsinki: demonstration for a raise in student allowance in 2006 (b)

two men and two women, and the 'leader' of the confrontation seemed to be the woman to the left, aggressively shouting at the police and bending towards them. The other three looked confused rather than aggressive. Hence, this was a rare representation of a 'Herculean' woman standing, if not alone, in the leading position against the oppressors. Although the gender conflict among the activists in Helsinki was an issue the politicization of which was next to impossible, two different femininities seemed to be possible in the visual representations of counter-democracy, whereas in the case of Lyonnais representations, these features were nearly absent.

Performing, working, and deliberating

The remaining three frames of the activist imageries, performing, working, and deliberating, displayed sceneries of counter-democracy that differed rather dramatically from the previous ones. Although especially the frame of performing was often connected to demonstrations, the primary emphasis of these frames was elsewhere: on the one hand, it was on the 'fun' side of activism – the festival, the party, and the spectacle – and on the other hand, it was on the 'serious' side – the working 'bees', the meetings, and the negotiations. These three frames, respectively in quite different manners, created bridges between the activist imageries and the city imageries.

If the previous frames offered insights into the masculinities and femininities in activist representations, the dominant frame of performing added in yet another keying: that of gender ambiguity. The frame of performing was dominated by either feminine, or explicitly gender-blending, ambiguous representations in which signs of neither femininity nor masculinity primarily oriented the meaning.

According to the environment of the performance, the representations differed in their degree of 'publicity.' Especially in the Finnish imagery, part of the frame 'happened' in nearly private scenarios. In these representations, activists often played music for other activists sitting as an audience. More commonly, though, performing happened before a 'wider' public. These public spectacles had features in common with the city magazines' frame of culture (see the following section), although the glitter and shine of the city magazines gave way to a more home-made, ragged, and improvised spectacle. Some performers were performing in a masquerade: they were disguised as clowns or other theatrical figures. Illustrations 6a and b show representations of 'clowneries' from the two contexts, keyed with gender-blurring secondary frames. These representations were a reminder of the tradition of fools and clowns

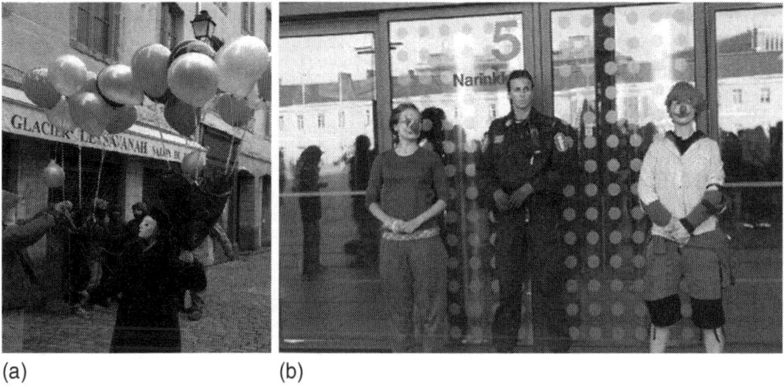

(a) (b)

Illustration 6 The frame of performing in Lyon: 'Non à Big Brother' activists cover surveillance cameras with balloons (a) and in Helsinki: the 'Clown battalion' hindering entrance to Kamppi shopping mall (b)

as subversive actors and 'truth-tellers' throughout the Western cultural history, and to carnival acts as truth-telling satire (see Bakhtin 1987). It is noteworthy that straightforward male representations were almost completely absent as central figures of the 'carnival aspect' of activism: the masquerades were feminine representations, or played with keys of homosexuality, or blurred gender (cf. Butler 1990, 50–2).

Why clowns, and why the gender ambiguity? Gender is a coercive performance: even if the scale of representations of femininity and masculinity, women and men, is a constantly changing one, gender remains a structuring principle for representations of humans that dictates rules concerning normality, acceptability, beauty, desirability, and credibility. Even though the rules can be challenged and changed, they are there. In the previous section I argued that analyzing gender representations was central to understanding the on-going mechanisms of counter-democracy in these imageries. Furthermore, in the frame of performing, the blurred signs of gender emphasized one source of counter-democratic power: the power of powerlessness, and thus the power to ridicule. Clowns are out of reach of the categorizing power of gender, as they are neither one gender nor the other. They are at the same time tragically powerless, and extremely powerful.

Finally, the dominant frames of working and deliberating consisted of the most 'civil' and 'peaceful' representations of the activist imageries. It was hardly surprising that these frames were primarily in use in Helsinki. There were examples of them in both contexts, though, and these two frames offered the clearest 'links' between the activist and the city magazine imageries. The frame of working depicted activists often concretely with tools in their hands. They repaired houses, dug ditches, and planted seeds. Unlike in the frame of performing, gender representations within this frame were unproblematic, and there were both women and men 'on the job.' The gender keying in this frame seemed to follow the 'official' norm of gender equality common to these kinds of activist groups. In particular, the Finnish imagery contained representations of women and men in similar working overalls, carrying out the same tasks, as in Illustration 7b.

These activist representations were somewhat analogous to the city frame of occupations (see the next section), although a secondary frame of performing twisted this analogy. Illustration 7a, for example, was a mixture of the two frames: the digging and seeding was part of a contentious performance against a GMO plant, as the drum left to lie in the foreground hints. The Finnish images, however, were less marked by secondary framings, even though the contentious aspect was present: the representation in Illustration 7b, for example, portrayed 'actual' work in a squatted house.

The frame of deliberating consisted of representations of meetings, seminars, debates, and other gatherings that differed significantly from those in the frame of demonstrating. In these images, activists sat in bare classrooms, meeting halls, or sometimes in squat or outdoor environments. The compositions, postures, and faces in Illustrations 8a and b portrayed decidedly civil debate or deliberation.

(a) (b)

Illustration 7 The frame of working in Lyon: anti-GMO activists planting non-GMO seeds on a factory yard (a) and in Helsinki: Orange activists building an underdrain for a squatted house (b)

(a) (b)

Illustration 8 The frame of deliberating in Lyon: *Robins des villes* activists evaluate the wheelchair accessibility of a residential area under construction (a) and in Helsinki: 'Sack the central tunnel' activists debate with members of the City Council (b)

In the French imagery, the deliberating parties always consisted of activists only, or activists and members of the general public, as in iIllustration 8a. The Finnish representations within this frame, on the contrary, often pointed out and underlined with explanatory captions the co-presence of activists and decision-makers. In Illustration 8b, the panel of discussants consisted of activists and City councilors. For the Finnish activists, this kind of connection was clearly beneficial and valued: it made sense to emphasize these occasions by publishing images of them. In a series of images from a local social forum in Helsinki, for example, the ex-ministers, local politicians, and members of the Parliament sitting in the audience were carefully pointed out by photographing them. Hence, the frame did approach the city imagery frames of engaging and representing, but mainly so in the Finnish case. To show these connections, or their absence, I next look at the frames of the city magazine imageries.

4.3 City framings

Culture and cityscapes

The most repetitive representations in both *Lyon Citoyen* and *Helsinki-info* (henceforth LC and HI) were those in which the dominant frame was either culture, or cityscapes. Together they framed nearly the totality of the magazine covers. They also emerged as secondary frames reciprocally, and intertwined in different ways. This way, they dominated the entire regime of representation, or the representational paradigm, of the city magazines rather strongly (cf. Hall 1997a, 232). The appearances of these frames were strikingly similar in the two contexts, even though differences also occurred.

The dominant frame of culture incorporated two main characteristics of representations that the broad title of the frame seeks to capture: 'culture' *for* the people, and *by* the people. The former refers to representations of cultural events – their stars, shows, and publics – and the latter to representations of 'ordinary inhabitants' depicted in beautiful, sunny sceneries of leisure activities and recreation. Evidently, the two characteristics also often merged. In these representations, urban life was beautiful, colorful, and unproblematic. Life in the cities was one big feast of creation, show, vacation, and good times. LC imagery in particular was dominated with glittering representations of performing arts, like the one in Illustration 9 below, referring to the opening of the *Biennal de la danse,* a biannual modern dance event in Lyon.

A crucial keying of the representation in Illustration 9 was movement. Typically, people represented within this frame were walking, dancing, jumping, running: These were representations of a very active, joyful, and energetic nature. In LC in particular, the movement stretched to captions and titles as well: *'Biennal,* it's gonna be dancing!,' like in Illustration 9, or a version or another of *'Une ville qui bouge,'* 'A city that moves,' a slogan-like phrase that occurred repeatedly in the magazine.

The frame of culture was also the one making the two magazines look the most alike, sometimes to the degree of nearly twin courses of motion, nevertheless with some differing elements.

Illustration 9 Dominant frame of culture in Lyon (LC 24/2004, cover)

(a) (b)

Illustration 10 Dominant frame of culture in Lyon (a: LC 17/2004, cover) and in Helsinki (b: HI 1/2006, cover)

In LC, the majority of representations in the frame of culture depicted performers, whereas HI emphasized more the 'ordinary people.' Juxtaposing the gender representations in Illustrations 10a and b, there are similar postures of 'action' by a man and a woman, except for the direction of their swinging foot, and their gaze: the man in LC looked up, concentrated on the movement rather than on being looked at, whereas the woman in HI, in her child-like posture, smiled to the camera. In addition, in the HI image a man stood by the jumping woman, with his hand raised, as if ready to catch her should she fall off balance (see Goffman 1979). These two images captured both some of the similarities and the differences in the two city magazines: the overall joyfulness and zeal on the one hand, and the LC emphasis on skillful artist performances versus the HI somewhat clumsier, homely performances of everyman and -woman.

Apart from the abundance of representations of the 'creators,' artists, and performers, the LC frame of culture also portrayed large crowds in ways that formed a continuum in which 'the people' and 'the city' merged into a representation of both, as in Illustration 11 below.

In Illustration 11, the caption[15] told, as any Lyonnais would recognize, that the image was about the new river bank arrangement the

Illustration 11 Frames of culture and cityscapes intertwined in Lyon (LC 29/2005, p. 8)

city took great pride in, one of the grand 'projects and actions for the city'. It was represented through people spending a sunny day by the river with the city both as the scene and as the topic, the two merging into a representation of 'life at its best'. 'The river bank emerges! The stiles of *La Guillotière* are accessible before the accomplishment of the ensemble,' promoted the caption. In this city, everything was nice and smooth and pretty, and people were happy and relaxed, like in the summer days of one's childhood. These merging representations evoked nostalgic interpretations: time stands still, fireworks go on forever, and conflicts have been forgotten long gone, if they ever existed at all. As such they join the tradition of French urban photography since the post-war era, in which 'Frenchness' is reconstructed as unified and undivided, and contemporary problems have been erased (Hamilton 1997, 148). The most famous examples of this tradition are iconic photographs of Parisian street life, lovers, and urban 'fiestas,' but the images from present-day Lyon joined the paradigm easily.

The cityscapes frame appeared more independently in Helsinki than in Lyon: landscapes and buildings were represented on their own right, and architecture and nature were the topics of the stories, as in Illustration 12.

Illustration 12 Frame of cityscapes in Helsinki (HI 2/2005, cover)

Nostalgia was explicit: an old building was represented as 'historic Helsinki'. History, often treated through the frame of cityscapes, was an important and repetitive topic of HI articles: buildings that used to be there and others that still were, in spite of the World War II bombings, or the havoc caused by the 1960s and 1970s ideas of modernization, appeared as valued and respected representations of Helsinki cityscapes.

Occupations, care, representing, and engaging

While the frames of culture and cityscapes somewhat dominated the representational regime of the magazines, the remaining four frames of the city magazine imageries were the ones that made the difference between LC and HI and tourist brochures or commercial magazines, as they consisted of representations directly linked to the basic functions of the cities *vis-à-vis* their inhabitants. Images within these frames represented workplaces, education, social and health services, municipal politics, and the local civil society.

The dominant frame of occupations included representations of people in local schools, universities, course centers, as well as all imaginable workplaces from offices to construction sites.

In LC, students studied dutifully, construction workers balanced on their scaffolds, architects bent over their drawing desks, and office workers raised their eyes from their papers. Everyone was occupied, busy, and industrious. These representations often formed a continuum to those of the frame of culture in their emphasis on movement – if not physical movement, at least the idea of moving forward. In Illustration 13 the man hammering on the scaffold was captioned by a progressive title saying 'The future takes form,' and the angle of view emphasized the vanguard position of this strong-armed future builder.

The rather modernist design of the image, together with the traditional representation of the working man – with the heavy duty of forging the future – gave this representation a somewhat controversial undertone. This kind of combination of modernistic representations of progress, and traditional representations of the (male) workers were remarkably repeated and emphasized in the frame of occupations in LC. The frame of occupations was surprisingly male and physical work dominated compared to HI, in which it was somewhat more varied. First, in HI, the frame of occupation emphasized mainly representations of education, and did so in ways that sometimes seemed to question traditions

Illustration 13 Frame of occupations in Lyon (LC 25/2004, cover)

or stereotypes, or at least to promote a less classical future direction than in the LC example above: in Illustration 14a, two women were represented as participants in a car mechanics course. In Illustration 14b, a school scene represented a multicultural group of students.

Illustration 14a's caption 'Vehicles as profession. Even girls are interested in cars. After high school, Elina Partanen and Hanna Rönkkö study as freshmen at the Helsinki mechanics institute,' revealed that the representation was no coincidence. There was a need to say *even* girls do this, since 'we all know boys mainly do.' To represent a car mechanics course with an image of two women is a promotional choice: it keyed the representation with a secondary framing of gender equality, and a suggestion that this, and perhaps the whole city, was an advanced case. At the same time, the slight awkwardness of the case seemed to require an explanation in the caption.

Similarly, Illustration 14b's representation of the school class was a persuasive one. The caption informed: 'Language immersion at school. In Myllypuro high school, nearly half of the students speak a mother tongue other than Finnish. You can hear Arabic, Italian, Bengali and Tamil in the halls. Does the multiplicity of cultures and languages make the school day different?' Here the frame of occupation was keyed with a secondary frame of 'positive multiculturalism.' It told a story of a city with new realities to come into terms with, such as the increasing immigrant population in schools: the representation was a negotiation. The obvious reaction to the rhetoric question of the caption would be

(a) (b)

Illustration 14 Dominant frame of occupations in Helsinki (a: HI 1/2004, p. 3; b: HI 2/2004, cover)

'different from what,' and the obvious answer 'a normal school day,' that is, one in a school with mainly Finnish-origin pupils.

There were representations of Lyonnais schools, too, but they did not emphasize immigration or multiculturalism in any similar way, for obvious reasons: there would be nothing new, and nothing 'innocent' to this degree to report. Also, a multi-lingual school would be a much more controversial topic in the French context, where the assimilatory treatment of immigrant populations is a several decade long, yet increasingly debated tradition. This debate was not the city magazine's cup of tea.

The above examples made the point that in LC, the frame of occupations was a continuum to the two previous frames in representing the 'wonders' of the city, its efficient students and workers and its bright future. In HI, in contrast, it portrayed slightly more nuanced themes and issues, not all of them self-evidently easy and resolved, even if some also gave the impression of 'forced optimism,' and negation of problems characteristic to the Finnish public culture.

In spite of these differences, there was also a converging keying within the frame of occupations: that of the frame of care. A ballpark description of this frame in both contexts could be reduced to 'caring for children.' Children, and people taking care of them were the principle and densest topic within this frame, and this was the frame children were mainly represented in. Children represented innocence and joyfulness, and the supply of protection and nurture available in the cities. Messages such as 'a child well in her/his city' – the headline of a LC cover (no. 26/2004) – echoed as strongly persuasive: if a child is well, all is well. Here again, the Lyonnais imagery joined French photographic traditions of for instance rebuilding the nation and reconstructing a sentiment of national solidarity in post-war France that was visualized in representations of children and the 'sanctity of happy childhood' – the hopes of a brighter future (Hamilton 1997, 115, 119; see also Luhtakallio 2003, 74–5). The Finnish tradition of representing children in the post-war years was even more emphasized: For example in 1955, children alone or with their mothers were the most common topic of general magazines' covers. Moreover, throughout the 20th century, 'mother–child' portraits form a paradigm widely in use in media representations in advertisement, propaganda, as well as 'factual' communication both in Finland and in France (Luhtakallio 2003, 63–6).[16] The city magazines made no exception: Illustrations 15a and b below show the visually converging representations of women and children that formed the core of the frame of care in both contexts.

In both examples in Illustration 15, women were holding small children in their arms, an age-old composition of mother–child imagery.

(a)

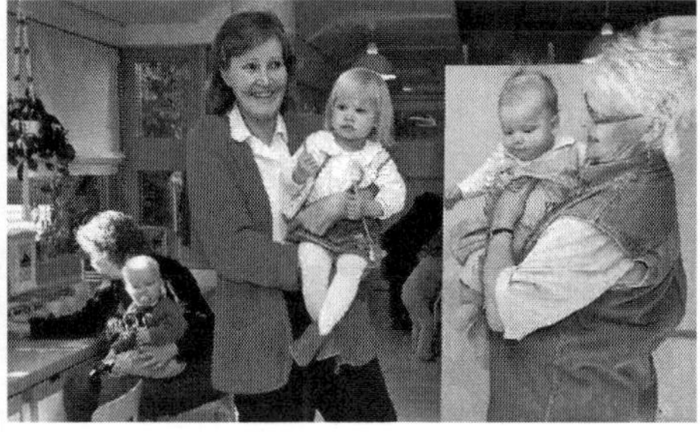

(b)

Illustration 15 Dominant frame of care, secondary frame of occupation in Lyon (a: LC 18/2004, p. 18) and in Helsinki (b: HI 5/2004, p. 12)

The adults represented within this frame were exclusively women in both contexts – female nursery workers or volunteers, mothers or grandmothers. However, whereas in LC, men were absent altogether, as even the title 'They look after them. Example: at the Boileau nursery' defined 'them' as female, in HI, fathers were mentioned in the title – 'A cottage for mothers, fathers and children' – and they thus were potentially present, at least in the context of this structure for family counseling.

Within the city magazine imageries, the dominant frame of representing was far more common in LC than in HI. In terms of the representational regime of the city magazines, it was, however, an important frame in both contexts. It was, in a sense, the most constitutive of the master frame of the city magazines: the frame of representing made the magazines different from other magazines most clearly. It tied the paradigm to local politics in a way unique to the city magazines. These were most likely the only (local) news media in which editorials were written by a mayor instead of an editor-in-chief, as in LC, and occasionally in HI, and in which mayors, councilors, administrators, and instances of local services and decision-making were depicted and quoted as abundantly. In LC in particular, the frame also included representations of material symbols of the municipality: tax sheets, city and district halls, or even light bulb storage for street lamps. These images illustrated articles about tightening economy, bright-looking accounts, or the city hall's Christmas wishes to the inhabitants.

The core of the frame in both contexts was, however, the representations of the municipal 'personnel,' divided into two principal categories.

The first one was keyed by the frame of occupations, and it can be summed as 'portraits of service,' shown in Illustrations 16a and b.

In these cases, the frames of representing and occupations merged, and the composition defined which was more dominant: it was often a question of nuances whether the image portrayed the person or documented her function, whether it represented work, or a public function. The titles of the images above, 'Can you help me? Receive, listen, accompany' (LC) and 'Service to the long term unemployed' (HI) anchored these representations to municipal services. In both contexts, these representations were the ones within the frame of representing in which women were most commonly in a 'leading' or 'guiding' position.

The second category was less affected by secondary framings, and it can be entitled 'portraits of power,' as the common denominator was the different keys of power. How is power depicted? What kind of power can we see, and how? The paradigm of visual culture studies has a long history of analyzing power and powerlessness (e.g. Berger 1972; Fyfe & Law 1988; Craig 1992; Nixon 1997; Cortese 1999). Power can be symbolized by physical size and strength (virile posture, height, muscles), perspective (from below), by clothing (the 'power suit'), by directions of gaze (directly pointed to the camera, challenging, often serious), and by so many other visual features that the process of meaning production is far from being easy to unravel. However, it was not only the visual keys that illustrated power, the captions and titles also helped to pinpoint it (see also Luhtakallio 2003).

Pouvez-vous m'aider ?

(a)

Palvelua pitkäaikaistyöttömille

(b)

Illustration 16 The frames of representing and occupations intertwined in Lyon (a: LC 25/2004, p. 10) and in Helsinki (b: HI 10/2005, p. 22)

If men were absent from the frame of *care* and less frequent in representations of civil servants, they were pre-eminent in representations of political leadership: mayors, councilors, and sometimes members of the administrative staff. In LC, the portraits of power almost exclusively represented political leaders and, in particular, one of them, the Mayor of Lyon, Gérard Collomb. His image appeared many times in each issue of the magazine, and representations of him marked the frame unlike any others.

A whole series of images similar to the examples above portrayed the Mayor 'leading the situation' in a variety of environments, and the mayor alone, closely cropped, looking directly at the viewer, and 'delivering' an influential message. In the caption of Illustration 17a, first, we learn that 'On an official visit in France, the President of Portugal, Jorge Sampaio, spent a day in Lyon. – As the previous Mayor of Lisbon, he was particularly interested in the river bank projects presented by Gérard Collomb,' and see the Mayor hosting the high-profile foreign group in a self-assured way. In all representations of this type, the Mayor's posture and movements were relaxed, sovereign, and his position in the images central. Illustration 17b, secondly, was one of the repeated, often only slightly changing portraits next to the mayor's editorial. These were representations of a city in good, paternal hands of a strong and capable leader.

In the Finnish imagery, a particular person or function did not dominate the frame. Leading officials portrayed more in the representations than in the French imagery. They were often seen in large portraits accompanied by a personal interview or a feature article of their responsibilities. These, as well as politicians' representations, were rather evenly distributed between men and women, and sometimes of both

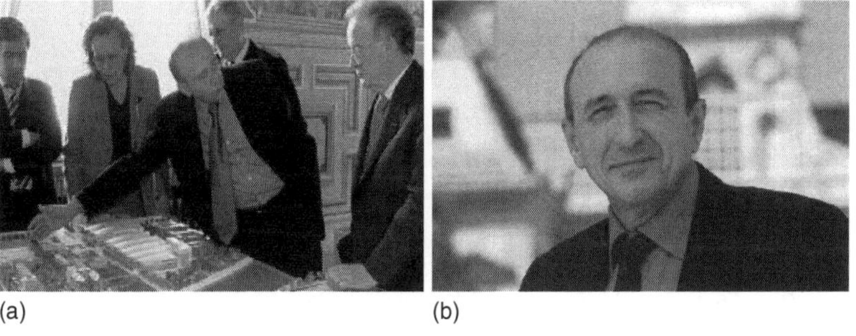

(a) (b)

Illustration 17 Dominant frame of representing in Lyon (a: LC 32/2005, p. 3; b: LC 29/2005, p. 7)

together, as in Illustration 18a. Symbols of power were quite equally shared, and the variety of depicted persons was wide.

The title and captions of these representations explained: 'The council kick-off. The new City Council elected Rakel Hiltunen as President. Jussi Pajunen continues as the President of the executive board.' This type of portrait in which a woman and a man 'shared' the power, was not the only one of its kind in the Helsinki imagery, whereas it was totally absent from the Lyonnais one. In LC, women appeared in this frame as well, but they were exclusively portraits of city district mayors, depicted alone beside their 'neighborhood column' the magazine published at the last pages of each issue. Women and men together were not a probable topic for illustrating representative power in the French case. In the imagery of HI, representations of power were overall more shared, whereas in LC, political power was a rather centralized feature, and it was especially in the Mayor's hands. This observation reflects local power structures in France and Finland: In the former, the continuously quasi-monarchic position of the mayor in local power structures, and in the latter, the increasing power of the officials, and the lack of a transparent 'center of power' have been noted with concern in many recent studies (e.g. Holli *et al.* 2007; Blondiaux 2008, 29; see also Chapter 5 in this book).

Illustration 18b with the caption 'the City Council sessions can be followed from the gallery of the council hall' was keyed to the frame of engaging that stretched the city magazine imageries towards the themes of the activist imageries – at least in theory. This frame was related to

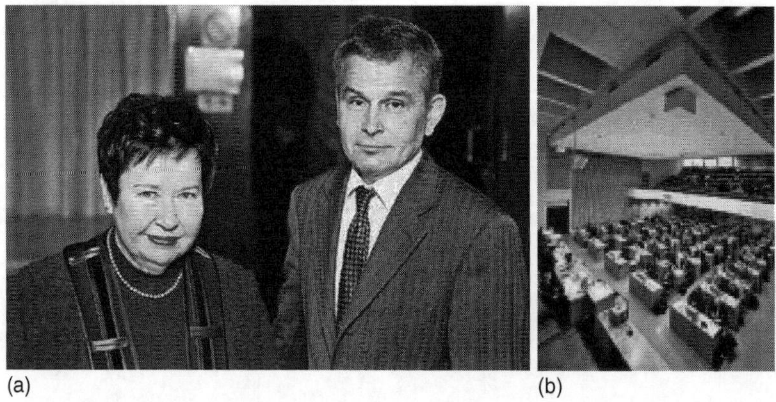

(a) (b)

Illustration 18 The dominant frame of representing in Helsinki (a, b: HI 1/2005)

local civil society: voluntary work, associations, or events of participatory democracy. These representations were scarce both in repetition and in representational weight: the images were rare, and they were usually small and not centrally placed. Furthermore, they represented a rather different civil society from the one seen in the activist imageries. In both magazines, however, some signs in these few images shared features and keyings with frames of the activist images.

In HI, the representations of the frame of engaging were always keyed by secondary frames, notably the frames of occupations and culture. There were volunteers at their tasks, sometimes performing arts, sometimes doing different kinds of manual labor. This way, the frame approached the activist frame of working: The images were representations of a 'useful' civil society with concrete achievements. In iIllustration 19b, 'With strength of dozens of youngsters' ('*Voimalla kymmenten nuorten*'), two volunteers posed in a municipal youth center with the computers they used to edit a youth magazine.

In LC, the depicted moments of volunteering were performances, or art works, like Illustration 19a that represented an installation of used shoes. It approached the activist frames of marking and performing – it was a mark left behind, but the meaning of the mark was primarily artistic, unlike the meaning of a banderol left hanging from a squat window, for instance. Illustration 19a was, however, a unique example: it actually reported the doings of a social movement, a Lyonnais branch of an international association against mutilating bombs and mines. It was the only image in the entire city magazine material, both French and Finnish that created a direct link between the cities and social movements acting in them.

Bellecour

Anti bombes

C'est devenu un rendez-vous... incontournable. Chaque année en automne l'ONG lyonnaise Handicap international érige sa pyramide de chaussures grâce aux dons des particuliers. Le 8 octobre de 10h à 20h30 sur la place Bellecour, elle espère un public nombreux pour la soutenir dans son combat contre les bombes à sous-munitions, mini-bombes regroupées par dizaines ou centaines dans des conteneurs, qui continuent de mutiler et tuer après la fin des conflits.

(a)

Voimalla kymmenten nuorten

(b)

Illustration 19 Frame of engaging in Lyon (a: LC 36/2005, p. 21) and in Helsinki (b: HI 6/2005, p. 10)

4.4 The dynamics of representing the local society

Activist and city imageries: framing worlds apart

What kind of representations of the local society did the activist websites and city magazines provide? They provided, first of all, representations of two very different societies in both contexts. Despite the intertwining, or resemblance, of certain activist and city frames, their general definitions of local societies were rather oppositional. The city magazine imageries represented well-to-do local societies, in which there either were no problems, or solutions to problems were ready and clear. The activist imageries represented local societies in constant turmoil, characterized by a struggle between the unjust power structures and counter-democratic efforts to resist them. Hence, these imageries provided an expression of a struggle over what the society was, should be, or was about to become. In order to sum up the analysis of this 'struggle,' I first look at the distances and interconnections between the activist and city framings in each context, and in the next section, I parallel these local 'dialogues,' or, rather, the lack of dialogue, with reflections on counter-democracy, and the conditions of politics and politicization these visual representations portrayed.

The first observation of the activist and city imageries is that they had very little to do with each other. They indeed looked as if they were about four different cities, not two. The most dominating and repetitive frames, *marking* and *demonstrating* (activist) on the one hand, and *culture* and *cityscapes* (city) on the other, created representational regimes astonishingly similar between France and Finland, and nearly oppositional within the two cities. Nearly, since there were connections, too: the frames of *marking* and *cityscapes* were both representations of the city environment, ownership of it, and the right to model and transform it. Equally, the frames of *demonstrating* and *culture* were in both contexts characterized by movement, moving, and action.

Furthermore, there also were features that directly connected or linked the imageries to each other – weak signs perhaps, but worth reflecting, as the fact that there were, indeed, not four different cities, was to the least a disturbing one before these images.

First, in Lyon, common to both imageries was movement: a constant, transformative movement. In the activist imagery it meant processing a new kind of society, and in the city magazines, a modernistic progress – or a constant neo-liberal change – was unstoppable. The only somewhat mutual connection between the imageries were scenes within the frames of performing (activist) and culture (city), in which the connecting feature was more the esthetics of performing than anything else, and the frames of working (activist) and occupations (city), although the former was so weak in the activist imagery that it cannot be regarded as a strong connection in any way. In addition, the frame of engaging in the city magazines made one allusion towards the activist imagery. These connections were, however, extremely rare and vague. The quasi absence of the frame of deliberating in the activist imagery, and the centralized power of the frame of representing in the city imagery were illustrative of the distance between the imageries. In the light of the enthusiasm for participative democracy in the French political debate, and the implementations of several practices of it in recent years, it is noteworthy that this phenomenon was almost completely absent in both imageries. Put in the perspective of the next chapter, in which the politicians' and activists' discursive framings of the issue will be analyzed, this absence seems revelatory – and logical. Something so controversial would not fit in the representational regime of LC, in which the insistence that 'everything is just great' was even more emphasized than in its Finnish twin magazine. The representational regime of the activist imagery, furthermore, was not particularly receptive for any kind of cooperation with the city establishment, especially not with the political powers. In this sense, the visual framings of the activist images were analogous to their group boundaries and conditions of cooperation I analyzed in Chapter 2.

Secondly, in Helsinki, the frames of working (activist) and occupations (city) were the ones that connected the two imageries both visually and, at times, thematically. Even though the logic of the representation was different – the former was about voluntary work and the latter about either paid work or studying – both carried the idea of building, more or less concretely. Furthermore, representations of the activist frame of deliberating made a rare connection to the city frame of representing. The former emphasized a willingness of the activists to include power holders in their discussions – and be included themselves. Similarly to the activists' faith in their possibilities of influence, and their permeable group boundaries observed in Chapter 2, connections to city politics and power structures occurred in the Helsinki activist imagery. HI's representational regime made, however, only few 'concessions' to the activists. Civil society representations were exiguous, the frame of engaging was weak, and no social movement or contentious claim or action appeared on the pages of HI during the time span of the study. Considering the corporatist pillars of decision-making in Finnish society, and the inclusive ideal of the municipal law, the quasi absence of the civil society in a magazine of a local administration is striking. It is as if 'the city' was suddenly separated from its context, the Finnish society in which civic actors play an important role. There was no place in this kind of a city for its civil society, except for those who worked so closely with the city administration that it was difficult to tell which was which. However, the analysis of the democracy framings of politicians and activist in the next chapter will emphasize the firm preference of Finnish politicians for the 'good old' kind of activism, with law-abiding repertoires and a humble attitude.

Thirdly, the most obvious connecting feature in both contexts was the presence of the police forces within the activist frames, mainly that of violence. This connection was not a flattering one to the cities, whose administration was represented at work in the often rather harsh images of the frame. The city magazines represented police officers in images that intertwined the frames of representing and occupations. Needless to say, these representations carried no indices of violence, but rather confirmed for their part the general vision of the cities in good hands.

Masculine and feminine dynamics of counter-democracy

What kind of portrayals of the 'age of suspicion', in which democracies need to come into terms with their citizens in novel ways (Rosanvallon 2006) the activist websites and city magazines represented in Lyon and Helsinki? In the following, I consider the similarities and differences in the French and Finnish imageries, and sketch both the politico-administrative and counter-democratic 'styles' the imageries illustrated. In the end, I suggest that taking into account gender in these styles has important implications to understanding the contextual struggles of representing the society.

In the city magazine imageries, happy-looking people in colorful pictures studied, worked, performed arts or attended cultural events, or enjoyed themselves in the city. Politicians and city officials appeared assertive, and urban landscapes represented the multi-faceted beauty of the urban environment. The visual contents of the city magazines were, generally speaking, a theatrical *mise-en-scène* of the results of good representation and governing, and the good reputation of the politico-administrative institutions and persons. Theatricality is a feature characteristic to politics, but in a situation where politics is in danger to be exhausted of *content*, as well as its source of legitimacy in the electorate because of the processes that fusion politics with governing and the market, the theatrical scenes become ever more crucial to the power holders. They are all the affirmation there is. Equally, the significance of reputation increases in a mediated, opinion-driven society, in which the legitimacy of the leader is, in fact, in a state of crisis (Rosanvallon 2006, 23, 240–1, 53–6). In the city magazines, indeed, the cities were represented as big, skillfully directed theatres, where the show went on in thousands of colors, and the assertive, trustworthy leaders with spotless reputations had the cities 'in good hands'. The role of politicians in the city magazine representations was emphasized in France more than in Finland, as if 'the ghost of the Prince' was sneaking on to the pages. In the Finnish case, civil servants often 'substituted' politicians in representations that dominated the imagery a little less than in France. Reputation was also at stake in the plethora of representations of happy schoolchildren dutifully learning, working men dutifully on their jobs, youngsters depicted practicing orderly hobbies, and all kinds of people enjoying their free time. In addition, urban landscapes contributed to this theatrical display of power and excellence. Architectural sights evoked ideas of a glorious and valued past, or a dynamic, promising future. The city magazines produced an image of the city as non-problematic, calm, and free of conflicts. All in all, the imageries of the city magazines were purified of politics, in the sense of open possibilities of politicization, and thus provided one illustration of the decline of politics, and the age of neo-liberal *impolitique*, non-politics, in representative democracies (Rosanvallon 2006, 258–61).

The activist imageries, for their part, displayed visual proofs of the ever more active and intervening, and in many ways a disappointed, skeptical, and even cynical civil society. The counter-democratic actors in these representations stated loudly and clearly that the process in which these local societies represented themselves had severe deficiencies. Active citizen surveillance, obstruction, and denouncement attained multiple visual illustrations, some more in the spirit of 'healthy' counter-democracy, some less, and some representations, at least at first glance, captured outright perversions of counter-democratic forces in frustrated, violent, and disillusioned manners (Rosanvallon 2006, 15, 258–9, 271–5). On the one hand, broken windows evidenced a frustrated and sinister presence of a citizenry that faltered on the edges of critique. The activists had their hand in the *cité* concretely, but the message was a disillusioned smash. On the other hand, the crowds that gathered in demonstrations cried out a message of obstruction: the 'people-veto' was in action, and it was clearly practicing its power of rejection and refusal. The active citizens forming a counter-democratic body were watching over the constitution of the society, and saying: 'We are here and we see your doings.'

The theatrical 'shows' of the activists depicted as clowns or other disguised figures performing carnival acts made reference to the traditions of fools and clowns as subversive actors of Western cultural history, and to carnival acts as truth-telling satire – or acts of exposing the powerful, and 'blowing the whistle' by means of ridicule and derision. Representations of police violence and other kinds of abuses of power can equally be interpreted as acts of revelation: 'This is what the society is made of, and this is how our exercise of fundamental rights is received.'

Despite the versatility of the activist representations, they portrayed two principle styles. These styles emerged through the analysis of the configurations of gender in the representations. Leading massive crowds of demonstrators, breaking windows, fighting against the police, and other use of force were marked by representations of masculinities. Deliberating, performing, doing voluntary work, and portraying the fun and pleasure of activism were marked by either feminine, both feminine and masculine, or blurred and queer gender representations. Thus, the repertoires of counter-democracy formed different styles that had different gendered implications – gender was the principle secondary frame that keyed the differences in the styles. Even if there were an example of a woman throwing a tile, even if all genders can be performed in endless variety, the representational reserve that links representations to the ones seen before, and enables the understanding of types of representation, constrains us to see physical violence mainly as masculine (cf. Goffman 1974; Hall 1997a; Nixon 1997).

Politicization requires critical and perhaps doubtful, but not cynical and hopeless sentiments as the driving forces of counter-democratic actions. The more perverse – in the sense of being non-political – the counter-democratic styles, the weaker are the hopes for politicization. These styles were not, however, dependent on the counter-democratic actors alone, but perhaps also on the politico-administrative systems they acted in. To sum up: like system, like counter-democracy.

In Helsinki, more varying styles of counter-democracy were 'worth' being represented, and the occurrence of different feminine styles was stronger than in Lyon. The axes of whistle-blowing, resisting, and building – in deliberation and in concrete action – produced alternative representations of the society, and the representations were marked as both masculine and feminine so that especially the latter were more diversely represented than in the Lyonnais imagery. In the Lyonnais counter-democratic imageries, on the contrary, masculine representations dominated the scene, and the representational regime of the activist imageries was bent towards a combination of firm resistance, sometimes more perverse and non-political, sometimes less, and suffering and despair of the oppressed citizens. Illustrations 20a–d below show these two stylistic extremes.

Illustration c and d, from the Helsinki imagery, illustrated counter-democracy with a lot of hope in the air: women and men gathered together to re-build and deliberate. A diversified repertoire of styles, and a lesser degree of violence among them, thus, alluded of the degree of hope; not of straightforward, factual inclusion of citizens, but of having a reason to hope. Illustration 20a shows counter-democratic perversion in its most sinister and lugubrious form. If grabbing a Molotov cocktail is the choice of repertoire, it implicates a deep disbelief that anyone 'on the other side' would be interested in hearing any message in other forms, forms that might result in dialogue for instance. When there is no more faith in the sense of passing a message, the Molotov cocktail is what is left. In the spirit of Goffman (1979), Illustration 20b is a

(a) (b) (c) (d)

Illustration 20 The two extremes of counter-democracy in the French (a, b) and the Finnish (c, d) activist imageries

representation of exception: it suggests that the possibility of feminine violence exists, even though its exceptionality was emphasized here by the fact that it was a photograph of an advertisement poster tuned into its new use, instead of a photograph of a living person.

This said, it is clear, however, that the styles of counter-democracy could only be analyzed within their contexts, and by taking cognizance of other accounts of the local struggles over representing the society. The French activists reported their concern over the increasing police violence during demonstrations since the beginning of the 2000s. They were scared, and female activists in particular said on several occasions that they had begun to avoid certain demonstrations due to their fear of being assaulted by the police. Furthermore, the activists' feelings on the responsiveness of the city to their claims were rather analogical to the absence of all conflict and disruption in the *Lyon Citoyen* images: there was barely any response at all. Thus, the French imagery – as representations with their two-way function of both presenting and producing a reality, not as mirrors of local society as such – were also a comment on the acts of the officials. This comment could be summed up as something like: 'This is what you get in return,' for not listening, and not including. Hence, a Molotov cocktail can be a politicized tool indeed, if no other choice against an oppressive power holder remains, or if other ways of politicizing go unnoticed. Indeed, had the revolutionaries in the 18th century stuck to a negotiation strategy, the world history might look very different today.

Similarly, deliberating and the use of other 'civil' repertoires may become empty and de-politicized, even perverted counter-democracy to different degrees, if the circumstances hinder politicization, like in a context in which the power holders dictate both the choice of repertoires and the 'acceptable' claims of counter-democratic actors. In the Finnish case, the two-folded situation illustrated in Chapter 2 was analogous to the visual representations of the struggle. There was both an attempt to 'be included' by assenting to various requirements of the power holders, with the hope of getting 'at least something through,' and an attempt to express clearer resistance through less consensual actions. The latter were closer to the French counter-democratic styles. Which extreme, then, proves actively counter-democratic, and which de-politicized, cynical, or violent non-politics, is not solely a matter of repertoires, but primarily that of context, the meanings given to the activity, and the political circumstances in which it is carried out. In conclusion, the analysis of this chapter suggests that assessing the conditions of politicization and active counter-democracy requires both a contextual regard, and in particular, a gender-sensitive reading of the forms of counter-democracy.

This chapter has showed the importance of juxtaposing the different 'parties' of the local struggle for representing the society. In the following chapters, I further emphasize this configuration. The next chapters will compare, first, the framings of democracy of local activists and politicians, and finally, in Chapter 6, the acts of justifying of representatives of 'counter-democratic actors', and of the 'cities' in local disputes.

5

Framing Democracy: Participation and Representation by Activists and Politicians[1]

Recent political theory has placed much emphasis on the ideas of inclusion, deliberation and participation as answers to the problems of existing democracies (e.g. Fraser 1992; Benhabib 1996; Young 1996; 2000; Rosanvallon 2006, 2008). These ideas seem to trickle widely, in various forms, into legislation and policy (Bacqué *et al.* 2005; Sintomer 2007; Blondiaux 2008). In both France and Finland, different participation practices and procedures have recently been introduced as remedies to the problems of representative democracy. Evaluations of practical endeavors to enhance civic involvement in decision-making indicate that citizens draw contradictory experiences from them, some empowering, but some nurturing the distrust between citizens and representative democracy (e.g. Niemi-Iilahti 1999; Carrel 2003, 2006; Rui 2004; Koebel 2006; Leino 2006; Talpin 2006; Bäcklund *et al.* 2006; Bäcklund 2007; see also Chapter 1 in this book). In this chapter, I put in parallel the ideas springing from current democracy theorizing with the ideas the local political actors put forward when they talked about democracy. The focus is on the perceptions and definitions of democracy of, first, the counter-democratic actors met in the previous chapters, and, secondly, the local politicians and administrators that held different positions of political power in Lyon and Helsinki.

How did different actors in the two cities perceive the state of local democracy, and how did they define and treat the tensions between the processes of representation and participation? The activists and politicians had different resources for talking about representation, participation, and democracy, depending on both the national political culture, the local political culture, administrative culture familiar to them, activist culture in their country and city, and a variety of 'micro cultures' guiding the doings of a specific activist group, party organization, and other significant contexts for their activities. Still, they all recognized the tensious dynamics of current local democracy, and located the key to understanding them within the processes of representation and participation. In order to enable a comparison of the articulations of these tensious processes, I related the local actor groups' perceptions and definitions of democracy to a scheme of four theoretical models of a democratic public sphere proposed by Myra Marx Ferree *et al.* (2002a): the representative liberal, the participatory liberal, the discursive, and the constructionist models. Through these models, the authors tackle a range of normative questions: what qualities should a democratic public sphere have, who should be participating and how, and what sort of outcomes should result from a well-functioning democratic process (Marx Ferree *et al.* 2002a, 289–90, 316). I use the models as a conceptual tool in tracing the local actors' ways of framing democracy, participation, and representation.

The models are theoretical ideal types that represent different directions of the academic and political debates on democracy. My use of them as frames that my interlocutors deployed in their talk about democracy is grounded in the idea that they are 'general' enough in order to resonate and make sense in both contexts, but at the same time the actors challenge, fracture, and contradict them in various ways. Thus, the focus is not on the detailed 'contents' of each model, but rather on their occurrences in the contextual realities, and their inter-relatedness in mundane talk about democracy. In the following, I describe the models briefly before giving the floor to civic activists, local politicians, and civil servants.

Crucial to the representative liberal model is its emphasis on elite dominance, technical expertise, and professional decision-making that leaves the citizens only a rather passive role, and is reluctant of expanding participation. The question of inclusion is solved through proportional representation. The exception to this rule is the figure of a 'citizen expert,' who, ideally, does not have a political agenda, but is solely willing to share her knowledge with the decision-makers. What logically follows is the demand of detachment and civility in repertoires of expressing ideas and, in particular, expressions of emotion are rejected in this tradition (ibid. 290–3).

The participatory liberal model has empowering objectives, and an inclusive idea of participation. It emphasizes maximal participation of citizens as something that improves the quality of the public sphere, and helps in developing the general will. It also has an educational dimension in the sense that participating will develop the capacities of individuals to act publicly, and it rejects the norm of expertise as a precondition for participation. The repertoires of political expression have a wide range in this model: emotional, polemical and conflicting speech acts are welcome. This tradition, also called 'strong democracy,' underlines the procedural nature of political decision-making, and the role of public deliberation in it (ibid. 295–8).

The differences between the participatory liberal and the discursive model are not self-evident, the most important distinction being probably the question of repertoires. Drawing rather exclusively from the Habermasian tradition of deliberative democracy, the discursive model emphasizes civility, enhanced by the norms of mutual respect and dialogue. In order to create the 'ideal speech situations' required by the model in which the best of arguments can win, a certain level of organization is necessary, and citizens have to be able to put aside narrow interests. Thus the 'who' question is to some extent at the service of the 'what' question: popular inclusion renders deliberative process possible, and this is the main reason for it. The discursive model more or less presupposes that participants of the deliberative processes share common values and are thus ready and able to participate in civilized dialogue (ibid. 300–3). The fourth category, the constructionist model, consists mainly of ideas criticizing the Habermasian tradition. The biggest difference between this categorization and all the others is perhaps the nature of inclusion: there is a specific concern for including those in marginal positions in a society. This concern stems from the idea of recognition politics, in which different standpoints and values are valorized as essential in order to create a democratic public sphere (e.g. Young 2000). As a consequence, styles and repertoires of political participation are totally dependent on the participants, and the differences between them. The 'who,' the 'what,' and the 'how' are intertwined in this model. The idea of the avoidance of closure includes rather different ways of thinking from an ever-widening realm of the political to an agonistic idea that all finalized decisions are a threat to democracy (Marx Ferree *et al.* 2002a, 307–11).

The representative liberal model plays a special role in the local actors' talk about democracy: it is the symbol of the dominating system of governance at the local level in both contexts. In the interviews, identically in France and in Finland, the local actors took this model more or less for granted, as the basis upon which other possibilities could be reflected. Nevertheless, the meanings given to the representative frame differed from a context to another, depending on its place in relation to the other frames and the emphasis put on different features of the models. Representation is a complex issue that does not concern the current 'representative system' alone, but is deeply embedded and influential in the historical development of different polities. In Pierre Rosanvallon's (1998) words, representation functions as the 'political figuration of the social' and as such it is illustrative of prevailing features of a political culture. Representation functions either as a constructive or a descriptive process, the former referring to representation as a dynamic process of a society in a constant state of creation, the latter to a 'mirroring' process of a supposedly complete, transparent, and throughout 'represented' society (ibid. 308). Risto Alapuro (2005a) has suggested that this division portrays the historical characteristics of representation as 'constructive' in the French, and 'descriptive' in the Finnish tradition.[2] The framings of democracy of current local actors in this chapter offer an empirically founded reflection of this historico-theoretical thesis: the inter-relations and frame dynamics result in understanding the mechanisms and conditions of politicization processes, and their differences in the two contexts, from the viewpoint of the idea of representation. The following sections identify different manifestations of the democracy frames, their intertwinement and overlapping, and fractures in them, in the talk of the local actors.

5.1 Activists' conceptions of democracy

Disillusioned antagonists in Lyon

The general atmosphere of talking about democracy among the activists in Lyon was rather pessimistic. Local democracy evoked bitter criticism and abrupt statements. They often explicitly abandoned the representative system as not democratic at all. However, they framed democracy – as it should have been, in their eyes – with various combinations of both the representative and the three other framings.

Two different ways of spelling out the grim climate of opinions were particularly articulate among the Lyonnais activists. In the first one, the representative liberal model framed democracy implicitly as the basis of the system. The activists judged the system to be hopelessly corrupt and dysfunctional, but estimated that its rapid or drastic change was not probable, the way Chazz did:

> 'Well, I don't have any solution. I'm not going to talk about a revolution because I don't necessarily believe in it. At least not a violent one, and not tomorrow. ... I find that [the current political system] installs a total intellectual indolence ... these guys don't call

> themselves into question ... when they fail or lose, they should leave their responsibilities [but they don't]. ... They make decisions that not one French person wants. ... Like the surveillance cameras ... [the Mayor] has never asked whether the Lyonnais population approved. No, it frightens me.'

The only way Chazz envisioned things could really change was through a violent revolution – which he did not believe in either. He framed the question of democracy within the representative model, criticized the actors of the system bitterly, and distanced himself from it altogether, ultimately by labeling it frightening. In many interviews, strong emotions flavored talk about democracy. In the following, Solange explained angrily why she had not even considered taking part in an opportunity of participation offered by the municipality, and why she had actually given up on practicing representative democracy altogether.

> 'You can say what you want, they'll do as they please ... me, I don't believe that at some point ... a consultative organ would have any real power. I mean, they can say "oh yes, ... we have heard what you had to say and we'll take it into account", me, I don't believe it one second. It's been years that I don't vote and it's not for nothing, I know very well that people doing politician politics don't take into account what we have to say, that's my conviction.'

These kinds of expressions of distrust towards the representative model often included a suspicion that participatory practices were, and would remain, a sham. There were, however, less extreme views as well. In the second predominant line of argumentation, the activists framed democracy in a more complex manner. The prevailing, often concomitant, frames were constructionist and participatory, the latter especially regarding the range of action repertoires. The notion of 'situated knowledge,' combined with private, small-scale action, and contentious attitudes were stressed especially when the activists framed democracy in a wider context than the representative system. Also, as Miriam described, short-term engagements and projects were seen as the most beneficial and important for democracy:

> 'I have the impression that every time when things happen that are actually worth it, it's these small initiatives of small associations who try to get people together to debate, to discuss, to make small propositions ..., I always have the impression that it's on a short term

> basis. ... I think more of this think global, act local thing. I really believe in small local actions ... because they respond to very concrete needs.'

Some activists framed their questioning of the responsiveness and inclusiveness of the current political system with ideas close to the constructionist model. They turned to 'small solutions,' away from the big, meaningless system, and stressed the potential of proximity (see Doidy 2005a). Some activists also used the proximity argument to dispense completely with the representative system and to call for a direct model of democracy instead, in which representation was to be replaced by a different process of collective decision-making and delegation. Léonore envisioned:

> 'I have the impression that people are asked to go and vote and after that not to put their noses in the affairs of the government anymore. And this system, well, it makes me laugh a little when they talk to me about democracy and that kind of things, but the only democracy that seems legitimate to me is direct democracy, with people who are not elected to make the decisions, but delegated to bring about a decision that has been made by the collective. ... This means that at a large scale it makes things very complicated ... and that's why I believe in smaller units ... that are auto-governed and autonomous.'

Even those who did not call the entire system into question – some even had enough faith in it to participate in neighborhood councils – were critical towards the current practices of participation, and the possibilities to actually deliberate with those in power. Christelle, who had rather positive insights about participatory democracy in general, described her anticipations and estimates of future developments:

> 'No, I don't have the impression that there would be a strong political will. I have the impression that ... what has been enforced as participative democracy has slightly an aspect of a fashion effect, there has to be neighborhood councils even though finally they don't have a big role. ... And so I'm not very ... optim[istic], hem, sure that it will ... have a very important role.'

The activists' criticism was, however, also directed towards their fellow citizens and even towards their own ways of acting in processes of deliberation. These criticisms often labeled the problems as relating to national characteristics – the 'French problem' – such as impatience, lack of long-term commitment, laziness, incapacity of coming to an agreement, and the like. Some activists saw that there was a need for change from within each person, and that this was the only way to renew and reform democracy as well.

In sum, in Lyon the representative model was, unsurprisingly, far from self-evident among the activists. The representative frame, however, often structured their ideas, too, through negation and refusal. The activists were eager to replace it by constructionist or participatory frames, but had little confidence in their own possibilities of having an influence, or making this shift actually happen. For them, the best of democracy was manifested in short-term and small-scale engagements and associative initiatives.

Watchdogs of democracy in Helsinki

> 'Q: So what would ideal cooperation with the city be like, in your opinion?
> A: Well, for example, they could ask statements from this [citizen] network. It could be thought that a representative of the network was asked to join a planning group, but they are political positions mostly, so in that way I understand that this kind of transversal network is a little inconvenient' (Marita).

> 'I think of this as a kind of acting as the watchdogs of democracy. Our point of departure is always that it is the Council that decides things in practice' (Pertti).

These excerpts captured well the framings the activists in Helsinki often put forward in the first place when I asked about their role in local democracy. They questioned neither the local political power structures directly nor the order of representative democracy as such. However, they had a lot of ideas about how to change democracy. They usually talked about these ideas only once they had positioned themselves within the representative frame. Also, many of the new practices they suggested, like the ones Marita put forward in the first excerpt, were quite easily imaginable: asking for the opinion of associations is an everyday procedure in many fields of administration in Helsinki, and most official advisory boards formed around specific policy issues include association members.

Despite the apparent approval of the local political system, the activists claimed that representative democracy 'needed its watchdogs,' to a point that it could not function without constant surveillance. They framed democracy as a rather fragile system that could not be left to stand on its own, as Siiri in the following:

> 'It's within the Pro Municipal Services network that I have actually come to realize what a horrible state this democratic system is in. It has somehow distanced itself from the citizens, so that I think it is absolutely necessary that there are these movements and pressure groups that are as close to citizens as possible, a kind of watchdog over these decision-makers. So it's a kind of citizen surveillance, like "what is it that you are doing now," to keep them in line.'

Unlike the French activists who put the blame rather openly on politicians, the activists in Helsinki founded their criticism particularly on the vulnerability of the political system *vis-à-vis* the tendencies of neo-liberalization of the state and the public sector. They talked about the decision-makers in rather paternalistic terms. They emphasized their own competence and expertise, and appeared confident that democracy needed their efforts of surveillance, and would benefit from their actions, if only the politicians listened to them. In a sense, they seemed to suggest that external forces – neo-liberalism in the first place – threatened the collective Finnish affair of 'building the nation,' and citizens should be let along to fix things, to bring democracy 'back' from the wilderness. It was as if the activists were, despite their criticism, avoiding views that would call into question their devotedness to the current system of governance: a watchdog is on the side of those it watches over for.

Nevertheless, the activists neither remained only within the range of the representative frame nor did they completely avoid expressing transformative views. In so doing, they seemed to smoothly slide form the representative frame towards other framings, like Irma:

> 'But if you ask who the city is, well that is us, through our representatives. I think that for this kind of [activity] ..., there is no folder there with the title "active citizens who contribute" ... so of course it terrifies them ... but the question here is, after all, of changing the ways of thinking towards real democracy. The kind [of democracy] in which both ... administrators and representatives understand that they are our representatives ... also between the elections and in all kinds of questions. Every citizen could have an influence on the municipality, and this should be seen as a possibility.'

While starting off with a 'representative' description of how things 'are,' Irma slid further to suggest a radical change: one towards a 'real' democracy. The latter, however, was framed with representation too: in a real democracy, the representatives 'understand that they are our representatives.' This understanding clearly implicated a stronger citizen influence and inclusion – but she still preferred to call it representative. With the help of this 'tactic,' as if thus secured to come up with more daring suggestions, Irma comfortably shifted from the representative to other frames of democracy, moving towards popular inclusion.

To a certain degree, the activists in Helsinki seemed rather confident of their capacities to 'do something' about the functioning and practices of local democracy. Although they groaned about the attitudes of the decision-makers, they were not as cynical as their French counterparts often seemed to be. They had more faith in the power of arguments, based on their idea of the rationality of the system. They framed democracy as a representative system with participatory, discursive, and even constructionist reshaping about to come up, or already in practice among the activists, as Jarmo explained in particularly sociological terms:

> 'So after all, there has been a profound change, a turning point in participation types. Okay, if I think of what's going on here, I would say that we implement this kind of Habermasian discursive idea that the best argument wins.'

In sum, the activists in Helsinki took the representative frame of democracy for granted, and yet called its exclusiveness into question and seasoned it with other framings in ways mostly unfamiliar to the politicians. They quite proudly emphasized their own expertise in political issues and their capacity to watch over democracy. They talked about democracy as of something belonging to them, just like they did with citizenship (see Chapter 3 in this book), and appeared rather confident that they were needed in making it better.

5.2 Politicians'[3] conceptions of democracy

Lyonnais promoters of democratic reforms

The Lyonnais politicians talked enthusiastically about citizen participation, and shared their ideas about how to organize it better. Representative democracy and citizen participation were often discussed alongside each other, and the frames of democracy in use were diverse, in particular, due to the relatively wide range of accepted styles of political expression. Many politicians were warmly in favor of citizen participation, although critical insights came up, too. In the following, a councilor shared his experiences of concrete situations of citizen participation that he had found somewhat frustrating, but concluded in the end:

> 'But we always have contradictions, it can't exist without contradictions. I would say, the more democracy is wide-ranging, the more there are contradictions. So it's not because there are contradictions that it [democracy] isn't a success. I would even say that it's a proof that listening is extended. ... I believe that a successful democracy is ... as open as possible' (Councilor, M, Left).

Conflict and contradiction thus came up as natural elements of democracy. The 'how' of democratic participation was not exclusively restricted to civility and detachment, and even the constructionist frame appeared in the politicians' talk at times, like in the above demand for open-ended democracy. The question of the interrelation of representation and participation was clearly something the councilors had been thinking about. In their talk, different frames of democracy appeared concomitantly, even if unequally: all the other framings were more or less subordinated by the representative frame. These actors supported participation in principle, but pointed out that the concretizations of all the other models except the representative one caused many practical problems waiting to be solved.

> 'We're experimenting in Lyon with forms of local democracy that we would like to be rather organized and, ... not knowing really how to put them into operation ... . When I think for instance about the neighborhood councils, I believe that we haven't necessarily found the good formulation yet. And the good formulation, it won't come just from the councilors to organize it ... I mean, that the question of participative democracy is a real question, it is evident that the choices can't be made without talking to our fellow-citizens, without taking the temperature, without taking the precaution of explaining where we're going. ... So yes, I believe that in the functional organization ... of how to be situated between participative democracy and representative democracy, I believe that the good formulation has not really been found yet' (Councilor, F, Left).

The interlocutor described the state of the art of the new forms of participation as not finalized. She posed several open questions: what should be done? How could the 'good formulation' be found? She stressed the importance of talking to the citizens, but on the other hand 'taking the temperature,' an expression in current use in French politics, implied that in her eyes, the politicians had a strong control over the whole situation. The representative frame was not expressed quite so loudly, it served rather as the maternal gaze controlling the other, subordinate and imperfect possible framings. The suggestion she made that the councilors were not the ones who should organize better participatory formulations was, however, an allusion to giving away power, even if it was only the power to 'formulate.'

Others went even further: especially councilors 'left of the left,' communists and the like, had radical ideas about changing the decision-making system. However, the representative frame was dominant even in their suggestions, like when a councilor explained the idea of a regional citizen participation program aiming at ambitious new decision-making practices.

> 'So the citizen ateliers will poll the people, whom ever wants to inscribe, and then they'll make the first report and send it to the 11000 people [who are on the list] to ask their opinion. And then the atelier will ... go to the Council ... to make propositions ... and the idea is ... to transform some these propositions into decision. So the idea is actually to go as far as sharing the decisions. That's pretty far in citizen participation. ... The last word will come from the Assembly, because ... we can't ask the citizens to decide in the Assembly's place, that's complicated, but ... even if the councilors will have the last word, some of the decisions will be citizen decisions' (Councilor, Left).

The interlocutor regarded the practice he described as an advanced form of citizen participation, even though it did not reach final decision-making. 'Citizen decisions' were, however, made real through a transformation process, in which mediating levels were needed: ateliers led by councilors, reports to be sent to the inscribed people, presumably some instance to treat the opinions thus gathered, and finally the Assembly that would make the final decisions.

In addition to procedural solutions, also the participating citizens posed problems to the politicians. The hopes they had of citizens' actions involved the idea that these should durably engage themselves to improve their own competences, and thus little by little become able to be more helpful to the decision-makers, and more capable of participating. In this respect, the politician's views resembled those of the urban planning professionals interviewed by Marion Carrel (2007a, 101–2): they saw participation as very much an educative process.

> 'I'd say that a successful deliberation is one that allows citizens to train themselves. I mean, it's not just for them to shout about, but to see the reality a little, the constraints, the finances, the technical problems, and so on. That is the goal of deliberation, to train people to the realities of administrative and economic functions. But that requires permanence' (Councilor, M, Left).

Training was necessary, as the 'quality' of the participants, their lack of patience, competence and long-term devotion was often seen as the biggest problem of participatory practices. The origins of these problematic features were partly in the citizens' lack of experience, but also in their 'Frenchness,' exactly like in some activists' opinions. The politicians highlighted impatience as the national vice and the one that explained many of the problems of French participatory democracy, in particular.

The politicians had other problems in mind that echoed French particularities as well. The problem of the mediating groups, a familiar troublemaker in French political tradition throughout the republican history, troubled Lyonnais politicians as well, and seemed to build firm confrontation between political groups. This feature also communicates with Carrel's findings. In her study, the local councilors often rejected citizen involvement in decision-making altogether by saying they were incapable of making collective decisions. Furthermore, citizens' associations and groups were also rejected, this time, by the planning professionals who otherwise promoted inclusive, open-ended participation. They feared that group voices and 'inhabitant-professionals' would prevent the inclusion and influence of the 'actual' inhabitants (Carrel 2007a, 99–101, 104–6).

Among my Lyonnais interlocutors, these two opinions collided with each other, but also with a third, rather unusual viewpoint for the French context. For a number of those, especially Right-wing representatives, who kept firmly and exclusively within the representative frame, participating citizens were not representative enough *vis-à-vis* the population. Those who moved within the range of other frames often suspected groups and associations of biased lobbyism. But on some occasions, especially politicians who were involved in participatory work, also praised associations and people active in them, acknowledging their efforts to engage in the political processes over time. The following excerpts represented the two extremes of this specter: in the first one, a Right-wing politician repeated the traditional view of French universalism, whereas in the second one, a (moderate) Left-wing politician made less common allusions towards the value of associations in the participatory process.

> 'Deliberation is discussing, and in the very end, in any case, it's us who choose. So ... it [participatory democracy] aims at satisfying those who ... are associated with the municipal work, but who are at the same time kept a little bit under supervision. But ... they have the tendency to ... fraction the electoral corpus, while in reality, especially in France, it's one of the fundaments of the French democracy that the people is not divided, that it is sovereign in its ensemble. There are no categories, no particularisms' (Party division secretary, M, Right).

> 'So it's the different associations, it's the people that work in the neighborhood councils for long term, active citizens doing collective work. ... For the individuals, well, it's more like ... the passions of the moment, "there's dog poo in front of my door, it's a scandal" ... but it doesn't go any further. Whereas the associations who reflect collectively, they have wider views, a bit more elaborated, and with them it is possible to exchange a little deeper views regarding the possible, the impossible, the constraints, the finances, and so on. Because the inhabitants often have very particular interests, the general interest is not their cup of tea. We're more interested in listening to people who work long term and have a reflective capacity: they entail much more interesting things' (Councilor, M, Left).

The latter interlocutor described an experience probably familiar to most professionals, politicians, and citizens involved in participatory democracy, to a certain extent regardless of the context. However, in the French context this politician still took a rather exceptional stand in emphasizing associations the way he did, even if he also framed the problem mostly from the representative perspective. In so doing, he approached his Finnish colleagues, who also stressed cooperation with associations as beneficial to democracy.

To conclude, the Lyonnais politicians talked about democracy moving within a range of different frames, although the representative model dominated their framings. The promotion of participatory democracy was, for many, a crucial task they wanted to engage in, although consensus over practical solutions was lacking, and the question of sharing power through participative processes was not high on the agenda.

Defenders of 'genuine democracy' in Helsinki

Contrasting with the variety of frames the Lyonnais politicians used, in Helsinki the politicians almost exclusively talked about democracy and representation as synonyms. The legitimacy of political institutions was, in their words, based firmly on representative mandates. The way they talked about democracy was often simultaneously confident and defensive – they could treat demands to reform the system as ill-based, but at the same time somewhat threatening – as one talks about an issue the importance of which is irritatingly unclear.

> 'Then what is democracy? The councilors have been elected by the inhabitants. But I think that in order for there to be genuine democracy, the preparations have to go on based on the basic decision of the council and not on these recommendations coming from the outside, because it is just one part of the people that don't quite have an official mandate' (Councilor, F, Right).

Genuine democracy served as a metaphor for an order of things firmly within the range of the representative frame, in which those without official mandates were 'outside', and should not have been trying to influence the decision-making. When talking explicitly about citizen participation, the councilors had mainly two lines of argumentation. On the one hand, they treated citizen groups participating spontaneously and independently with cautiousness and in some cases with straightforward reluctance. Associations that cooperated with the municipality in service production, on the other hand, were rather unanimously praised as important and good partners. The attitude towards citizen participation seemed to vary depending on the kind of participation the interlocutor had in mind. They rejected especially those contentious groups whose activities and motivations could be placed within the participatory or deliberative frames. These rejections were tied notably to the question of action repertoires, and more so to 'the Finnishness', or not, of the repertoires. The prevalence of the code of detachment and civility was strong and the mere idea of challenging it provoked angry reactions among the politicians I met with.

> 'Of course social movements have to call all things into question. But if we start thinking, for example, about the reform of the city financial structures, you can influence it only through elections and getting into

> the council. ... Because we have these ways of democracy. And it's not good enough for them, they want to raise some kind of rebellion. ... In Finland we have a rather good average level of education, so people have the possibility and ability to consider things. These kinds of currents and movements running outside democracy, they stem from those cultures, I think, where the general level of civilization is not so high. There they function. ... Now that the Internet makes it possible that the same comment is copied three hundred times ... in the end the issue ... turns against itself, absolutely. And then these revolt movement people try to teach us things that every councilor deals with for several hours a month. It's totally pointless' (Councilor, F, Right).

This Right-wing councilor promoted the idea that certain action repertoires were unsuitable in the Finnish context by labeling them as stemming from cultures with lower level of civilization than Finland, thus placing the activists acting this way outside the Finnish society, almost as outlaws and barbarians. In addition to this, she jeered at the activists' claimed belief to be able to teach the councilors something. In sum, the councilor expressed a strong defense of the intactness of the representative frame. She also echoed the foundations of the Finnish political culture in her call for order, right procedures and education: rebellion was something very un-Finnish in her view (see Stenius 2010).

The undesirability of certain kinds of citizen activity and attempts to participate was a recurrent feature among the politicians. Even mild mockery of citizen activities occurred:

> 'What they have in common is that they are against something. When it reads pro-, it means anti-. Thus one can coolly draw the conclusion that if a group's name is pro this or pro that, it probably opposes to something. There's a whole legion of these all right' (Councilor, M, Right).

> 'And what will come of it if civic associations all of a sudden start deciding, where is democracy, then?' (Civil servant, F).

Compared to the Lyonnais politicians' pedagogic concerns about how to organize participation better, and how to teach people to become good participants, the hostility of the politicians in Helsinki towards wider citizen participation was striking. Deviations – even if only in the form of ideas – from the representative frame of democracy indeed provoked a lot of emotions among them. Enlarging citizen participation, and thus applying practices within the range of the other frames of democracy, often seemed an unthinkable idea to them. The heavy emphasis on formal political activities in the context of municipal institutions is reminiscent of the traditional state orientation of the Finnish way of doing politics (see e.g. Palonen 2002; Stenius 2010).

The negative insights on citizen participation were, nevertheless, not the whole picture. Some politicians were very concerned with the quality of decision-making and the adequacy of information on which it was based. In order to manage well in these respects, the help of citizen participation was welcome, even indispensable. A well-functioning, democratic public sphere was one where elected representatives made decisions, and occasionally got information from certain citizens or citizen groups with specific expertise on a chosen issue. The advantage of citizen participation was in widening the information basis for representative decision-making, and thus promoting the common good and better decisions for all.

> 'Q: So ... how do you feel, what do movements and voluntary associations have to give to decision-making?
> A: Maybe there will be ... more information in the reports [prepared by the administration]. Sometimes it happens so that when we get the report, it has been prepared rather quickly and the main issues are there, but there can be some crucial thing missing that is important to an association and that would be really important in the ... decision-making, and especially if the introducer submits a negative decision. ... So this way I think it's good that the background information comes in ...' (Councilor, F, Left).

It was through the themes of quality, information and expertise that other framings of democracy did appear, although always laminated with the representative frame. The idea of a deliberative process co-framed the talk of some politicians, but it was almost never directly linked to decision-making. For most, the appropriate place for inclusive deliberation was a consultative organ. However, some allusions were also made to a rather 'constructionist' future direction with an emphasis on dialogue and mutual respect that could be achieved through an exchange of ideas and listening.

> 'There could be open meetings with the boards, yes. Yes, there should be, and they could be held in different parts of the city. But when decisions are made, so it is, I mean, this current system feels quite good. Interaction with the inhabitants[4] ... there are surely

> different opinions about them, all representatives can't stand those situations. I have noticed that the more difficult the situation, the fewer board members show up. When you once experience it, after it is no longer so uncomfortable, and people are friendly deep down. And the inhabitants also show their satisfaction of being listened to and met. ... I feel that when one can speak and discuss, well certainly that's the course that should be taken' (Councilor, M, Green).

This councilor moved between the representative, discursive, and constructionist frames, leaving room, quite exceptionally in the Finnish context, even for not-always-so-civil political interaction. Deep down people were friendly, he said, so he was ready to bear even some uncomfortable moments. Trust in the friendliness of the adversary may stem from a personal belief in people, but it also reflects a political culture in which conformity is seldom threatened. In sum, a strong image of elite dominance based on representation with an emphasis on expertise framed the democracy talk of politicians in Helsinki. Detachment and civility were virtues they placed on themselves, but also on the 'good' citizens from orderly groups and associations providing them with necessary, additional information. Ideas within the range of the discursive frame came up in some Green and Leftist politicians' emphasis on dialogue and mutual respect as means of influence, and widened deliberation. Conflict and contradiction, however, were not seen as the natural elements of democracy like among the Lyonnais politicians, but quite exclusively as deranging, external nuisances.

5.3 Comparing the framings of democracy

Juxtaposing local activists' and politicians' talk in French and Finnish contexts showed, first, that different frames of democracy intertwined and overlapped in the actors' talk about democracy, representation and participation. Secondly, it showed that the frames were not used equally: the representative frame was dominant in the talk of all groups, although in different ways. Thirdly, the construction of the 'problems' of democracy that emerged often within the representative frame but were further laminated with different combinations, shifts, and fractures of framings, brought up contradictions concerning the French and the Finnish local democracy worth further reflection.

In Lyon, the range of frames in use was rather wide among both actors, yet the representative frame was the point of departure to the sometimes opposite directions the argumentations took. The historically emphatic problem of mediation was decidedly present, but the role of associations seemed a paradoxical issue. It provoked opposite viewpoints from the traditional universalistic attitudes to praising associations as partners in participatory democracy, and, among the activists, as the only factual possibilities for meaningful democratic action. There was further disagreement between the two groups: the French politicians promoted a reform of democracy rather self-confidently, despite some reservations about the current participatory practices, whereas the activists talked mostly in pessimistic and disillusioned terms, expressing frustration and anger. Yet both politicians and activists defined democracy as an open and collective process self-evidently marked by struggles and conflicts.

In Helsinki, by contrast, the representative frame permeated and more or less dominated the talk of both groups of actors. However, especially in the activists' talk, it also served as grounds for criticism and space for fracturing the frame from within. The Finnish actors in both groups were at ease with the idea of associations participating in democratic processes, but especially the politicians had different reservations on the matter. They wanted the associations to be of a certain kind, and to include people acting in a certain way. Furthermore, politicians often rejected the 'problem' of democracy, and clung to their positions in the representative system, whereas the activists seemed, despite their circumspection, rather confident about the upcoming changes, and their own influence on them. Still, in defining 'good' democracy, or good practices, both groups emphasized quality, legitimacy, and efficiency.

How to explain these differences? The answer lies in focusing on what kind of a problem, and whose problem, the problem of democracy was in the two contexts. In defining the 'problem' of democracy, the actors in Lyon and Helsinki framed their views emphasizing different questions. Their choices seemed to depend on what was the most suitable starting point considering the cultural 'tools' they felt the most comfortable with.

The French seemed at ease with questions concerning the repertoires of participation, and the potential outcomes of the process, but less so with issues such as what qualities the participation should have, and what should be the composition of the participating group. Hence, Lyonnais politicians eagerly talked about suggestions of 'how' to enhance democracy and participation, and the activists pulverized the offered means with equal zeal. The outcomes – be it the sixth republic or a revolution – were also discussed. These features, for their part, implied the politicization of participation. However, both the Lyonnais politicians and activists regretted the 'characteristics of Frenchness' that made changing things difficult. Instead of a reduction to national 'personality traits,' the problem perhaps lay within a political culture that, despite the effervescent surface, characteristic to the 'constructive' style of representation, had great difficulties with the problem of who should participate – under what mandate, defending what kinds of interests – and what qualities should participation include.

The Finns, on the contrary, defined democracy as questions of qualities and participants, but lost their track with questions concerning repertoires and outcomes. The Finnish tradition of 'plurality in the unity,' in which different opinions are allowed as long as a stable frame of common values remains, makes questions like what should participation be like, and who should take part, tangible (e.g. Stenius 2010). Expertise and efficiency, the civic qualities emphasized equally by both local groups, echoed the old nation-building imperative. The collective responsibility over the best possible ways to promote the common good of the Finnish society lay in the hands of legitimate representatives and educated, well-informed citizens who efficiently fulfilled their duties, and participated through their associations. All of the above underpinned depoliticization of participation: these rationalistic, matter-of-factual, even technical characteristics were not prone to lead towards contention and new options. Furthermore, questions concerning the repertoires and outcomes of participation were troublesome for both actor groups, despite their efforts to safeguard the mirror-clear, 'descriptive' representation. Their framings fractured when confronted with questions such as should conflicting, clashing, even uncivil participating repertoires be accepted and. whether, and how, citizen participation actually should influence the decisions taken, and change the political power structure. Both groups were, nevertheless, rather confident of their capacities and position.

In the following chapter, the dynamics portrayed above will be further analyzed by looking closer at the local controversies as they were represented in the local news media, and the ways of justifying the solutions different actors suggested in them.

6
Justifying on the Local Public Sphere: Newspaper Representations of Encounters between Citizens and Cities

In the previous chapters, I have analyzed citizens' encounters with their cities – with various representatives of 'the city,' as well as with the city space and environment – by considering locally embedded group styles and the different levels of engagement they display, different actors' views on democracy and citizenship, and visual representations produced and published by both parties. An important part of the local public sphere has hitherto not yet been considered: the news media. The role of the media – and newspapers in particular – for democracy and the public sphere has been widely emphasized (e.g. Anderson 1983; Dahlgren & Sparks 1991; Calhoun 1992b; Garnham 1992; Oliver & Myers 1999; McNair 2000; Marx Ferree *et al.* 2002b; Croteau & Hoynes 2003; Habermas 2004[1962]). In this chapter, I extend the analysis of the processes of politicization of the previous chapters to another level of the public debate, to the communication between citizens and policy-makers in local newspapers. Instead of concentrating solely on protests, or on one particular topic of disagreement, I analyze an overview of local encounters and conflicts during a time period of six months (January–June in 2005) in *Le Progrès* (LP) and *Helsingin Sanomat* (HS).[1]

In local newspapers, the coverage of local encounters – between citizens and cities, inhabitants and officials, activists and politicians – is daily bread and lifeblood. The coverage differs from that of national news media due to the close linkage to local interest groups. Many protests make it to the local news only, or make it there before becoming national news, and receive a broader treatment than in the wider news media (Oliver & Myers 1999; Neveu E. 2003). And apart from protests, local newspapers have a particularly strong role in providing their readers with tools to imagine and re-imagine the community they live in, and representing the 'common' in terms of both disputes over the common good and the 'normal,' habitual course of people living together in a city (cf. Anderson 1983; Thévenot 2006).

Therefore, in order to grasp the definition struggles concerning the common good in Lyon and Helsinki, I first ask what kind of disagreements attracted public attention, and how they were represented. A glance at the two newspapers gives the following impression of local conflict issues: construction plans and sites, zoning, and different public services were common sources of conflict, but also more abstract questions such as minority rights, interpretations of laws, and grounds for decision-making raised enough discord to be reported upon. However, the themes of dispute differed between the contexts, and the time period undoubtedly played its role, too. In Helsinki, the big issue of the winter of 2005 was budgetary cuts targeted at the school network that threatened to result in the closing of several schools. In Lyon, the scoop of the spring was less clear, but there were three topics that gained particular attention: the installation of parking meters – and thus the abolition of free-of-charge parking – the living conditions and right to education of the children of illegal immigrants, and the continuing disappointments and difficulties met in the work of the neighborhood councils.

The topics of dispute were, nevertheless, not the most captivating point of comparison in the newspapers. Instead, it was the ways in which different positions and opinions were justified in the local public sphere in Lyon and Helsinki. To give a quick example: when a French group of inhabitants opposed to the installation of parking meters in their district, they claimed that the plan was unfair and created inequality between inhabitants of different city districts. A Finnish group of inhabitants protesting against the closing down of the neighborhood school, for their part, claimed that the decision was based on erroneous statistics. These arguments did not stem from journalistic styles, or differences in the newspaper distribution. What were they about? For the French, the argumentative logic often stemmed from vocabularies of equality, solidarity, and fairness. The Finns seemed to rely – in this example as well as in many others – on arguments based on scientific knowledge, expertise, or calculations of efficiency.

The first, and primary, question of this chapter is, then, what were the differences in the justifications local actors in these two contexts used to legitimize their arguments, and why? What kinds of arguments, and by whom, were represented as justifications to differing views in local conflicts? I examine these questions by analyzing newspaper articles concerning local conflict situations with the help of Luc Boltanski's and

Laurent Thévenot's theory on justification (1991; 1999). The analysis is built on a methodological tool, the Public Justifications Analysis, adapted from Boltanski's and Thévenot's theoretical work, and developed to address public justifications in empirical material, such as newspaper articles (Luhtakallio & Ylä-Anttila 2011; Methods Appendix in this book). Equipped with this tool, I analyze the justifications different actors judged as legitimate in solving local controversies. In which worlds of justification – *inspiration, domestic, renown, civic, market, industrial,* or *Green* – (Boltanski & Thévenot 1991, 20–3; Lafaye & Thévenot 1993) did the French and Finnish actors find suitable arguments for making claims, how, and why? Furthermore, I analyze the tensions between different justifications, their combinations, and thus the 'generalized' arguments, referring to 'different sorts of values, principles, or models for judging what is good, worthy and right' the local actors in these contexts used (Lamont & Thévenot 2000, 236).

However, conflicts are neither the only thing making news nor the only context of citizen-city encounters – and the other way round, not all conflicts make it to the news, or to any kind of publicity. The second task of this chapter is to look at how and when the local communities were portrayed as harmonious and stable, and what or who was left out in these occasions. What were the terms of 'business as usual', whose voice did not get heard? In order to grasp these issues, I take a look at, first, the local activists' views on the newspaper coverage of local topics, and secondly, what else, apart from disputes, happened in the news reportages of encounters between citizens and the cities.

In his work after the justification theory, Laurent Thévenot (2006; 2007; 2010) has suggested that in order to understand how societies hold together, looking at 'the crisis', and justifications operationalized to solve them, are not enough. Instead, we need to consider three levels of engagement that actors have with the world and each other. The level of justifications is the most public and general regime of communication. But situations that do not reach this level of generality, or in which actors do not reach for the purpose of common good, need to be considered differently. In Thévenot's terminology, they are either pursuits of individual interests and fulfillment of plans, or expressions of familiarity and intimate engagement (Thévenot 2010; 2011). In terms of local news, these pursuits and expressions were represented, for example, in reportages of hearings and participatory meetings, collective flower planting, and different events for minority groups, organized by the city.

Thus, the second question this chapter addresses is how do the local news media represent engagements on the levels of individual interests and personal, intimate concerns in citizen–city encounters. Addressing these themes in the analysis of newspaper representations is both controversial and crucial: it is controversial because it is an attempt to examine under- or un-publicized issues using a public source, and crucial because it is in these reports that we may deepen understanding on the 'normal' course of citizen–city encounters, but also on possibly silencing, oppressive mechanisms of the public sphere. Even though the actors we have met in the previous chapters do not have a leading role in these encounters, I will also bring forth their views on the local media sphere. As I will show in the analysis of justifications in local conflicts, the equal standing of different parties in arguing about the common good is all but self-evident.

6.1 Justifications for the common good in local newspapers

Public justifications analysis and local conflicts

In the local newspapers in Lyon and Helsinki, conflicts concerning the definition of the common good translated into a wide range of disputes by a wide range of actors. In Lyon, a citizens' collective claimed that the installation of parking meters would put the inhabitants in unequal positions and violate the rights of the neighborhood's inhabitants (LP0116). A group of parents put pressure on the authorities against the deportation of one of their children's immigrant classmates, claiming that their deportation would violate republican values (LP0523). In Helsinki, a neighborhood association resisted the construction of a homeless shelter claiming that the homeless have the right to habitation, but the neighborhood is not a suitable location for it (HS0109). A residents' collective argued for keeping the public library branch in its place because closing it would not bring important savings to the municipality (HS0524). The representatives of the cities – mayors, councilors, officials, managers, consultants – either admitted to the citizens' demands but argued, for instance, for more money from superior levels of governance, lamented the malfunctions of this or that political process, or defended their cases, accusing the citizens of particularistic, erroneous and poorly based, or simply wrong views.

In order to analyze justifications in the newspaper articles, I organized them by identifying the claim, the claim-maker, and the justification(s) used to justify the claim (Luhtakallio & Ylä-Anttila 2011; see also Koopmans & Statham 1999; Koopmans & Rucht 2002;

see also Methods Appendix in this book). Table 6.1 illustrates the dimensions of the data from the number of articles to that of claims, the proportions of claim-makers, and finally to the number of the justifying acts I detected, and their division according to their performers, the groups of citizens on the one hand and the representatives of the two cities on the other.

The primary unit of analysis, justification, often required a reconstruction of the context of the conflict: justification was not a mere argument, and not built of words alone, but instead a chain of things, actions, ideas, and words that also included the physical environment of the conflict, the non-human objects, machinery, and other circumstances, in addition to the human claim-makers and adversaries of the situation. Thus, in a conflict concerning an incineration plant to be built, the technical details of the plant, the piece of land it was planned to be built on, the tools, machinery, and work needed, as well as the junk to be burned, were all organic parts of the conflict and justifications made to solve it, not just the context in which the conflict took place (Boltanski & Thévenot 1991, 21, 177–9). Thus, one claim could include justifications from different 'worlds': real life conflicts tend to be complicated, and even though newspaper representations surely are simplifications of the actual situations, they nevertheless portray a complex picture of a situation or a chain of situations, material components, institutional contexts, and a variety of actors.

The following example demonstrates this complexity, and how the Public Justifications Analysis approaches it, by laying out a fictitious, yet in both Lyon and Helsinki very possible case of claim making. I am going to illustrate a case of citizens' possible acts of justification in one single claim. In this case, the claim-maker is a group of worried parents. Their claim is that contrarily to a plan suggested by an imaginary city, a small daycare center in their neighborhood must not close. Arguments

Table 6.1 Newspaper data dimensions

	Articles total (N)	*Claims by citizens %*	*Claims by city (%)*	*Claims total (N)*	*Justifications by citizens (%)*	*Justifications by city (%)*	*Justifications Total (N)*
Le Progrès	102	72	28	127	75	25	213
Helsingin Sanomat	96	73	27	140	73	27	205

based on the seven different worlds of justification would form, for example, as follows:

Inspiration: The children's creativity flourishes in this center, as the devoted employees make great efforts in arts education and in creating an inspiring atmosphere.

Domestic: The daycare center has decades of tradition in the neighborhood, and the director is a respected 'mother figure' in the community. Many parents cherish their own childhood memories of the center.

Renown: A famous, awarded pediatrician and a number of other celebrities oppose to the closing of the center.

Civic: Good daycare is children's right, and if this center closes, the children of the neighborhood will not be treated equally with other children. A petition signed by over 200 people objects the closing.

Market: Daycare in small units is cheaper than in big centers.

Industrial: Professionals are responsible of the daycare center planning, and their expert knowledge confirms the effectiveness of proximity daycare with small groups of children in preventing childhood stress syndromes.

Green: If the daycare center closes, the parents will have to drive their children to a daycare center far away, which will produce more greenhouse gases and promote the climate change.

This example shows the way in which inspirational justifications were grounded on esthetical or emotional values, creativity, and expressivity (Boltanski & Thévenot 1991, 201). Domestic justifications based their force of argument on tradition, hierarchy, generations, an appeal to a superior power, or a need of protection due to inferiority, relations of confidence and authority (ibid. 1991, 207–8, 212–15). The renown-based justifications were founded on fame, success, visibility, communication, and numbers of followers (ibid. 223–5). Justifications based on the civic worth stressed collective organization and mobilization, representation, solidarity, and legality, and the general will (ibid. 231–3, 237, 240). Justifications of the market worth were the ones prioritizing competition, price, financial value, selling and buying, and free circulation of goods, both in terms of making money and saving money (ibid. 244–5, 250). Industrial justifications emphasized productivity, control and viability, efficiency, scientifically (or, for instance, statistically) analyzed facts, technical measures and objects, and the quality of work (ibid. 252–4, 259). Finally, Green justifications stressed environmental values and the protection of the environment above other values (Lafaye & Thévenot 1993).

The fictitious example is a clear one – the newspaper representations rarely were. A real-life claim could combine all of the above: parents claiming the center should not close could come up with all this in response to the initial conflict, the municipality threatening to close down the daycare center (with the help of a very compassionate reporter who would give them enough space). In order to grasp the complexity of the real-life justifications, the issue of overlapping of the worlds of justification must be considered.

In many cases, the claim-makers did not justify their claim with a justification of one world, but moved from one to another within one act of claiming. They used different justifications side by side to back up one claim from different points of view – as if making sure that the claim was as well armed as possible against any imaginable opposition. This feature stems from the nature of newspaper representations: these justification acts were somewhat frozen images of complicated conflict situations, in which sequences of the conflict may have followed one another for long, and continue to do so after the article has been published and read.

Returning still to the daycare center example, the parents could have come up with a cluster or hybrid of justifications, combining two or more of the justifications illustrated above: the daycare center must not be closed because the municipality has to fulfill its statutory responsibilities (civic) *and* organize accessible and good-quality (industrial) daycare *and* promote the protection of the environment (green) in its democratic decisions (civic). Furthermore, they could have built their argument so that it would denounce the counterpart's real or expected argument: a civic justification leaning to the rights discourse would judge the market world in this type of matter altogether by claiming that rights and equality cannot be measured in money. Also, the parents could have claimed that administrative and economic effectiveness is less a viable standard in this case than effectiveness in promoting children's well being, and in this way remain 'within' the industrial world, but nevertheless question the arguments favorable to the closing of the daycare unit.

After all this fiction, the next section moves on to examining the reality of public justifications in Lyon and Helsinki. First, I make a comparison of predominant justifications, and then zoom further to the micro-level of public disputes: the encounters between power-holders and citizens, and the ways in which they communicated their views on the common good in what ever matter was at stake.

French and Finnish modes of public justifications compared

In this section, I compare the acts of justifying in the newspaper coverage of local conflicts in Lyon and Helsinki. Table 6.2 illustrates the proportions of different justifications in the analyzed set of claims.[3]

The most significant quantitative result of the justification analysis was the prevalence of civic and industrial justifications in both Lyon and Helsinki. This axis also included one of the biggest differences between the French and Finnish justifications, as the French used civic arguments significantly more than the Finns. The civic world was by far the most common basis for justifications in Lyon, whereas in Helsinki, while frequently used, it was less insurmountable. The claims were slightly more dispersed between different worlds in the Finnish data, even if the industrial world was the most commonly used base for justification. Although minor in a number of cases, the biggest difference between the two contexts was the appearance of market justifications, which the Finns used more than double the times than the French. Domestic justifications were more common in the French material, whereas the differences were less important regarding inspiration-based, renown, and Green justifications.

It is no surprise that civic arguments proved common in the argumentation especially by the citizen groups of both contexts. In its purest form, civic justifications were demands for rights and/or lawful procedures by civic actors, as in the following two examples:

> 'The demonstrators denounce an attack against the liberty of expression.'
>
> The demonstrators protest against police violence, arbitrary arrests and abusive imprisonment in recent demonstrations, because

Table 6.2 Justifications in claims of local conflicts in LP and HS (%)

Justifications in claims	*Le Progrès (%)*	*Helsingin Sanomat (%)*
Domestic	24	17
Inspiration	17	14
Civic	66	40
Renown	8	3
Industrial	39	45
Market	9	19
Green	5	8
Total *N*	127	140

> they are attacks against the basic right and liberty of expression (LP0519).
>
> 'The tenants of [the city of] Helsinki worry about their rights.'
> The tenants' associations of Helsinki oppose the city's plans to change the legislation concerning tenant democracy, because the reform would narrow the rights of the tenants and it has been drafted without hearing their opinions (HS0216).

In these two examples, a very straightforward claim for civic, i.e. 'democratic' procedures built up the justification. The legitimacy of the claim leaned entirely on the presupposition of shared democratic values, and not only values but also, in fact, collectively set and accepted rules. Civic justifications were, however, often combined with other arguments, and this did bring up more differences between the two contexts. In the Finnish case, the most common combination appeared with the industrial world, with an emphasis on efficiency and quality.

> 'The teachers' union would like to inspect the legality of the school savings in Vantaa.'
> The local teachers' union insists that the legality (civic) of the planned cutbacks in schools have to be examined (industrial), and the City Council must return to the issue (civic), because saving money through cutbacks leads to impossible working conditions (industrial), and possibly practices that would violate the law on primary education (civic) (HS0427).
>
> 'The airport's environment permit does not need to be changed'
> Associations of the inhabitants of Vantaa campaign for changes to the airport environment permit (civic), because airport activities should be regulated by noise detectors (industrial) (HS0305).

The civic–industrial somersault in the first example was very typical to the logic of the Finnish justifications. In the fashion of an oppressed party, the teachers' union seemed to choose to leave no stone unturned, while sticking to the back-and-forth between the civic and industrial worlds. In the second example, the civic justification seemed to be more of a decoration for a claim that essentially relied on an industrial case.

In the French case, civic justifications combined often, similarly to the Finnish case, with industrial arguments, as well as often with domestic justifications, and sometimes with the two at the same time.

> '19 cameras of video surveillance installed at the Pavillons square.'
> The Non à Big Brother collective opposes (civic) the installation of new video surveillance cameras, because they have not proved to be an effective way to prevent crime (industrial), and they are a danger to the rights and liberties of the individuals (civic) (LP0313).

> 'Petition against a deportation – The mobilization for Carnelle gains strength.'
> Pupils' parents (domestic) put pressure on the authorities (civic) against the deportation of a young immigrant student, because the deportation would be against republican traditions (domestic) and values (civic) (LP0523).

> 'Croix-Rousse and parking meters: "Refusing a fatality".'
> A citizens' collective claims (civic) that the installation of parking meters (industrial) would put the inhabitants in unequal positions and violate the rights (civic) of the neighborhood's inhabitants (domestic) (LP0116).

In the first example, the combining civic–industrial justification resembled the one in HS0427. Yet, different from the Finnish examples was the introduction of the domestic base of legitimacy into the civic–industrial logic in the second two LP examples.

Furthermore, civic justifications seemed to gain different substantial emphasis in the Finnish and the French cases. The Finns primarily stressed legality, contracts, and decisions taken in representative organs, whereas the French called for equality, solidarity, and rights. Arguments leaning on the opinion of the majority, often claimed by the use of a petition or of statistics, and hence in the 'middle ground' between civic and industrial, were common in the Finnish material. Also, the use of industrial justification, apart from being more common, was more 'independent' in the Finnish case. In the French case, the industrial world almost never appeared alone, without a civic or other combining feature. In HS, however, there were claims by citizens that were justified solely with industrial arguments that played 'the expert card' to the full.

> 'The Greens of Vantaa chafe at the falling down of the gas plant plans.'
>
> The Finnish League for Nature Protection and the local environment association claim that the city's proposition of a gasworks cannot be built as a power plant as planned, because recycling junk in this way turns it into an incineration plant, which requires the installation of specific types of filters (HS0118).

Proving technical expertise by meticulous details and technical facts, as well as by frequent references to scientific studies and statistics, was often on the agenda in the Finnish claims, whatever the issue or the other worlds of justification in use. This was so even if many justifications, like the example above, implied a civic understanding of common rules, and abiding by them. In the French claims, on the contrary, industrial justifications appeared mostly somewhat subordinated by other arguments, especially ones grounded in civil rights and liberties.

The encounters: justifications by citizens and city representatives

The main differences in performing public justifications between the two contexts left open the question of the citizen–city encounters, as well as situations in which a justification would be judged upon, and denounced, from within another position. Juxtaposing the justifications used by the citizens and the city representatives in HS and LP offers answers to these questions, but first, a few words on the people behind these acts, and the comparative 'design' of the case.

The claim-makers on the 'citizen' side were very much alike in both contexts. Considering the important differences in the role of associations in French and Finnish political cultures, it was somewhat surprising that associations were represented as 'the voice of the citizens' nearly as commonly in both newspapers. In HS, 33 per cent of the citizens' claims were performed by an association or a representative of one, whereas in LP the share was 23 per cent. Given the difference in the numbers of associations in the two countries, as well as the historical role of associations in Finnish corporatist governance model, and the traditional 'allergy' of the French political culture towards associations, this feature of local claim-making was slightly surprising (see Chapters 1 and 5 in this book). It was perhaps indicative of a process in which the position of associations becomes increasingly similar, as the hopes for their partnership in public service production increase (see e.g. Holli *et al.* 2007). However, in both contexts, the most common claim-makers on the citizen side were by far groups of 'the inhabitants', or a variety of similar expressions derived from this term.

I included in the notion of the 'city' claim-makers all public bodies and institutions, whether they were, strictly speaking, municipal or regional, in order to avoid differences due to the structures of local decision-making instead of the logic of local conflicts in each context. The most noteworthy difference concerning the claim-makers of 'the city' was the dominance of officials in HS – two-thirds – compared to LP, in which local politicians presented half, and officials a fair third of the claims. In some cases, other parties took part in these conflicts as well. For example, private companies sometimes appeared as the only opposing party to the citizens' claims. I included the majority of these cases as well, since all construction projects, environmental issues, and the like, provide for the implication of local public structures, and decision-making, whether or not immediately present in the article.

Table 6.3 illustrates the division of justifications by the two groups of actors in HS and LP.

The juxtaposition of the justifications reveals that in both contexts there was a 'common ground' of very typical acts of justification. In HS, common ground was firmly located in the industrial world. In LP, industrial arguments on the one hand, and civic ones on the other, were justifications both claim-maker groups used abundantly.

Table 6.3 Justifications made by citizens and citizen groups, and by city representatives

Justifications	*Le Progrès (N=213)*		*Helsingin Sanomat (N=205)*	
	Citizens (%)	*City (%)*	*Citizens (%)*	*City (%)*
Domestic	16	9	13	7
Inspiration	12	4	12	2
Civic	**38**	**42**	**34**	**9**
Renown	6	2	4	–
Industrial	**21**	**28**	**25**	**47**
Market	**3**	**15**	**6**	**31**
Green	4	–	6	4
Total	100%	100	100	100

What does a 'common ground', then, mean in these media-represented citizen–city encounters? I suggest it indicates at least the most obvious common denominator of the respective (local) political cultures – the tool everyone knows how to use, or at least knows is the important tool, the language everyone understands, if not shares, even in the midst of the bitterest conflict of interests. In the French case, the tool was that of civic rights, deliberations, and solidarity. In the Finnish case, it seemed to be the language of efficiency, work, and requirements of quality and expertise. Common ground did, however, not indicate an agreement, but rather the observation that these modes of justification were possible for both parties, and also provoked reality tests in which the adversary's justifications were questioned 'from within.' In the Finnish case, the following example illustrates this usage of industrial justifications.

> 'There is a wish for clear calculations of the economies made by closing schools.'
> The representative of the municipal education department asked for constructive suggestions concerning the reduction of the number of schools – if the school spaces cannot be objects of cutbacks, something else will have to be cut, because as the number of pupils will decrease in the future (industrial), the price per capita cannot rise (market) (HS0309a).
>
> The citizens called for more clarity in the calculations (industrial) and actual need for savings (market), as the statistics and prognosis concerning the number of pupils are currently controversial (industrial. (HS0309b).

The citizen group questioned the validity of the industrial argument made by the officials by stating that the calculations and statistics it relied on did not hold. The market argument was treated less directly, but the claim for clarity indicated distrust in the durability of the presented argument. Thus, the citizens' justification produced a reality test within the industrial-market combination that denounced the city representative's case by at least an attempted revelation of the false groundings of the latter.

In the French case, civic justifications were used similarly, as the following example illustrates.

> 'Urban planning of Gerland: An encounter between inhabitants and councilors.'

> The inhabitants of Gerland demand that the decisions concerning the area's urban development have to be made in accordance with their demands, because in a democracy, the representatives must follow the will of the people, and listen to what they want, and the citizens' words have to be taken into account (LP0421a).

> The councilor in charge [of the citizen participation procedure] states that a consensus has to be found, and that the councilors have to make the basic decision after which the citizens can be consulted, because the councilors have been mandated for decision-making (LP0421b).

In the above case, the councilor called into question the citizens' use of the civic worth, and concluded that it was not justifiable. His own way of using a civic justification in producing a hierarchical order (first the councilors, then the consulted citizens) would probably call for yet another reality test – had the citizen group had another chance to argument, they might have claimed that this kind of hierarchy was not democratic, but autocratic. Thus, they would have denounced the councilor's argument as not civic, but domestic. However, the story did not go further here, so the case ended with the councilor's suggestion of a 'purer' way of justifying the situation from within the civic world.

The extension of the previous example was, however, not far-fetched. The French use of the civic justifications by both the citizens and the city representatives became more nuanced when the cases of denunciations were compared. Both parties denounced the domestic worth from within civic justifications, often accusing the other party of 'un-civic' behavior: autocratic and hierarchical (and sometimes 'scandalous'; cf. Doidy 2005b; Rosanvallon 2006) in the case of the city representatives, as in the first exemple below, and self-centered and particularistic in the case of the citizens, as in the second example.

> 'Parking: A neighborhood council brawls. Croix-Rousse: the parking meters will not pass'
> The association *Croix-Rousse Citoyen* denounces the total lack of dialogue between citizens and councilors regarding a plan to install parking meters in the neighborhood and accuses the Mayor of functioning like an autocrat (LP0308).

> 'The councilors answer to inhabitants. The general assembly of CIL [*Comité d'intérêt local*] of Montplaisir brought up several agendas including the A. Courtois market place, the project of the zone 30, the parking fees...'.

> The representative of the transport and sewerage board responses to inhabitants' critique of the market place planning by saying that the problem is a complex one and that there are numerous professional interests to be taken into account. He strongly denounced the inhabitants' demand that the city hall should take a 'commanding' position by saying it could not in any case take a decision without hearing all parties concerned in the affair (LP0306).

Another aspect that Table 6.3 showed was that the justifications based on the market world appealed mainly to the city representatives in both contexts. In addition, the market world was in use by the Finnish city representatives twice as often as by their French counterparts. The market world was habitually combined with industrial justifications, as the following example illustrates.

> 'A golf course proposed for Turvesuo in Mankkaa.'
> The head of the technical department claims that the zoning of the area of Turvesuo into a golf course has to be commenced, because a change in the city plan has to be worked through (industrial), and because the golf course would raise the value of the surrounding lots (market) (HS0330).

In this example, as well as in many others, it was easy to make the interpretation that money was the 'real' base of the claim, and the industrial 'back-up' was there to enhance the legitimacy of the market world, the denouncement of which could be easy in these cases. The public officials were mainly acting with taxpayer money, so would not a denouncement concerning the use of this money, or the purely financial evaluations of public, i.e. deep down civic, concerns always lurk in the background? Indeed, the citizens were not completely detached from the market world: they denounced it, especially in the Finnish case, with all possible ways they could come up with – most prominently with industrial or civic arguments. They claimed that there was no base for justifying from within a market world in situations that could not be measured in money, such as children's education, or basic services. In addition, the citizens did, in rare cases, also make use of the market worth, as in the following example in which the market justification was almost desperately turned on the lathe.

> 'The inhabitants of Viherlaakso defended their library.'
> The inhabitants of Viherlaakso state that the area's library has to be preserved, because its annual costs are not high, and its discontinuation would not bring big savings (HS0524).

This rather extreme case illustrated the particularly Finnish characteristics of 'desperate' acts of justification that occurred exclusively among the citizen claim-makers. 'Desperate' in the sense of not making use of arguments that logically come to mind in the first place, for instance in the case of defending a public library: that the library is a public services and that citizens all over the city have the same right to near-by services, or that libraries are the worst imaginable source of savings in bad economic situations, as they benefit everybody in the same way and prevent social exclusion. Instead, the inhabitants of this neighborhood claimed that the savings the municipality would make by closing down the library were insignificant. Implicitly, they also played the expert card, as they referred to the annual costs of the particular library and showed understanding of the importance of this sum in the municipal budget. However, this kind of act of justification can also be interpreted as that of an 'oppressed party,' forced to join the world of the opponent, as otherwise there would be little hope that any attempt of justifying a different solution would be successful.

In the French case, the city representatives' use of market justifications did not provoke this kind of reactions from the citizens, but to the contrary, bold denouncements from within the civic world. Curiously, the civic world sometimes offered a scene for the above types of justifications: cases in which the 'city' justified its claim by legitimacy of the requirements of participatory democracy, for instance, and the citizens, although disapproving of the case, felt obliged to justify their disapproval anyway they could within the civic range of arguments – instead of saying, for instance, that the structures of participatory democracy functioned so badly they could not form a base of legitimacy (a claim the Lyonnais also made on some occasions). In these cases, it seemed that the citizens felt obliged, in the context of talking to the news media, to enter a 'common ground' defined by the city representatives, instead of relying on values that would perhaps be closer to their agenda.

6.2 Absent conflicts, silent voices?

The love–late relationship of social movements and local news

> 'I can search *Le Progrès* as much as I want [for information on a demonstration]. And then these media that call themselves a little bit alternative, like *Lyon Capitale* that calls itself the journal of free spirits, and it's a total rag. But independent communication in Lyon, you'd need a freaking good pair of eyes' (Chazz).

> 'Q: How well have you succeeded in gaining publicity?

> A: Well, otherwise we've been really successful, but as *Helsingin Sanomat* does not discuss these matters, it means that we stay out [of publicity]. The alliance between *Helsingin Sanomat* and the city executives seems unbreakable' (Jarmo).

Eric Neveu (2003) has emphasized the particularity of local journalism *vis-à-vis* social movements and civil society in general. In his account, the local press is often more attentive to social movements than national ones, both in regarding their claims earlier, and in treating them in more depth, and often more favorably (ibid. 457–8). However, he also recognizes the phenomenon that Jarmo above is speaking of: local journalism is dependent on, and in many ways intertwined with local power structures and interest groups, as they need to stay in good terms with their sources – i.e. not make anybody too upset (ibid. 449). The activists I interviewed in Lyon and Helsinki described, quite bitterly, how the local news media were tied to the apron strings of those in power. The activists in both cities criticized the newspapers for not covering alternative visions of the city, and for conforming to the opinions and claims of the city leadership.

From the activist point of view, local newspapers were indeed dependent on and connected to the local context in its variety, but in cases where the conflict broke out between local power holders and citizen groups,[4] they were obviously more dependent on, and connected to the former. In this sense, some parties were treated 'more equally' (sic) than others.

In comparison to the conflicts displayed in the local newspapers, those brought up by the activists and the ones I observed during my fieldwork were rather different. In the few cases in which the newspapers treated a topic close to the activist groups, the interpretations differed from the ones the activists put forward. For example, above, Chazz talked about a clash between the police and the activists during the contention about free billposting that had been reported exclusively from the police's point of view. The activists had been accused of a quasi-ambush even though, according to Chazz, it was the police that deliberately caused the confrontation. Equally, Jarmo brought up details concerning the newspaper coverage of the case concerning the profits of the local power company. According to him, *Helsingin Sanomat* had, despite the desperate efforts of the social movement to correct the information, blindly followed the argument of the City Executive Board – that claimed the profits could not be disbursed to other units of the city – until the day the national competition official made its opposite decision. Then the newspaper, in Jarmo's terms, 'ate its words' and reported the opposite with no remarks whatsoever (see Chapter 2 in this book).

However, the very common accusation of activists in this study[5] that newspapers disregarded them and their causes and claims completely, was exaggerated. In the previous sections, the reportage of local conflicts represented primarily citizen views on the issues (over 70 per cent of the justifications in both newspapers were expressed by citizen actors). There were, however, only a few examples in the newspaper data that directly concerned a conflict in common with the previous chapters. One of them was the reportage in *Le Progrès* concerning the *Non à Big Brother* (NBB) collective's arguments against the installation of video cameras (see above, example LP0313; see also Chapters 2 and 4 in this book). When the coverage of *Le Progrès* was compared with the collective's website for instance, the conclusion would obviously be that the newspaper reported the movement's argument quite loyally, very much in the spirit Eric Neveu (2003, 450–1) described to be characteristic to the local press: factual, descriptive, and respectful reportage of local affairs. Nevertheless, in the interviews, the activists of the NBB collective stated that local media had ignored their claims, and put forward only the Mayor's view on the matter. They had perhaps not done their reading very thoroughly – or, maybe the activist style required criticism towards mainstream media, even if there were occasionally exceptions to the rule.

Nevertheless, the activist accounts of the media differed in Lyon and Helsinki. The activist groups in both cities described the local media as a many-sided field, and pointed out the importance of the alternative media, such as independent, often voluntary-based radio stations, web journals, and small-circulation publications of different groups. In addition, Helsinki had something Lyon did not: the *Voima* magazine, a freely distributed nation-wide alternative monthly, with a 60 000-copy edition. The nationwide French alternative news sources were not originated from Lyon the way *Voima* was from Helsinki (see also Chapter 2 in this book). At the same time, there was also a difference concerning the mainstream media. In Lyon, the importance of the local media was somewhat overwhelmed by the importance of the national press, much more consumed by most of the activists than the local one, whereas in Helsinki, the local press was the national press. Clearly, the position of *Helsingin Sanomat* in the local public sphere of Helsinki was significantly stronger than that of *Le Progrès* in Lyon. It was a foregone conclusion among the activists in Helsinki that if *Helsingin Sanomat* ignored a topic, it did not exist. In Lyon, the activists did not seem to bother themselves very much with the coverage of their actions in *Le Progrès* – instead, if a claim or an action made it through to the national news media, it was considered a great, yet rare, success. In this sense, the activists in Helsinki were more dependent on their newspaper than the newspaper was on them.

Difficult articulations of personal attachments

Apart from the conflicts that were the focus of the previous sections, both newspapers reported extensively of various peaceful encounters between the citizens and the cities. In addition to representations of conflicts and critical voices, representations of harmonious, unanimous, and consensual encounters were an important type of reporting the encounters in local news media. These articles reported, for example, that citizens came in droves to plant daffodils on the railway station square as the city of Helsinki provided seedlings and organized this spring-like happening, or that in Lyon, the new concept of citizen-picnics in a park initiated by the city hall's democracy project was immensely popular.

These representations were not about conflicts – more likely, they were representations celebrating a common ground, sometimes even a *commonplace* in Thévenot's (2010; 2011; see also Chapter 2 in this book) sense, or, sometimes they were about *avoiding* conflicts (Eliasoph 1998). In these scenes of harmonious encounters, despite the absence of a dispute, the division between the 'civic French' and the 'industrial Finns' seemed to be repeated as well. These representations also dealt with the dynamics between the different levels on engagement: They treated the moves between different degrees of public with more intensity than the representations of conflicts.

Hence, the local processes of defining 'the good life' did not happen only in conflict situations. The local newspapers abundantly reported how 'all is well.' These were representations celebrating the harmony and smoothness of the citizen–city dialogues, representations of the absence of conflict, and sometimes, more or less implicit efforts to repress or conceal a conflict. Furthermore, some of the latter seemed to be about certain conflicts – and, in particular, conflicts that were rarely issued in the actual 'conflicts' at stake in the reports of the local disputes. This feature stresses the importance of analyzing absences: sometimes there is more to be learned about problems that have not been spoken out than the ones that are screamed on the streets.

Instead of justifying – a process that may help solve a problem, but at the same time makes a conflict apparent – the local actors were now represented in the midst of situations and issues in which citizens and policy-makers came together to 'work on a common project', and situations in which citizens were acting on the public sphere without making actual claims. Rather, something less articulate than claims was often communicated through these accounts.

First of all, reports that can be resumed by *happy occasions* were common in both newspapers. The examples I mentioned in the beginning of this section – planting daffodils and 'citizen picnicking' – were examples of this feature. These reports resembled in many ways the articles of the city information magazines, *Lyon-Citoyen* and *Helsinki-info* (see Chapter 4 in this book). It was as if the time and pace of urban life had halted in them, and harmonious, smooth dream of a city in which everybody was happy had suddenly come true, even if only for the few hours of the event. In these stories, the politicized level of justifications was absent, and instead people's personal attachments and 'normal,' habitual ways of engaging to each other and the city were brought forward. The city representatives rarely figured actively: the citizens played the leading roles.

In contrast, the city representatives had an important role in reports that concerned *satisfactory communication*. These articles, more emphasized in HS than in LP, represented communication events between citizens and city representatives that had succeeded, in a certain sense. In these cases, the officials or politicians were giving out information to the citizens, the citizens were receiving information (and, in some cases, giving it, too), and mainly, everybody was happy about the information that had circulated, or at least of the fact that it had circulated. These representations were surprisingly similar in both contexts, and sometimes almost touching in their overwhelming assurances of how good it was to inform and be informed in return. In HS (2005-05-12) for instance, a report of this kind stated that on an organized walk around the neighborhood, the inhabitants of the Ruoholahti neighborhood had given their opinions to the city planning officials on how to make the area more pleasant. The officials, according to the article, were willing to hear citizens' opinions, and after the event, both the citizens and the officials were pleased by the information that had circulated. The evening ended with a collective cup of tea in a nice, mutually understanding atmosphere.

In *Le Progrès*, a variation of the former theme were articles that reported on *successful participation*. The theme of these reports was participation in itself: events of which the only thing to learn was, basically, that participation 'took place.' These articles provided meticulous reports on the number of people that participated, on the contents of the participation, on the length of the event, or on its different parts, such as the speeches and the coffee service, and on the good course of the participation, the latter very much in the same spirit as the information reports above. Also, LP sometimes covered the efforts of those who worked to enhance participation – be it an association or the officials. In its extremes, the 'successfulness' of participation was represented rather minimally, like in the case of an event of participation for people in wheelchairs, who according to the article were 'happy to be able to show they existed', even if they were not 'waiting for a miraculous healing' (LP0406). Without taking a normative stand on what participation should actually be like, reading these reports gave an impression of something forced down. How 'successfully participating' did the people sitting in the audiences of neighborhood councils, eating canapés after receiving zoning information, or, indeed, showing they 'existed' in their wheelchairs, really feel, was something the newspaper reports did not transmit. These cases were hints of the difficulty, and potential hazards, of communicating individual interest on one hand, and intimate, personal concerns on the other, to the public level.

Finally, in both LP and HS, articles that seemed to be about *avoiding conflicts* represented encounters or events often explicitly pointing out that a conflict did not occur, sometimes in a style implicating a sense of relief. In an article in HS, for example, it was reported that the parties in charge of the construction of the railroad tunnel organized a gathering for the inhabitants in order to provide information about the building site and to answer questions. The main point of the article was that the evening went off peacefully, and 'no emotion-outburst-glazed inflammatory speeches against the project were heard at the Savio school' (HS2005-02-10). This example, as well as many others alike, echoed the speech and action norms in the local organizational styles (in Chapter 2): the way of reporting about the peacefulness of the encounter implicated a statement against emotionality, and protest in general. In fact, the article ridiculed protesting by means of the metaphor – inflammatory speeches –, and drew the boundaries of 'good' citizenship strictly to exclude those styles of expression. At the same time, the tone of the article gave the impression that a conflict was not a far-fetched idea and that perhaps a bad one had been narrowly avoided. The avoided conflict related to the predominant style of the Helsinki 'imagined community': the conflict to-be-avoided was, to begin with, a situation in which someone would cease to be civil. Regarding the strong prevalence of 'peaceful' repertoires in the tradition of Finnish collective action, it was somewhat disproportionate that the fear of a deviation of this norm evoked such 'fixing' operations.

Similarly in LP, there were articles that seemed to treat a conflict 'between the lines.' An article reported on 'The Youth of Lyon' association that had carried out a survey of young people and politics, stating: 'For Fakri, Jayandra, Rochdi, Samia, Anissa and Wassim, politics has an importance,' and quoting the afore-mentioned youngsters who said that the experience of collecting the survey information had been an extremely pleasant one (LP2005-03-16). This example drew implicit boundaries quite explicitly, and is as such an example of the 'hazards' of articulating the individual and intimate in the public that I pointed to above. The first names listed in the article – a maneuver that already implies the 'human interest only' type of importance granted to the people mentioned – were all names of young Muslims. This act positioned them not as political actors to be taken seriously, but as targets of power, both as 'young,' and as not-quite-French, and possibly without full citizen rights for both reasons. However, this, or the evident background fact of young Muslims being the 'politically problematic' group, was carefully diluted by the overall positive tone of the article. Indeed, in the French case, some of the most evident 'avoided conflicts' concerned ethnicity-related and multicultural issues, particularly regarding the Muslim population. This (non-)conflict challenged the boundaries of the local 'imagined community.'

In sum, the *raison d'être* of this kind of articles seemed to be, at least partly, an often rather forced dilution of a more or less implicit conflict. Instead of offering an arena of politicization, the newspapers took part in the process of de-politicization of certain topics. The double bind of the local press (Neveu E. 2003, 451) portrayed in these cases in all its powerfulness. Despite the different journalistic and organizational styles, the newspapers in both contexts had the same power to raise certain conflicts to the agenda and to dilute or disregard others. Which ones they raised and how, and which ones were tamed were context-bound solutions, undoubtedly subject to change: in spite of the power of the mainstream media, other means and agents of politicization also existed, as I have shown in the previous chapters.

6.3 Politicization and engagements in the local media

The civic French, the industrial Finns?

In this chapter, I have examined representations of different encounters between citizens and their cities in local newspapers: conflicting encounters in which the parties justified their claims, operating with justifications they judged legitimate for their arguments; missed encounters that social movement actors complained about, accusing the newspapers of either absent or slanted reporting of the themes they fought for; and harmonious, happy encounters in which the citizens and the cities came together in unproblematic terms, or in which the possible conflict and crisis threatening the situation were more or less tactfully faded out.

The analysis in the previous two sections concerned representations of justification acts in two local newspapers. This object of analysis has two main consequences for the use of the justification scheme as a methodological tool. First, it does not reach the complexity and volatility of real life conflict situations, as the newspaper representations, once printed out, stay the way they are. Thus, there is necessarily something static and frozen about them compared to, for example, an analysis of justifications in an ethnographic setting. Secondly, however, these justifications have made it to mainstream newspapers, occupying an important position in two local contexts. Thus, with some level of certainty, they do represent modes of 'culturally successful' justifying in their respective contexts.

In France and Finland, very different justifications proved successful. In the Finnish case, civility, rationality, and expertise, themes familiar from previous analysis concerning public debate and the political culture, seemed to be the citizens' best bet (see Kettunen 1997; Raevaara 2005). There was a strong tendency to treat political conflict as 'neutral' technicalities, or purely economic questions (see Palonen 2002). Even in claims that were of a civic nature, the Finnish citizen groups emphasized laws over solidarity and rights. Thus, a successful claim in the Finnish public sphere was justified by efficiency, rationality, expertise, and scientifically proven knowledge that promoted primarily efficient and high-quality solutions for a given societal problem. Nevertheless, the Finnish representations of local conflicts were also bitter contests of the best arguments between industrial-, market-, and civic-based solutions.

In the French case, the rise in the level of generality from particular, local problems to public questions of rights and solidarity within the range of civic justifications seemed to be an unbeatable choice. Perhaps somewhat surprisingly, this tendency was stronger in the arguments by the city representatives than those of the citizens. The denunciations of domestic modes from within the civic world echoed the republican tradition of universalism, and the justifications by the city often stressed the position of the claim-maker as a legitimate representative, a claim-maker in the name of democracy. Both groups of claim-makers preferred rights- and solidarity-based solutions that denounced privilege and hierarchy, and stressed solidarity and democracy. However, the French representations of local conflicts were also full of controversy and distrust within the civic world. Both the citizens and the city representatives accused each other of not being sufficiently civic-minded, and the toughest tests took place within civic justifications. The importance of the civic world was shared, but it offered both 'common ground' and a battlefield: the claims of the city representatives seemed to colonize the range of civic justifications in a way that was without doubt frustrating to the citizen groups.

In the light of previous studies, the popularity of the civic argumentation in the French case was no surprise. For example, in a comparative study between France and the United States, Michèle Lamont and Laurent Thévenot (2000, 310–12) emphasized the salience of solidarity, common good and collectivity-based civic arguments in the case of a French environmental movement, in contrast to the prevalence of market justifications in the American case. In my analysis as well, for the French, civic arguments were the corner stone for a great range of arguments: it could be stretched to almost anything, and combined with almost any other world of justification in more or less holding clusters or compromises. The prevalence of the civic world also parallels with the importance and weight my interlocutors gave to democracy in Chapter 5 – even if only to disagree about what to do with it.

When juxtaposing the French and the Finnish cases, other dimensions also emerged. First, it seemed that industrial justifications could barely 'stand alone' in the French case. Instead, they were often used as a supporting justification, mainly to the civic world. The industrial logic on its own was often awkward and quickly denounced from within the civic world. Secondly, both actor groups usually avoided the market world, as if it would not really offer a publicly defendable justification in affairs that touched democracy and publicity. This feature also resonates with tacit cultural knowledge, as well as with previous comparative studies: in France, talk about money is a difficult thing, whether in the context of paying for a collective dinner, or defining the practices of voluntary philanthropy (see e.g. the excellent analysis in Camus-Vigué 2000), so why not in the context of discussing the fate of public services?[6] The relative awkwardness of both industrial and market logic perhaps in part explains the stronger resistance towards the processes of neo-liberalization of governance in France than, for instance, in Finland. One of the most sinister examples of what happens when an industrial-market combination is imposed upon the society in France were the horrid consequences of the privatization of *France Télécom* in 2008–2009. The privatization resulted in a flagrant, yet globally very typical to this type of processes, mistreatment of the staff, and in consequence, a wave of employee suicides,[7] with explicit suicide notes concerning the restructuring of the company that shocked the entire French society.

With a little practical experience of Finnish culture, it is easy to see that the Finns tend to react very differently to industrial-market constraints. The 'elasticity' of the Finnish society, when confronted with change, has a long history: Henrik Stenius (2010) has pointed to Finnish society's relatively smooth passage to modernity that, in his account, is mainly due to an associational culture that encompassed the entire civil society. It became an extraordinarily consensual and 'adjustable' entity, easy to govern for leaders who had matter-of-factual, rational arguments for their claims. The same phenomenon largely holds today, and it fits particularly well into the demands of neo-liberal governance. Thus, the passage to the latter as well is quite 'smooth and easy,' even though the processes entail equal amounts of pain and suffering as the ones on-going in France. But their logic is culturally intelligible: as illustrated in the justification analysis, the industrial world was the 'common ground' on which the parties understood each other, even if there was no agreement. This result is in concordance with the conclusions I made in Chapter 5 of the Finnish actors' ways of framing democracy through expertise, and evaluating it on the grounds of finding the 'best solutions' for governing the society. The overlapping of civic and industrial justifications in the citizens' claims seemed to indicate that civic justifications, within which the legal and orderly features were strongly emphasized compared to the 'French civic,' were, in addition, judged as 'sufficient' in only a few cases. Instead, these claims were intertwined with the industrial arguments of 'the best way of carrying out a project' or 'the most effective means.' These combinations resonated with the strong emphasis on expertise both in Finnish politics, and in collective action repertoires (e.g. Raevaara 2005).

Publicizing individual interests and familiar engagements?

What do these accounts of citizen–city encounters tell about the processes of politicization in Lyon and Helsinki? First, politicization and justification are, at least in the case of media representations, interdependent: if someone gets to, or is forced to, justify something in a newspaper, the topic has already been politicized, or is on the edge of politicization. If it were not, there would be no need, and no room, for justifying.

The case of justifications also brings up the question of how politics is defined in different contexts: is it a strategic game of power, is it an arena of conflicts of interest, or is it, as a common Finnish expression states, about 'handling common affairs'? The implication of this analysis concerning consensual politics is rather curt: no conflict, hence no justification, hence no politicization – and hence, following Rosanvallon (2006), de-politicized politics, and a deepening crisis of legitimacy for democratic leaders.

However, the question of politicization is far from being simple. First, some justifications seemed to be more politicizing than others, and as the contextual analysis showed, some justifications can also be outright de-politicizing. The analysis in section 6.1 illustrated that industrial and market justifications in particular, and especially in the Finnish case, were often used in ways that tended to close down options of politicization. They directed the debate towards industrial technicalities or financial necessities that opened few possibilities for fruitful politicization.

Secondly, the failure of social movements to publicize and justify their claims in the media was undoubtedly a blow to their project, but by no means a deathblow. As I showed in Chapter 4, the power of counter-democratic actions can function in many ways, and there are multiple channels social movement actors can use to build up politicization, and thus their project does not depend exclusively on the mainstream media. Nevertheless, the cynical conclusion, often drawn by social movement actors themselves that in order to get mainstream publicity to cover their cause, they just needed to be spectacular enough and get the cameras on the spot, seemed to get support in the newspaper analysis.

Thirdly, if the public sphere in the two former cases was a space of conflict and struggle, it was also something else. In these representations, attempts to communicate 'joint projects,' and even 'commonplaces' to the public level were visible. Especially the latter, the level of close affinities, remained more or less unarticulated, and led rather to a somewhat awkward ritualization of the people in question – such as the ones in wheelchairs, or the immigration-originating youngsters – rather than giving them a voice to tell what they actually needed or wanted (see Thévenot 2010; 2011). The happy and harmonious encounters, as well as the sometimes narrowly avoided conflicts, represented, nevertheless, the important reproductive function of the media: ritualistic reproduction of the shared and the common by the community. It can be argued, in fact, that in order to exist as the arena for non-violent conflict solving, the public sphere also requires this on-going ritualistic community building. These rituals were, however, also a means of avoiding, not only conflicts, but politics and politicization altogether, and thus the benefits of these rituals to the 'community' were at the least somewhat contradictory (see Eliasoph 1998; 2011). In the next, concluding chapter, I reflect these themes further and discuss them together with the themes arisen in the previous chapters.

7
The Souvenirs: Politicization and Local Civic Practices in France and Finland

I began this book by re-introducing a traveling metaphor: doing comparative research takes a lot of traveling, both concretely and in abstraction. It is not clear where the journeys end exactly, if they ever do, but just like in less scholarly traveling, there are moments when sharing the souvenirs is appropriate. The preceding chapters have all been moments like this, but there is one last session of snapshots and keepsakes to come. This chapter will place the souvenirs of this journey on the same table, and take a look at the ensemble: what did we learn, how did the preliminary ideas about the destinations (and perhaps about the road itself) change on the way, what do the souvenirs signify, and what does it matter? First, I take a small detour as a reminder of the starting point of this set of questions.

Arundhati Roy (2009) throws in a big and politically incorrect question in the opening of her recent book by asking 'Is there life after democracy?' She hurries to explain that she does not suggest a possible return to totalitarian forms of governing, or giving up democracy as an ideal. What she suggests is that the 'working model' of democracy, the Western liberal representative democracy as we know it, urgently needs restructuring. In its current state, in her words, it no longer warrants societal justice and stability: it is too much representation, and too little democracy (ibid. ix–xi).

Different variants of this diagnostics have become recurrent during the past two decades. Social scientists, political philosophers, civil society actors, and some clear-sighted policy-makers who have presented parallel ideas, also note the same paradox as Roy does: at the same time as being more widely accepted and more commonly exercised worldwide than ever before, democracy is failing its promises. It is being hollowed and emptied of meaning. This emptying has taken place through a variety of processes: the globalization of the market economy and its increasing power to dictate political leadership and impose profit-oriented logics, the bureaucratization of political power, the ceremonialization of the political public, and many other developments that Pierre Rosanvallon (2006) describes as phenomena of the 'age of generalized suspicion' in which democracies have to come into terms with the fundaments of their legitimacy, and with their citizens, in new ways.

I agree with Roy and Rosanvallon, among others, that the questions concerning what happened to democracy and what should be done with it have to be asked in countries that already 'have' democracy, even if 'having' has to be put between quotation marks. France and Finland are such countries: both of them proudly present themselves as model students of the graduating class of flourishing and well-functioning democracy. The 'official' France claims copyright of both the creation of modern European democracy and the most advanced forms of new participatory democracy, whereas the 'official' Finland prides itself on the inclusiveness, transparency, and trustworthiness of its democratic institutions, backed up by this and that international rating. Obviously, and as I have showed concerning the local level in this book, the democratic realities are far from being this simple, and they are perhaps quite far from matching such self-satisfied outlooks altogether, depending naturally on the definition of 'democracy' deployed. In terms of a broad, process-oriented definition of democracy, both model students have failing courses. Thus, it is necessary to look at what is going on right there where democracy is supposed to function and have all necessary conditions and requisites to flourish. This opens the route to finding answers to the challenges that democratic ideals face in different contexts, and to the challenges citizens face in practicing democracy in different contexts. So, the question is, how did they practice democracy, what were their ways to politicize things, and how did the processes go in Lyon and Helsinki?

I have approached these questions by tracing the processes of politicization on different levels of the public spheres in two local contexts. Politicization is a strong illustration point in analyzing democratic practices, as it carries the keys of transformation, renewal, posing new questions, and keeping the wheels turning – it is, in sum, the driving force that democracy needs in order to be alive, and resist the 'hollowing' and 'emptying' tendencies and forces. At the same time, it is not a simple concept, and even less so a clear empirical object. The processes are not easy to detect or interpret. In order to detect and interpret at the best possible ways, I explored the local democratic practices in Lyon and Helsinki close-by from five different angles.

7.1 Five comparisons of democratic practices and politicization

The five cases of comparison brought to light the same theme – processes of politicization and the practicing of democracy – in form of different variations. These variations each highlighted particular features both empirically and conceptually, while also contributing to the question of politicization and its links to people's engagement to each other, their understanding of the form of society they took part in, and the meanings they gave to different representations of the latter.

First, I compared the grass roots civic practices of local activist groups in Lyon and Helsinki. I looked at the organizational styles of these groups and the kind of engagements the activists had with each other, and the local society around. The first case of comparison in Chapter 2 showed that the Lyonnais activists tended to engage through group bonds that were very concretely embedded in their environment: the neighborhood, both symbolically and as concrete walls, streets, and (commercial) spaces, was a collective commonplace, a base of familiar belonging and personal attachments. The activists in Helsinki, in contrast, were in the first place bound together by the networks of associations that formed the backbone of virtually all contentious activities in the city. They shared first and foremost an engagement in the collective projects of the local civil society.

The case comparing squatters in the two contexts focused on the groups' relations to the 'outside', and ways of managing conflicts also inside. The Lyonnais squatters drew, on one hand, rigid boundaries between their group and the institutions – the city, the police, and the media – and there was no place for negotiations in these relationships. Rather, the continuous, insolvable conflict was at the heart of the squatters' practices of politicization. On the other hand, conflict within the groups was not avoided either. Instead, also inner conflicts could function as vehicles of politicization, even if sometimes also vehicles of dissolution and the end of a group. Conflict was, nevertheless, the driving force of the squatters' actions. Instead of permanent establishment, or a successful media campaign, the squatters aimed at continuous politicization of the city space. Their ways of reaching for this goal translated, once again, their immediate surroundings, and perhaps immediate emotions, into political action. In Helsinki, the conflict with the 'outside' was managed with the help of significantly more 'permeable' group boundaries, which resulted in many more or less successful negotiations with the city. This had, however, also consequences on the groups. They followed the Finnish custom of becoming registered associations, and balanced between consensus and contention. There was a tendency to avoid also inner conflicts to a point of denying differences existed, and thus keep the group from dissolving, which was surely, at least in part, due to the engagement in a project that negotiating with the city tied them. Conflicts and discords would have taken energy, and weakened the group in face of the struggle of getting recognition (and occasionally, getting a house squatted for them) from the city. What they needed was a unanimous group, even at the expense of ignoring certain conflicts.

The pair of cases portraying speech and action norms of two groups of activists shed light on yet another aspect of the levels of engagement predominant in the two contexts. The Lyonnais No to Big Brother group held expressions and performances of resistance as the preferable ways of acting. Their understanding of politicization was more of a continuous flow of consecutive actions, situations, and topics, than a successfully executed project. This did not mean that they were not serious about what they did, but rather that their understanding of politics was not primarily tied to issues as such, but rather to the translations of these issues onto the political level. In contrast, the Pro Municipal Services network in Helsinki understood politics very firmly as a project of pushing through a particular issue. They engaged in politicization by means of gaining and claiming expertise, and strategizing to get their project through. And they did get projects through – but in the end they were always a little disappointed, despite their success.

Secondly, in Chapter 3, the ideas the activists had of citizenship showed that the historical and cultural burdens of the concept were important to the self-understanding of civic actors. Citizenship is, naturally, about rights and responsibilities, and it is today in many ways a multi-layered construct of intersecting identities, as has been suggested in the extensive literature concerning the concept (e.g. Soysal 1994; Yuval-Davis 1999; Beasley & Bacchi 2000; Faulks 2000; Wind 2008–2009). But what actually are the changes in citizenship produced by change in political regimes, where, and how? Instead of predefining the scope of citizenship in the two contexts, I have used it as a contextual set of meanings, practices and processes (for a similar definition, see Neveu C. 2003; 2004). In spite of the risk of conceptual imperfection, I preferred to conduct an analysis of the current, contextual political meanings of citizenship, and local practices the activists attached to the concept themselves.

The refusal of the republican ideal of a universalistic, undivided citizenship set the ground in the French case, whereas the consensual, harmonious, and even apolitical understanding of citizenship dominated the Finnish activists' ideas of citizenship. As a concept-in-use, citizenship was a more politicized set of dimensions in the French context than in the Finnish one. For the Finnish activists I met, acting as a citizen, *kansalainen,* was a duty, a service to the common good that they carried out by participating in local social movements, by voting, and by paying taxes. They were fond of the concept, and at the same time took it pretty much for granted. Citizenship was a clear and unproblematic notion that they felt was 'theirs' to define and realize in the ways they pleased, and yet they rather unanimously defined it in ways that are proper to the Finnish political culture, since the concept of citizenship was created in Finnish and into the Finnish politics (see Stenius 2003).

For the French activists, being active in the society was a way of being in the world, and a necessity for resistance and political struggle – but being called a citizen, *citoyen-ne,* did not become them. It was the republican concept par excellence, spoiled and stained by the wrong-doings of the French state, and the extreme Right groups that in recent years had somewhat colonized the use of national symbols. In addition, it was perhaps spoiled also by the excessive promise it held. The republican, universalistic, egalitarian and unmediated bond – almost like a commonplace – between the individuals and the state was too far from the actual experiences of 'the state' the people had: the excluding immigration policies, the power abuses of the local police, or the disappointing functions of participatory democracy. Furthermore, the history of the concept, and the debates over it, as well as the even currently valid, solemn political rhetoric concerning citizens, distanced the subjects of citizenship from the concept (cf. Duchesne 1997). They did not recognize it as 'theirs'. Still, it was important to them. The discussions over citizenship were far longer and more intensive with the French than with the Finnish activists, who took the concept more as a given, and did not really care to reflect on its possible dimensions.

I also wanted to know how the somewhat abstract understandings of citizenship reverberated in 'doing citizenship' in the two contexts, and chose to look more closely at the gender dimension of these doings, as it had seemed to be a point of divergence already in the case of the squatters. The French activists thought that dealing with gender-based discriminations and implicit attitudes was crucially important in civic groups. The activists by no means agreed about how to deal with it, or even what gendered citizenship was, nor did they agree on the ways to solve the problem in practice. The debates on the topic were frequent and heated, and the activists described them with lengthy reflections on their own position. Many male activists went through a lot of trouble trying to figure out why discriminatory practices existed – as they recognized – even if they felt that nobody really meant to be discriminatory. The Finnish activists, in contrast, saw almost no gender differences, not to mention conflicts or gendered discrimination, within their groups. Even if some noted that tasks tended to be distributed unevenly among women and men, and that somehow ones often got a lot of space for their ideas and others less, they did not think these problems were due to gender, or did not want to talk about them in such terms. They joined rather unanimously the Finnish mainstream idea of achieved gender equality, a stable state of affairs that requires no further reflection (e.g. Korvajärvi 1998; Holli 2003).

The French activists' rather open-minded and at times even sensitive take on gender created open spaces for observable politicizations within the groups, and sometimes trickled outwards as well. Paralleled to this effervescence, the Finnish way of sticking fast to an image of all-embracing, more or less unquestioned gender neutrality, was depoliticizing and fore-closed the debate rather than enhanced politicization. The unease and 'trouble' concerning talk about gender and gendered practices was, in fact, illustrative of the very organizing principle that was defining the place of politics in the Finnish context. The French orientation towards conflict made it possible to bring up the gender conflict like other conflicts, whereas the Finnish orientation on (gender) consensus made conflicts something to be avoided.

The third angle to comparing politicization and democratic practices concerned the visual dimension of the local public spheres. I analyzed the representations of the two local societies through frames of counter-democracy in images published by activist groups, and frames of good governance in images of city information magazines, *Helsinki-info* and *Lyon Citoyen*.

The activist website representations echoed different forms of 'counter-democracy,' as described by Pierre Rosanvallon (2006), and illustrated the local civil society in action. These images were accounts of politicization by means of demonstrating, claiming spaces, exposing police malpractices, and deliberating, among other things. It should be stressed that despite the identical frames, the 'same' forms of counter-democracy were not the same in different places. The strong similarity of the French and Finnish representations concerning particularly the frames of marking, demonstrating, and violence in the activist imageries is of particular importance to the Finnish context. It indicates a change in the repertoires of activism in Finland. Finnish demonstrations have followed a significantly different logic compared to the French, for example, even though certain forms of action were 'imported' as early as the 1960s (Alapuro 1989, 22–4). Secondly, frame analysis of the contradicting representations illustrated how gender interplayed and co-created meanings with counter-democratic framings. In both contexts, the activist imagery included powerful representations that were disruptive to the heterosexual matrix by means of complex or blurred signs of gender: the juxtaposition of two very different masculinities – the muscular, violent, macho police versus the skinny, feminine activists – and the gender-blurring, even queer representations of the satiric, performative truth-tellers and whistle-blowers, as well as the mainly Finnish representations of aggressive, masculine women. Counter-democratic struggles, thus, did not only call into question the legitimacy of the respective politico-administrative orders but also the conformist gender orders. In addition, these examples indicate that 'practicing democracy' is very much dependent on contextual gender structures and that gender is a key feature in understanding the contextually different configurations and consequences of processes of politicization.

On the other side, the city information magazines offered an illustration of two thoroughly governed and ceremoniously led local societies, virtually purified of politics. However dynamic the representations of the local society portrayed, they mirrored a transparent, unproblematic and well-governed (and all-governed) society that left no room for controversy. These images represented two beautiful, well-taken-care-of, well-led cities with happy inhabitants, but with not that much politics. Juxtaposing the activist and the city magazine frames was an exciting trip to four (sic) rather different cities, and led me to conclude that the visual dimension of the public sphere is indeed revelatory: it displays something that words rarely express this clearly. The activist representations ranged from the bitter, cynical, and at times completely disillusioned practices of street politics (more predominant in France) to the deliberative, autonomous practices of politicizing and building the society (more predominant in Finland). The city representations, in contrast, ranged from barely concealed promotion of elite power and market-driven neoliberal governance to diligent service provision and esthetics of the urban 'good life.'

Fourthly, I listened to local activists and politicians talk about democracy. The conceptions they used to analyze the tension between democratic representation and participation showed how differently the more or less recognized 'crisis of representative democracy' was treated in the two contexts. In Lyon, the activists were for the most part pessimistic and cynical about the possibilities of participatory democracy as proposed from above. The Lyonnais politicians very eagerly promoted these possibilities, but they were reluctant, nevertheless, of truly sharing power through these means. The activists from Helsinki saw themselves as the watchdogs of democracy, and wished they would be listened to more, and perhaps granted possibilities to participate in the local deliberations and decision-making, but they rarely questioned the hierarchical relationship between political representation and citizen participation. The politicians in Helsinki were reluctant, sometimes even hostile, towards most citizen-initiated forms of participation, and welcomed mainly the kind where citizens answer when asked. They did not seem to be very comfortable with new, increasingly inclusive forms of citizen participation, and even less so with active interventions of citizens in the decision-making processes.

These dynamics of conceptualizing democracy completed the picture that had already begun to emerge in the previous chapters. The Lyonnais activists and politicians, despite their rather opposite views on many things, 'agreed' on two things (at least): the emergency of changing the democratic system, and the necessity of conflict in politics. The activists and politicians in Helsinki mainly disagreed about the former and disregarded the latter, but agreed on at least one thing: the importance of expertise in politics.

Finally, the justifications citizens on the one hand, and city representatives on the other, came up with in newspaper reports of local disputes that portrayed the different grounds for predominant moral arguments about the common good. This analysis showed that in the French case, the most popular justifications were grounded on civic values of collective solidarity and equality, enhanced by arguments basing on traditions, but also industrial efficiency. In the Finnish case, on the contrary, the most viable, and habitual, justifications also to the citizens were based on industrial efficiency, functionality, quality, and rational expertise, often endorsed with allusions to profitability and lawfulness. Be it a library threatened of closing, or heavy savings targeted to preliminary schools, the Finnish mode of argumentation often rendered them questions of a purely technical nature. The French, for their part, used solidarity-based arguments to justify their opinions ranging from the just treatment of illegal immigrants to the opposition of parking meters. The different grounds of justification provided for different grounds of raising the level of generality, and politicizing. The civic justifications seemed to be closer to the arenas of politics altogether, whereas the technical facts the Finns argued about were sometimes neutralized to a point in which it seemed it was a mere misunderstanding between two experts whether a library should be closed or not.

So, in the newspaper representation of local conflicts, the crucial conflicts resided in different worlds – in France, in the civic world, in Finland in the industrial world – making them very different conflicts with very different consequences altogether. The matter-of-fact, engineering-like industrial worth was the 'common ground' on which the parties of the Finnish local disputes understood each other the best, whereas the civic world with its groundings on solidarity, equality, and fairness were the most common 'meeting point' in the French conflicts – the city representatives used civic justifications even more abundantly than the citizens. This analysis drew portraits of 'the civic French', relying on solidarity-based justifications, and 'the industrial Finns,' trusting in rational–functional justifications. In both cases, however, the citizens seemed to be somewhat 'forced' to justify on the shared grounds. The French were stuck with continuous 'reality tests' within the civic world, accused of being too 'domestic', or civic in a wrong way by their adversaries. The Finns were prone to back up even the strongest and most obviously insurmountable civic justifications with industrial 'facts,' and however much they were capable of expert argumentation, they still were at their defenses. Thus, in both cases, even if the citizens got their voices heard in the newspapers, they were the underdogs that had to try all possible arguments in order to convince the opposing party.

The conflicts of Chapter 6 are the purest examples of politicization in this study: in order to get justified in a newspaper, an issue has already been politicized to a certain degree. Comparing these politicizations by means of the Public Justifications Analysis results in, inter alia, a reflection of the idea of rise in generality in different contexts. The way Camille Hamidi (2006), as well as Luc Boltanski and Laurent Thévenot (e.g. 1991; see also Koveneva 2010) use the expression is extremely illustrative of the French style of civic justification; as I showed in the beginning of this book for Hamidi, in particular, rise in generality is one of the conditions of politicization. The justifications used by both actor groups constantly took the issues to the level of general principles of the common good in civic terms, i.e. a collectivist, solidarity-based common good, and opened new spaces for politicization. Now, each world of justification has its own definition of a common good, and a rise in generality is thus technically possible however one justifies an argument, but when the question is about a rise in generality that politicizes a confrontational issue on a public sphere marked by a democratic self-understanding, the civic world constitutes a meta-frame within which the debate takes place. In this sense, arguing on the public sphere requires a certain collective understanding of reciprocity and equality (even if this does not mean that public conflicts would eventually be fair or equal in any ways). In the Finnish justifications, where correct calculations, rational deductions, and – at their ultimate civic-ness – relying on lawfulness reigned, the general principles referred to were about efficiency, expertise and good quality solutions for the society, but the common good they promoted was often de-politicized, emptied of possibilities of further politicization. Technical facts opposed to one another easily remain mere contradictory technical facts, if not accompanied with arguments based on collective responsibility, solidarity, and justice. Hence, rise in generality necessary for politicization is probably possible only when the public is on the edges of 'recognizing itself' as a public (Dewey 1927), which seemed to occur in the French case more often than in the Finnish one.

This section has resumed some of the main comparative findings this book has put forward. Politicization proved to be differently grounded in the two local contexts. Indeed, the concept itself, the way I discussed it in the beginning of this book, went through multiple translations, and perhaps also transformations.

If we focus on the conflict linkage of politicization, we can say that, briefly put, in Lyon, politicization was almost daily routine, while in Helsinki, de-politicization was more prone to take place. The French actors' readiness to open a conflict and deal with it was apt for making politicization possible, whereas the Finnish actors' tendency to avoid conflict and prefer consensus rather hindered than supported politicization. If we look, instead, at the few cases in which the entire process of politicization could be followed, it seems that the Finnish activists managed to open 'playable' spaces in a wider public than the French, and even 'win' some cases. They relied on expert knowledge and arguments based on technical, statistical, or legal facts, and at times managed to influence even the highest levels of municipal decision-making. The French activists, in contrast, rarely got favorable responses to their actions that they based mainly on the logic of resistance and contention, justifying their arguments on grounds of solidarity, citizen rights, and equality. And finally, if we concentrate on the aspect of raising the level of generality, and the 'translations' of issues between different levels of engagement (Thévenot 2010; 2011), it becomes clear that politicization was – also – inherently situational, difficult to predict, and affected by complex layers of micro and macro contextual, historical, general, particular and case-specific features. Hence, politicization is a process inherent to political culture, to organizational styles, and the predominant modes of engagement and modes of raising the level of generality.

What's the use of a concept with so many faces? The definitions of politicization in the French and Finnish local contexts illustrate the importance of the way I have suggested to use concepts in a comparative study (see Chapter 1), and to expose them to translations and transformations. In comparing French and Finnish styles of politicization, the broad international comparison of features that characterize large cultural entities becomes possible by analyzing in what kind of processes the 'general features' actually exist, and what is it that makes them general. At the same time, important fractures and weak signs of change – that mainly escape the eyes of policy analysis-based models – become apparent, and seeing these seemingly insignificant features of political engagement makes it possible to get beyond two-dimensional comparisons.

7.2 What the souvenirs tell about the destinations

Two historical 'diagnoses' illustrate the fundamentally different roots of understanding politics in the French and the Finnish context. In the 1920s, Reinhold Svento wrote in Finland: 'In national and societal life will be established, over time, the kind of rules of behavior deviating from which in the name of the common good is allowed only extremely seldom. Politics educate at the same time the whole people, teaching them to behave according to predetermined rules' (Svento 1928, 38–9 cited in Palonen 2002, 502, my translation). A very different account was formulated by Alexis de Tocqueville: 'In the political world, everything is agitated, contested, uncertain; ... independence, contempt of experience and envy of any authority [reign in the world of politics] (de Tocqueville 1835, 91 cited in Palonen 2002, 500, my translation). Today, these accounts sound slightly caricaturesque – but they still manage to represent the stereotypes of Finnish and French styles of political action. The former emphasizes the commonly recognized rules of the game, while the latter imagines a game that constantly 'renegotiates' its rules.

Stereotypes exist because we need them, because we have the habit of repeating and reproducing them, and because they are sometimes useful in maintaining status quo. In France, on the one hand, the ever-moving, effervescent imagery of the political culture is part of a political '*imagined dynamism*' that conceals the hierarchical, even 'monarchic' sources of power that have in no way given up their position. Michel Koebel has suggested that the current developments of participative democracy at the local level in France, in fact repeat and consolidate traditional power structures, and that participatory instruments serve to enhance the legitimacy of the political leadership in place (Koebel 2006, 11–12; see also Blondiaux 2008, 9). Enhanced citizen participation overlaps with two rather contradictory trends. First, the over-representation of the privileged levels of the social strata in the local representative bodies (as in all other representative bodies in France) has increased strongly during the past forty years. Secondly, the practices of neoliberal governance have overrun much of the local political space, hence innumerous decisions concerning the local level are made on other levels, notably that of inter-municipal governance. It makes sense to question whether participative democracy in France has more to it than a managerial logic disguised in the clobber of uplifting democracy, within which citizens are persuaded to participate and play their part as customers of the 'public governing firm' (Koebel 2006).

Underneath the changes brought about by both the neoliberal trends and the 'participative imperative,' roam the disappointments caused by participatory practices, installed with solemn words but given no significant power resources what so ever (Blondiaux 1999, 404; 2008, 15; Carrel 2006; 2007). The French activists and politicians were more distant in their diagnoses of the society, but they still seemed to agree upon the necessity for change and renewed democratic governing. Many politicians, whether enthusiastic or not, and whether from the left or the right end of the political spectrum, stressed the importance of 'taking the temperature' among the citizens, the French expression for assessing the electorate's feelings and attitudes, and hence affirmed the idea of an inherently unknown, and constantly changing social configuration of the electorate.

The activists, on the other hand, were cynical and pessimistic – in their view, representative democracy was largely in peril, and they saw no quick remedy to it. Even if the recent decades' developments in structures and mechanisms of participatory democracy are remarkable in France compared to Finland, local activists saw no real hope of enhancing democracy through them – mainly because they did not believe in the sincerity of the politicians' will to truly transform democratic decision-making, let alone share power. The developments 'promised' change, but in the local reality, this change was more theater than true transformation. In sum, the French contentiousness, when examined close up, in interactions between activists and decision-makers, included activists' implicit knowledge that they were contending with stagnant, out of reach hierarchies that kept the power configurations intact. To resume the Lyonnais activists' standpoint, they were very suspicious of the decision-makers, and the entire political system. This general attitude created positive politicizing energy and boosted their critical capacity to generalize topics close to them to political topics in public, but it also worked in the opposite direction and nourished hopelessness, cynicism, and even somewhat anti-political anarchism.

In Finland, on the other hand, the presumption of transparency and inclusiveness are part of a political *'imagined unanimity'* and a prevailing of consensus that have probably never been as thorough as is often suggested. It has become the predominant understanding of the political culture since the 1960s and President Kekkonen's reign, but has always been and still is only a part of the story. Rather than by unanimity, the Finnish history is marked by the combination of consensus and controversy (Kettunen 2004). The culture of consensus is more like a fake-calm surface under which the society is bubbling with a thousand unsolved conflicts, and non-transparent power structures.

In Helsinki, it seemed that in the politicians' eyes, the legitimacy of the representative system was based on a descriptive, 'mirror-clear' representation, in which the social configuration of the society is known down to the detail, and mediating structures – associations, representative organs – function as direct channels between the levels of the society (cf. Alapuro 2005a). The fragility of this constellation emerged, however, when it was confronted with demands for more inclusive and influential citizen participation: these demands, as well as experiences of direct, or even just a little less mediated citizen participation, such as public hearings in planning issues, fractured the picture. The confusion of the politicians facing new forms of participation, generally regardless of their political affiliation, was not only characteristic of the politicians in Helsinki, but seems a more widespread trend (see e.g. Holli *et al.* 2007). For a country with general governing traditions and legislation as 'inclusive' as in Finland, the weak and unsophisticated current state of participatory democracy, and the lack of political enthusiasm concerning it are remarkable, and in many ways an implication of the perplexed state of the political culture.

The examples of the dynamics among activists, and between them and the decision-makers in Helsinki showed that the Finnish culture of consensus and inclusive decision-making included putting a lot of effort into quelling conflicts. This often led to depoliticizing issues of controversy, instead of dealing with them through a political process. Nevertheless, political processes did take place, and they were primarily marked by the use of rational arguments stemming from expert knowledge, and by a raise in generality, habitually from the level of a project or a plan rather than that of a grievance on the level of close affinities. The activists in Helsinki had confidence in their power of influence, by using the latter means. In spite of their critique on the state and functioning of democracy, they also had confidence in its institutions, including the place and role granted to associations within the system. Similarly to suspicion in the French case, this confidence was both 'good' and 'bad' to the activists' capacities to politicize. It was good in the sense that they confidently addressed the institutions with their (expert) claims. It was 'bad,' i.e. often de-politicizing, in the sense that in trusting the institutions, they got trapped. First, in the consensual and conflict-avoiding modes of action that by far did not guarantee that their voices were heard, and secondly, as in the case of the media disputes, in a logic of justifications defined by someone else.

Politicization was, in both contexts, a wavering process requiring contingent conditions and producing uncertain outcomes. Why, finally, does it matter so much, why bother trying to understand something so vague? What if it never occurred at all? Lack or complete absence of politicization is a state of apathy, perverted counter-democracy, or frozen, de-politicized consensus in which nothing truly moves, and no injustice can be fixed (see Eliasoph 1998; Palonen 2003; Rosanvallon 2006). This state is the ultimate tragedy of democracy – and it is an on-going one in contemporary Western democracies. They are less threatened by traditional dictatorship than perhaps earlier (although these threats by no means have disappeared worldwide), but they are extremely threatened by forces and processes that empty politics of meanings, and albeit through deceiving vocabularies of constant change and restructuring, congeal politics and representation. The elements of the 'age of generalized suspicion' are anti-public, politics-killing, and have dangerous impacts: when politics freezes over, apathy steps in. This impact is detrimental to everybody and the societies as whole. Practicing democracy is messy: its forms are never pure, but always carry the possibility of perversion, malpractice, and misunderstanding. But a true mess is better than a false order.

The historical essence of democracy is to be at the same time a promise, a problem, and a process – and to remain unaccomplished (see also Dewey 1927, 148–9; Rosanvallon 2006, 10). Understanding the challenges of current democracies requires contextual analysis, as change never has but one direction, and it never lands identically on different grounds. Several questions have certainly been left open concerning the current process of change, and the consequences it will eventually produce on different levels of politics in different contexts. This study has shown that democracy is practiced with different tools in different places – and that in different contexts, people have different means, 'tool kits' with which they deliberate, resist, and politicize (Swidler 1986). Also, the results of these analyses suggest that different cultures could learn from each other. This does not mean importing practices from a country to another, but it means allowing new perspectives in discussions and actions (Eliasoph 1998, 259–60).

I began this book with a story of an encounter between French and Finnish citizens, politicians, officials, and researchers. They had the chance to learn from each other even in that brief meeting, so immediately emerged the intriguing, puzzling, and even troubling differences in working out a better, more legitimate and more inclusive democracy between, and even within the two contexts. Did they learn something? – the story does not tell. At many occasions during this journey, and increasingly when finally writing the preceding chapters, I have felt privileged to have these dimensions before me simultaneously. Looking at the troubles and hopes in the cases I have analyzed, actors in these two, as well as in number of other polities, could learn a lot from each other, as I have learned from both of them, by comparing and sometimes contrasting them.

Most importantly, I have learned that there is a great diversity of groups in these two societies that resist the emptying of politics, depoliticizing consensus, and perverted counter-democracy, and, instead, strive for active, positive political action. These enclaves consist of people who are concerned about the common good, and about increasing fairness and decreasing injustice. The more multiple the tools and repertoires they have at their disposal, the more possibilities for politicization, the more chances to open new areas of questioning – of thinking and doing differently – the more room for more people to come along and take part, and hence, better ideas, and better decisions. At the same time, good intentions are not enough. Politicization does not in any assured way lead to a better world. It is, nonetheless, always an opening, and the point of departure for a new journey.

7.3 The road ahead: towards pragmatist political sociology

The five angles to politicization I listed in section 7.1 represented also the design of this study, composed of four corpuses of empirical material – ethnographic observations, interviews, images, and newspaper articles – and different conceptual and methodological approaches to them. With this design, I have also wanted to make a disciplinary point, and show why I think sociologists should study politics. This book has compared practices and representations of politicization in two local contexts. This kind of approach has not been the daily bread of traditional political sociology, let alone political science, apart from the focus on comparisons. However, in recent years, interest and concern on actors, practices, and micro-level processes of politics and democracy has grown in different academic contexts (e.g. Lamont & Thévenot 2000; Joseph *et al.* 2007; Hamidi 2010; Nash 2010; Eliasoph 2011).

These developments are closely linked to the so-called 'pragmatist turn' in current sociology (e.g. Silber 2003; Gronow 2011). It is no coincidence that pragmatist theoretical foundations and ethnographic approaches to the empirical world are closely interwoven in this current. Reaching the level of everyday situations and tracing processes of politicization are a promising way of grasping habitual action, but especially the points of crisis in which habits need to be adjusted or changed – and vice versa, the pragmatist theorizing provides tools that meet the sensitivity of ethnographic research, unlike the majority of theoretical tools commonly used in policy analysis and social movement studies.

In a world where 'glocalization' has become a coffee table term, there is an increasing need for political analysis that is at the same time sensitive to the most micro level social processes, and yet capable of grasping broad trends and including wide comparisons. Local is never only local, but it is always shadowed by wider historical and geographical reference points. Likewise, 'global' or 'international' are no more available for examination than the 'state', for instance, elsewhere than in the localized practices that bring them into concrete existence (see Gupta 2006).

The key question in understanding these processes, and their different grounds in different contexts, is the question of moving from one 'level' of generality to another, and transforming people's personal and particularistic attachments into issues of higher degrees of publicity. Carrying out this kind of an analysis makes it clear how the 'how' and the 'why' are related: to learn how a process of politicization takes place, or how a democratic practice fails or succeeds, opens a channel to finding out why it does.

Politicization is one of the embodiments of the critical capacity Boltanski and Thévenot (1999) say we people have. It is a process in which a collection of shared habits of 'doing politics' help in constantly seeking new solutions to (public) problems. It is both the nature of the problems and the solutions that make politicization a tricky object of study: dynamic, effervescent, and constantly changing. One solid way to study is long-term ethnographic work (Lichterman 1996, 2005; Eliasoph 1998, 2001; Carrel 2007; Hamidi 2010; Charles 2011; see also Luhtakallio & Eliasoph 2012), another one is what I have done in this book. Making use of the 'mirror' provided by the comparative perspective, and approaching the theme from different angles, with the help of different materials and concepts, has helped me to 'lure' the processes of politicization to reveal their different faces.

As a consequence of this choice of approach, in this book the results of the processes of politicization have been left to less attention. Where did this or that politicization lead to, in the end? How did the configurations of power, the articulations of engagement, or at the end of the day, the social structures of a given society change? These questions remain open, for the most part, but they also point out something characteristic to the challenges of current political sociology. As Dorian Warren (2009) reminds us, history never 'freezes,' but is a series of endless path-dependent events (see Luhtakallio & Eliasoph 2012). As we have seen in this book, exactly in this fashion, politicization escapes closed definitions: it does not look the same everywhere or every time, and it never really 'stops,' or 'freezes' so that it could be taken to the pathologist's table and opened up. Instead, politicization is a chain of habits, practices, events, and their articulations and representations that we need to examine situation by situation to see where the path is headed, without forgetting to look back at the previous curves. Sometimes it seems that there is a map to be followed. Sometimes it is more like a trail in the wilderness, and it is hard to think of any other way to find out why this turn or curve is taken, than to look at how the path slowly gets trampled, evens out and broadens.

Methods Appendix

I Visual frame analysis

Erving Goffman wrote Frame Analysis (1974) much within the framework of face to face interaction. *What is it that is going on here?*, Goffman's famous basic question, aims at pointing out that in their everyday life, people need to do a lot of analyzing about how they should understand one situation or another in order to navigate in the world of social interactions and encounters. According to Goffman, framing is an activity typical to human beings, through which we try to make sense of the world and situations we are thrown into (ibid. 8, 11). Switching frames, then, is a necessary skill, as all situations typically include several different framings, a definition of a situation – the frame through which it is understood – may change instantly when a new detail or additional information appears (Goffman 1974, 25; Peräkylä 1990, 19). Also, frames influence each other, overlap, and appear intertwined. Although one frame might dominate the overall definition of a situation, other framings direct the interpretations by adding new layers of signification and understanding that format both the interpretation itself, and the previous framings (Goffman 1974, 82).

The purpose of frame analysis for Goffman is twofold: first, frame analysis seeks to attain foundational framings in society that make understanding of events and situations possible and, secondly, to analyze the vulnerability of these framings, fractures and transformations in them. Transformations of framings take place in *keying* which is '– a set of conventions by which a given activity, one already meaningful in terms of some primary framework, is transformed into something patterned on this activity but seen by the participants to be something quite else' (Goffman 1974, 43–4). Hence, keying alters the frame by creating new interpretational connections, even between situations framed by familiar frames. Keying is neither static nor is it permanent; it can be followed by an indefinite number of re-keyings that always alter and re-alter both the foundational basic framing, and the previous keyings (Manning 1992, 125; Heiskala 1997, 261–24).

Cultural texts, be it speech, images, or printed words, always speak from within a certain world, objectifying something collectively observed or experienced. This 'world' or worlds also incorporate interactional elements in themselves. Within these worlds, framing is a process structuring experience, in which meanings are produced in communication with the contexts of a given situation. A frame connects a phenomenon into a space and a time. Framings are, however, never definite, since a continuous process of reframing moves and transposes the meanings. Nor are frames exclusive, but appear in different positions, intertwined and/or within each other, and thus the meanings they carry are mobile. They also provide for analysis of change, and analysis of mobile and fluctuating meanings that flee strict classifications, as mostly is the case when images are concerned (Goffman 1974, 13, 82; Peräkylä 1990, 19; Törrönen 1999, 7–8, 11).

Although the leap from face to face interaction and Goffman's prolix anecdotes of everyday events towards analyzing activist website imagery may seem long, I argue that Goffman actually did something of the sort of a leap himself. In *Gender Advertisements* (1979), although without spelling it out as frame analysis, Goffman analyzes advertisements and the framings of gender in them as those 'sources of exemplary representation' of which everyday life 'often seems to be a laminated adumbration of a pattern or model' (Goffman 1974, 562). In the following, I illustrate a spelled-out version of this perspective to frame analysis of visual culture.

First, when studying visual culture sociologically, it can be argued that we seldom encounter a situation in which the source and the general purpose of the images to be analyzed would be a complete mystery. Certainly, it is sometimes hard to tell a TV show from a commercial, but with a larger brush it still is more or less clear what it is that we are looking at. Thus, it is obvious that a *master frame* usually directs our interpretations. For Goffman, master frame means, for example, awareness of natural phenomena, such as rain and sunshine, or perhaps the recognition of basic emotions, such as anger or joy. Thus, a master frame guides our interpretations and gives frame analysis the basic setting where to take place: visual representations linked for instance to selling something, to telling a fictional story, or to reporting 'true' events, all of the above being of course raw and simplified examples only.

Secondly, the basic principle of frame analysis is its dynamism: frames transform and are elastic in different ways. These characteristics make applying frame analysis to visual analysis fruitful. Different shades of meaning and mobility of interpretations can be brought out through the two key functions of framing activity: *lamination* and *superimposition* (Goffman 1974, 82; Manning 1992, 121). Thus it is possible to analyze how visual representations simultaneously create meanings within many different, and differently functioning, frames. Typically, when we look at a social interaction situation or an image, one primary answer to the question 'What is going on in here' does come up. It is, then, often accompanied by other interpretational possibilities that may either slightly alter or color the uprising meaning, or redirect or change it profoundly (Goffman 1974, 25). For the sake of terminological clarity and methodic usefulness, neither of which perhaps is among Goffman's most praised strengths, I have applied the functioning of the frames into visual analysis by defining two ways of manifestation of the frames: the *dominant frame* and the *secondary frames*.

Dominant frame is the primary analysis of a situation the image offers. *Secondary frame* is an alongside significance that directs and focuses – and sometimes transfers or even switches – the meaning created in the communicational process of looking at an image. The number of secondary frames may vary in principle from one to infinite, whereas there usually is only one dominant frame – even though several meanings and interpretations, even contradictory ones, may arise from one image, a primary interpretation, the first idea of what is going on, can usually be detected. The idea of a secondary frame corresponds, therefore, by and large to what happens in Goffman's model through means of keying and lamination.

If working with a large set of visual data, the definitions of dominant frames enable quantification of the data simultaneously with ballpark interpretations of its general characteristics. A qualitative analysis can then be carried out based on the same framings. This way, a number-based and a qualitative analysis of the data can be integrated, and used supporting each other. The emphasis is, however, on the qualitative analysis. In my suggestion for a 'visual' application of frame analysis, the data at stake is always the point of departure: what kinds of framings stem from this particular set of images or other visual elements. It therefore functions in terms of the data, instead of striving to adjust it into readily named and defined categories.

Frame analysis does not offer general, pre-defined framings to be applied in all possible situations and data, but it challenges the researcher to structure the analysis according to her data. There is no pattern of either the general course of events – as in Greimas' actant model – or of the different levels of signification – as in methods based on the model of Barthes' codes, neither will the analyst loose herself in the statistical demands and often static classifications of content analysis. Hence, the definition of the dominant frames in a given set of data is already part of the analysis.

The defined dominant frames often function as secondary frames for each other when the set of images studied has a somewhat strong and clear master frame: the same framings appear and reappear in different ways. In addition, there are always an infinite number of secondary frames, stronger or weaker signs that affect the meanings that can be brought out in the analysis with the degree of subtleness needed to meet the objectives of a given study.

In this study, in concrete, I asked Goffman's opening question 'what is going on in here?', and wrote down the answers (the different steps of the analysis are described more in detail in Chapter 4). In addition to answering the questions myself, I also submitted my preliminary analysis to a test: a group of students looked at a sample of the images and described 'what was going on' in their interpretation. I then compared my own descriptions to theirs, and adjusted the definitions of the frames somewhat, but the general result of this test was that their interpretations were extremely similar to my own. There have been discussions concerning the roles of researcher interpretation on the one hand, and reception studies on the other, in the field of visual culture studies (see e.g. Seppänen 2001, 2002). My position is that carrying out an analysis of several hundreds of images is sensible only through the means of researcher interpretation following criteria of critical visual analysis. The latter stresses simultaneously the importance of reading both the image and its context with care, reflecting on the social conditions and consequences of the images, and emphasizing conscience of the viewer position (Rose 2001, 15–16). Although reception analysis is certainly an appropriate method for answering some research questions, it cannot replace researcher interpretation, both for the sake of theoretically and methodologically grounded analysis, and that of research economy.

II Public justifications analysis

How to interpret representations of claims and acts of justification? As a result of collective work with Tuomas Ylä-Anttila, I suggest[1] adjusting the theoretical scheme concerning justifications to empirical analysis basing loosely on the method of Political Claims Analysis (PCA)

(Koopmans & Statham 1999; Koopmans & Rucht 2002). The Political Claims Analysis was created to bring methodological standardization to social movement research on protest cycles, social movement impact, and other macro-scale developments in the print media, and to create a tool to carry out large international comparisons (Koopmans & Rucht 1999, 124). PCA integrates the level of political discourse into the analysis, and particularly emphasizes a multi-organizational claims-making by different actors and activities. It is mainly used to analyze a particular issue – such as public mobilization of migration and ethnic relations, a project used as an illustration of the method (Koopmans & Statham 1999). PCA is based on the definition of frames, and thus follows the same analytical tradition as numerous social movement studies (see Gamson 1995; Benford & Snow 2000). PCA mainly relies on a rather sophisticated statistical analysis of the framings, claims, and claim-makers the newspapers portray on a particular topic.

When treating newspaper material such as the one at hand in this study – comparative and extremely heterogeneous – the definition of interpretative frames and statistical analysis of them seemed an unsuitable approach. Also, the nature of the inquiry – the comparison of local controversies – required a qualitative reading of the material in order to answer the study questions in satisfactory ways. Thus, in order to develop a better functioning tool for studying public disputes and justification acts in local newspaper representations, I rather make use of an adjustment of the Justification theory by Boltanski and Thévenot to the methodological ideas of PCA: Public Justifications Analysis (PJA) (Luhtakallio & Ylä-Anttila 2011; see also Ylä-Anttila 2010). The PJA approach enables a quantitative overview on the representations of local conflicts, although the main focus is on a qualitative analysis of the justifications of the claims presented by different claim-makers.[2]

Luc Boltanski's and Laurent Thévenot's theory of justification (1991) studies the principles of common good put in to play in conflict situations. The theory takes the situations of everyday life as a starting point, and claims that unlike in normative theories on social action, people do not stand in ready-made roles and categories, but instead possess a critical capacity to justify their arguments (also Boltanski & Thévenot 1999). The universal categories of justification – stemming from the worlds of inspiration, domestic, civic, renown, industrial, market and green[3] – that are based on differing ideas of greatness, yet a converging idea of a common humanity[4], form a theoretical approach to the critical capacity people employ in conflict situations. This critical capacity allows people to deliberate and eventually come to a justified solution when confronted by the smaller and bigger everyday crises in which the habitual course of action is disturbed (Boltanski & Thévenot 1991, 12, 28–9, 39; Lamont & Thévenot 2000).

Thévenot *et al.* (2000) apply the justification theory to a series of studies comparing France and the United States as an analysis of 'the frequency of certain types of arguments and 'modes of justification', as well as the dynamics of their use in national and cultural contexts, paying particular attention to argumentation that involves combining various modes of justification' (ibid. 236). The starting point of the following analysis is similar: I use the seven-order-of-worth range of justifications both concretely in categorizing and organizing my data, and in drawing analytical generalizations. However, instead of combining different sources of debate and data, and studying a variety of sites of conflict, I tackle one public arena, the local news media, and strive to systematize the use of the justification theory as a methodological tool. My objective is, however, similar to Lamont and Thévenot's, as using the range of justifications aims at comparing the array of justifications and their overlapping, and eventually, at providing understanding on the cultural repertoires guiding public debate in two countries.

Due to the different scope of the two newspapers, the Finnish data was collected from the 'City' section of *Helsingin Sanomat* that concentrates only on the greater Helsinki region, while *Le Progrès* was covered in its entirety. The data includes all articles that concerned local conflict issues, participatory democracy, social movements, and in sum, all kinds of encounters, deliberations, disagreements, or exchanges between citizens – individuals or groups – and any representatives of the municipal institutions. The articles were collected both by using the digital archives of the two newspapers, and by going through the manual archives (microfilmed in the case of *Helsingin Sanomat,* and bound in the case of *Le Progrès*). The digital archives were searched with a set of keywords related to local issues and participation, and the analogical archives were read through at the level of titles. This double check was necessary both because of the difficulty of coming up with keywords that would cover the local controversies as a whole, and because of the apparent deficiencies of the digital archives: test searches carried out both digitally and 'by hand' showed that the archives would not find all articles containing the key words.

All articles have a 'citizen point of view' in them: I excluded articles that reported conflicts within the City Councils, for instance. While aware of the slight arbitrariness of this choice, and its implications of rather narrowly defined 'citizens', in order to adhere to the general research design of this study in which the principal focus is on civic practices instead of on institutional politics and governance, I judged it necessary to exclude the municipal politics as such from the material.

Only reportage and news articles written by journalists were included. Opinions written by the readers were excluded because there were none in the French data source, as well as commentaries and columns by journalists, because their logic of argumentation resembled more 'opinions' than 'reportage' (cf. also Koopmans & Statham 1999).

I coded the newspaper articles by giving each article a running case number and using the acts of justification in them as primary coding units. In some articles, only one point of view was represented – for example, reporting the claims of a local citizen group – in others, there were several, equally represented views – for example, describing the views of both a citizen group and a local official or politician on the same matter. In the latter case, the claims of the different parties of a given conflict were coded as separate claims under the same case number.

A *claim* was presented in the form of an opinion, a demand, an accusation, or, if the article cited a demonstration, even a scream (or a banderol) by crowd. Furthermore, a claim could also be a reconstruction of one side of an entire dispute.

A *claim-maker* was a person or a group that, according to the newspaper article, made a particular claim and stood for it, presenting argument(s) to justify it.

A *justification* was the argument or arguments that formed the claim: why the claim-makers estimated they were entitled to make the claim.

As justifications are, according to Boltanski and Thévenot (1991), not built from words alone, but from the chains of things, ideas, actions, and words used to justify an argument in a certain way, I also included these aspects into the coding grid. With these guidelines, I analyzed the newspaper articles by defining the claims, the claim-makers, and the justifications. Sometimes they were manifestly presented, sometimes understanding what was claimed, by whom, and how it was justified required 'building' the case from the elements given in the article. Due to the variation in the presentation of these elements in the newspaper articles, as well as my concern for the impacts of stylistic and rhetorical differences in the French and Finnish newspaper text, and the difficult issues of translation, I decided to build the coding matrix by extracting the acts of justifications from the articles into cases I then coded.

In other words, I wrote a summary of each case, i.e. each act of justification, and used these summaries as the basis of coding and writing the analysis. Therefore, the examples I present in the following are not direct citations from the newspapers, but citations from the cases I constructed from them.

In Boltanski's and Thévenot's understanding, the different worlds of justification are by definition not compromising, but exclusive. There are many ways in which the different worlds can, however, figure in relation to each other.

A *compromise* between two worlds is, thus, not a conflict in which justifying acts between the worlds are possible. A compromise is an uneasy, awkward situation, or at best a frozen composition of two worlds that rarely holds. In the newspaper articles, compromises occurred particularly in the nature of many claim-makers, and the larger settings of some conflicts. A neighborhood association could be seen as a domestic–civic compromise, as it is something bound to a locality and standing for the interests of the 'home', and at the same time an association, by definition a creature of the civic world. Many claim-makers were compromises as such: the local parents' (*domestic*) association (*civic*), the bus drivers' (*industrial*) union (*civic*), and the local (*domestic*) collective (*civic*) of environmentalists (*Green*) – or the head of the council's (*civic*) technical board (*industrial*), the financial (*market*) manager (*industrial*) of the council (*civic*), and the head of department (*industrial*) of the ministry (*civic*) of the environment (*Green*).

Also, a conflict concerning the construction of a school would form a complicated compromise between the industrial, market and civic worlds, with the simultaneous implication of construction workers, planning, and machinery, construction business, and public school network and political decisions concerning it. Furthermore, it can be argued that the entire empirical material stems from a fragile compromise between the worlds of civic (the public sphere), opinion (journalism and communication), industrial (work of the journalists, printing machinery, distribution channels, labor, and equipment), and market (newspapers make profit) justifications (Boltanski & Thévenot 1991, 277–80). However, I mainly set aside these types of compromises, as emphasizing the different combinations of justifications was more illustrative on the contextual differences concerning the definitions of the common good.

In the daycare center example given in Chapter 6, the children's parents could have come up with a cluster of justifications, combining two or more of the justifications illustrated above: the daycare center must not be closed because the municipality has to fulfill its statutory responsibilities (civic) *and* organize accessible and good-quality (industrial) daycare *and* promote the protection of the environment (Green) in its decisions (civic). These justifications, in my interpretation, would have to be treated not as a compromise, as the worlds do not penetrate each other and pursue to alter the original order of greatness within a world, but as *combining* modes of justifications.

Justifications of different worlds do permeate into each other in *reality tests* (ibid. 168–74). In some cases, reality tests occurred within one article, or even within one claim. In the latter case, the opposing party was not cited in the article, but the claim-makers were evidently aware of their claims. In the daycare center's case, a reality test leading to *denunciation* between worlds could be built as follows: a civic justification leaning to the rights discourse would denounce the market world in this type of matter altogether by claiming that rights and equality cannot be measured in money. A test within one world could, for instance, claim within the industrial world that administrative and economic effectiveness is less a viable standard in this case than effectiveness in promoting children's well being.

III Variations in methodology

The results of this study stem from an interwoven theoretical and methodological framework. The design I started out with was not a simple one: the amount and variety of empirical material was rather overwhelming. Hence, particular attention to 'triangulation' and, in many cases, development of suitable methods, was needed. Both empirical and methodological triangulation was necessary in order to carry out the study, modeled as a roundtrip between the theme of politicization and its many variations.

The group styles theory, originally put forward by Nina Eliasoph and Paul Lichterman (2003), is an attempt to combine in itself several approaches to analyzing culture. The Swidlerian toolkits, alongside the extended case method proposed by Michael Burawoy (1998), were the grounds Eliasoph and Lichterman took as their starting points. Their original idea was to develop an approach more prone to actually analyze interaction in group settings. Instead of, first, only telling illuminating, yet sometimes hazily expansive stories, or, secondly, instead of losing touch of the micro-social setting in generalized talk of toolkits, and thirdly, instead of taking for granted an underlying 'oppressive structure', Eliasoph and Lichterman took into account the benefits of these approaches and constituted the idea of studying culture '*in* interaction'. I understood this very literally so that it directs to studying culture as we can grasp it, where it is created: between people communicating with each other, and acting in groups. Through the hermeneutic division to bonds, boundaries and speech norms, they also made it easier (especially than Goffman ever did) to understand what they actually did when applying this approach to their vast ethnographic analyses, and also facilitated both the use of the approach and its further developing.

I am, both by reading sociological work of ethnographers, and by conducting my own study partly following ethnographic guidelines, convinced of the salience and increasing importance of doing ethnographic research. In a world and age in which especially globalization of the markets, and actors and mechanisms connected to the latter constantly persuade us to believe that cultural and contextual differences decrease at a breath-taking pace, and that all that is already not very solid melts into air, it is all the more important to conduct studies on a level where both the differences and the genuine similarities of human cultures and social action reside. In the midst of the deliberately – and wrongfully – standardizing, reductionist and regulatory powers (see e.g. Sennett 2007), context-sensitive micro-level analysis should be at the center of a sociological knowledge interests.

At the same time, I claim that the group styles approach also has strong potential outside the strictly ethnographic study designs. The way I have used it in this study illustrates that apart from face-to-face settings, also more mediated situations and empirical materials benefit from the sensibility of the analytical tools provided by the group styles theory. The extension of the range of the group styles is one of the building blocks of a closer connection between political sociology with its characteristically 'public' empirical objects, and cultural sociology directed at everyday practices.

Frame analysis, then, is an abundantly frequent methodological label under which very different approaches have been placed (cf. e.g. Snow & Benford 1988; Morreale 1991; Steinberg 1998; Benford & Snow 2000; Luhtakallio 2005). It is based on the initial work of Erving Goffman, and the basic idea that frames define social situations and experiences. Frames are needed as the organizational principles according to which we make interpretations of what happens to us and around us (Goffman 1974; 1979). I have used the approach in ways that I anchor rather firmly in the original Goffmanian starting point, even though the empirical environments I apply them in differ from Goffman's own studies.

First, I used the framing vocabulary to illustrate the 'definitions of the situations' the interviewed actors used. These 'situations', instead of being occasions of face-to-face interaction, were the actors' ways of making sense of the conceptual, at times fairly abstract situations and experiences of democracy, citizenship, and gender. I processed and named the interpretative frames they used when talking about these issues with me afterwards. In this sense, they are *my* definitions of *their* situational interpretations. But so it is in Goffman's work, too: he observes people in everyday situations and explains their ways of interpreting them. However, it sometimes feels both frustrating and uncertain to come to terms with the fact that it is not possible to get inside people's heads, the best we have to offer is the knowledge of a large amount of parallel situations of which different people make the same kind of interpretations.

Secondly, I used frame analysis in the analysis of visual representations in Chapter 4. The application of visual frame analysis is my own, one that I have developed for the needs of sociological research on images (Luhtakallio 2003; 2005). When conducting visual analysis within the field of sociology, the question of methods and methodology is unavoidable. The need for functioning and pertinent sociological methods for the study of visual culture is a topic that urges developing and new contributions. My application of Goffman's frame analysis is one possibility to analyze images in their social context, as representations. The assessment of the application is perhaps best achieved by time and the number of possible other users (see Homanen 2011). In the work I have done in visual sociology, it has, in my view, proved a functional tool by doing what a method should do: helped me in organizing, analyzing, and interpreting the messy empirical world.

Finally, the third variation of frame analysis I have made use of is based on the theoretical ideas put forward by the current labeled as 'French pragmatism', notably the theory of justification by Luc Boltanski and Laurent Thévenot (1991; also 1999; Lamont & Thévenot 2000). Like Ilana Friedrich Silber (2003), I am convinced of the connections between this line of thinking and the one that Silber calls the theory of cultural repertoires. I have introduced the latter through Ann Swidler's toolkit metaphor, and further developed it in the discussions of the group styles and the different uses of frame analysis. The Public Justifications Analysis is the result of combining the two approaches. It has the same fundamental idea Silber sees in the relation between cultural repertoires and justifications: it is a set of morally laden frames that have certain specific ways of relating to each other. In sum, the justification theory is a construct of specialized, finely detailed ways of framing. The most distinct character of this construct is that these frames are morally binding.

Both Silber and Boltanski and Thévenot ignore Goffman's work almost entirely. I have tried to show there is no good reason for that, and that on the contrary, Goffman provides one of the most salient and obvious links between cultural sociology and pragmatism. His work is, above all, about habitual interaction and its crisis situations in which collective work and effort with mutually recognized tools and styles is needed in order the course of things to be restored, and social life with its continuous flow of smaller and bigger ruptures to go on.

The objective of this methodological work has been two-fold. On the one hand, I have pursued it to meet the practical needs of the empirical material I have collected in order to compare local politicization the best I could. On the other hand, the objective of strengthening the bridge between political, cultural, and pragmatist sociology has guided my methodological choices and developments.

Data Appendix

I The interviews

The interviewees

A majority of the interviewees had a college degree or were university students at the time of the interview. One of the French and four of the Finnish activist interviewees said they were members of a political party (all were members of a party on the left of the political map, except for one Green in Finland). As the local groups were mainly rather small and the interviewees often had visible positions in them, I have had to limit the information I give in order to protect the informants' anonymity, and thus the personal and group details are not brought together.

Table DA1 Description of interviewees

Interviewees	Women	Men	Activists	Politicans/ officials	Born 1930s–1950s	Born 1960–1980s	Total N
Lyon	10	10	14	6	5	15	20
Helsinki	17	10	17	9	12	15	27
Total	27	20	31	15	17	30	47

The groups

('x' signals the groups I was ethnographically involved with.)

Lyon

Radio Canut (x)

Alternative, voluntary-based Radio station, important for the local activism both as a connecting point of different activist groups and as an information channel.

Cabiria

An association helping foreign prostitutes to integrate by means of language courses and help in dealing with the municipality.

La Fonda

Association facilitating processes of participatory democracy, working closely with the Regional parliament and its projects of citizen hearings.

APUS

Association helping substance abusers, prostitutes and convicts, especially in health and habitation issues.

Tiens bon la Pente

Neighborhood Association brought together by the neighborhood meal tradition in la Croix-Rousse and working for a more "convivial" and self-organized neighborhood.

Conceil de quartier de X (x)

Neighborhood Council of X, a statutory neighborhood council of a Lyonnais city district.

ATTAC Rhône

Local branch of the alter-globalization movement, active in organizing local social forums.

Non à Big Brother (x)

Activist group resisting surveillance cameras, specialized in 'revealing' the present and future cameras both on their website and concretely on the streets by means of colorful performances.

Squatters (x)

Different groupings squatting houses, living in squats, organizing activities and parties, as well as solidarity actions in case of evictions.

Les Lyonnes

A Socialist-Party oriented feminist organization.

Robins des villes

Association mediating city planning and arranging citizen–city exchange, often seen as too close to the municipality by more radical activist groups.

Ateliers de la citoyenneté (x)

Activist group organizing discussions on new forms of citizenship, mainly by means of self-reflection and talk marked by frustration of traditional politics, but also by 'traditional' activism.

Helsinki

Lähiradio

Alternative, voluntary-based Radio station hosting many programs by activist groups; loose organization and rather 'disintegrated' as a 'group', the radio mainly provides a channel for different groups.

(Sörkan) ATTAC (x)

Alter-globalization movement's local branch that is involved in a wide variety of activities in the city, including the organization of the Finnish Social Forum.

Pro Kuntapalvelut (x)

Activist group resisting the outsourcing of public services and criticizing the city budgetary politics, for example by claiming the city deliberately 'under-budgets' social and health services in order to later justify reducing the services.

Kenkää Keskustatunnelille

Activist group opposing to the building of a tunnel through center of Helsinki; the group members were mainly environmental and Leftist activists brought together by the project of lobbying against the tunnel, which they did with considerable success.

Reumaliitto

Association representing people with rheumatic illnesses, involved in the Pro Municipal Services activities.

Tapaturmainvalidit ry

Association representing people handicapped in accidents; involved in the Pro Municipal Services activities and an important Left-wing action group of mainly the elderly generations.

Oranssi ry

Squatters' Association founded in the 1980s, nowadays a well-established actor in Helsinki youth housing politics.

Vapaa katto ry (x)

Squatters' Association founded in the 2000s during the 'new wave' of squatting aiming at establishing social centers and anti-capitalist urban spaces, whose inspiration stemmed from squatting in Germany, Denmark, and Southern Europe.

Dodo ry

Environmental Association including many architect activists interested in environmentally oriented city planning.

Helka ry

Umbrella organization of neighborhood associations in Helsinki.

Six interviews from Helsinki were originally made in a previous research project, and were added in this corpus due to the thematic similarity of the projects (see Holli *et al*. 2006; 2007).

Original Interview questions (in French and Finnish)

(Indicative)

Activists

Grille thematique/militants

1 **Parcours militant**

Comment êtes-vous entré dans le champ militantisme?

Quelles étaient les premières motivations qui vous ont emmené à militer ou contester?

De quels groupes militants et/ou de quelles action avez-vous fait partie?

Qu'évoque pour vous la notion d'action citoyenne et/ou citoyenneté?

Quelle est son importance ?

Qu'est-ce que cela vous apporte?

Un militant a-t-il besoin de qualifications spécifiques selon vous? Les quelles?

Les femmes et les hommes militent-ils/elles de façon identique ou différente? Selon vous pourquoi?

Quel point de vue avez-vous sur la politique institutionnelle – êtes-vous par exemple un électeur (et qu'est-ce que cela veut dire pour vous)? Participez-vous aux activités des partis politique ?

2 **Engagement actuel**

Comment ce collectif/mouvement a-t-il débuté?

Quel est le but de ces activités?

Pourquoi a-t-on besoin de militer pour cela?

Quelles sont les actions typiques de ce collectif, qu'avez-vous fait jusqu'à présent pour obtenir des résultats?

Comment le groupe finance-t-il ses activités? Reçoit-il des subventions de la ville/de l'Etat?

Comment êtes-vous engagé dans les activités actuelles?

Que faites-vous dans ce collectif/mouvement, quel est votre rôle?

Quelle est l'importance de ces activités pour vous?

3 **Les militants**

Combien y-t-il des militants actifs dans ce collectif?

Qui sont ces militants, d'où viennent-ils/elles?

Y-a-til de femmes, d'hommes?

Les rapports sociaux de sexe ont-ils une importance au sein du collectif?

Quelle est la nature des contacts entre les militants – officiel, officieuse, amicale, fréquent, pas fréquent – quel genre d'affinité existe-t-il entre les militants?

Où rencontrez-vous les autres militants?

Avec qui avez-vous le plus de contacts? A quoi cela est-il dû selon vous?

Ce collectif a-t-il des contactes avec d'autres collectifs/mouvements locaux? Les quels? Quel genre de contacts? Existe-t-il de la coopération? Sur quels sujets?

Contacts avec groupes/mouvements ailleurs? Niveau national? International? Quel genre de contacts, quel genre de coopération?

4 **La ville**

Comment décririez-vous la réception des actions aux quelles vous avez participé par les structures de la prise de décision de la ville?

Quel type de contacts et/ou de coopération avez-vous eu et/ou tenté d'avoir avec les structures de la ville?

Qui avez-vous contacté? Avez-vous été en contact direct avec des élu-e-s? Des administrateurs?

Vos argument ont-ils été écouté? Ont-ils eu de l'effet dans la prise de décision?

Qu'espériez-vous au mieux des relations entre la ville et votre groupe?

Que pensez-vous de la politique locale?

Avez-vous fait de la connaissance avec des projets de la démocratie de proximité mis en place par la ville? Avez-vous participé ou pensé à participer aux conceils du quartier? Pourquoi?

Le changement des mandats a-t-il de l'impact? Après les dernières éléctions? Et les prochaines, qu'en pensez-vous?

Que voudriez-vous changer auprès des institutions de la ville de Lyon?

Comment imaginez-vous la situation dans deux ans?

5 **La sphère publique**

Quel est le rôle des medias dans vos action? Quels médias?

Avez-vous essayé d'intéresser les médias? Si oui, comment?

Quel genre de publicité avez-vous eu?

Quel genre de publicité souhaiteriez-vous avoir?

Quels sont les facteurs qui influencent la médiatisation ou non des activités, selon vous?

Votre groupe publie-t-il des matériaux/des informations lui-même? Où, comment, par quels moyens?
Quelle est l'importance pour vous des médias locaux/nationaux/ internationaux?

Information personnel
Année de naissance
Sexe
Situation familiale
Formation
Structure
Parti

Haastattelurunko/aktivistit
1 **Toiminta**
Kerro liikkeen toiminnasta
- miten se on alkanut
- mitä tavoitteita toiminnalla on
- minkälaisia toimintatapoja

Miten olet itse tullut mukaan toimintaan?
Miksi tällaista toimintaa tarvitaan?
Miten toiminta rahoitetaan? Saako yhdistys tukea kaupungilta/valtiolta?
Mikä on oma asemasi nykyään, mitä teet?
Mikä on kansalaistoiminnan merkitys itsellesi?

2 **Oma tausta**
Kerro hiukan taustastasi kansalaistoimijana – miten se on alkanut, miksi olet lähtenyt mukaan toimintaan?
Missä ryhmissä olet toiminut?
Mitä kansalaisuustoiminta merkitsee sinulle? Mitä saat siitä?
Entä kansalaisuus? Mitä se sisältää, mikä sen merkitys sinulle on?
Kysyykö aktiivikansalaisuus jotain erityisominaisuuksia? Kenestä tulee kansalaisaktiivi?
Ovatko miehet ja naiset samalla tavoin aktiiveja? Onko heidän toiminnassaan kansalaistoimintakentällä eroja? Miksi?
Mitä ajattelet politiikasta? Äänestätkö? Toimitko puolueissa? Miten poliittinen järjestelmä paikallistasolla mielestäsi toimii?

3 **Aktiivit**
Kuinka paljon aktiiveja liikkeellä on / toimintaa osallistuvien määrä?
Keitä he ovat – miehiä/naisia, ikäryhmät, etninen tausta, koulutus...?

Onko sukupuolten välisillä suhteilla/sukupuolten tasa-arvolla merkitystä toiminnassa?
Minkälaiset suhteet aktiiveilla on toisiinsa, kuinka usein tavataan, millaisissa merkeissä?
Missä itse tapaat muita aktiiveja? Keitä eniten?
Onko liikkeellä/yhdistyksellä kontakteja/yhteistyötä muiden paikallisten liikkeiden/yhdistysten kanssa? Minkälaista yhteistyötä?
Entä muihin kuin paikallisiin liikkeisiin? Kansallisesti/kansainvälisesti; millaisia yhteyksiä?

4 **Kaupunki**
Minkälaista palautetta olette saaneet toiminnastanne kaupungin edustajilta?
Minkälaisia kontakteja/yhteistyötä teillä on kaupungin kanssa? Oletteko yrittäneet tehdä yhteistyötä, miten olette onnistuneet?
Kenen kanssa olette olleet yhteyksissä? Minkälaisia kokemuksia sinulla on näistä kontakteista – valtuutetut/virkamiehet?
Kuunnellaanko ehdotuksianne/argumenttejanne?
Onko toiminnallanne ollut vaikutusta päätöksentekoon?
Millaiset yhteydet yhdityksellä parhaimmillaan voisi olla kaupunkiin?
Mitä mieltä olet paikallispolitiikasta?
Oletteko osallistuneet kaupungin osallistumishankkeisiin? Entä muihin projekteihin? Mihin? Millaisia kokemuksia niistä on saatu?
Mitä Helsingin kunnallispolitiikassa ja hallinnossa pitäisi muuttaa? Mikä toimii hyvin?
Miten luulet tilanteen kehittyvän tulevaisuudessa?

5 **Paikallisjulkisuus**
Mikä on median merkitys toiminnassanne? Mitkä mediat ovat merkityksellisiä?
Pyrittekö toiminnallanne herättämään mediahuomiota? Miten? Oletteko onnistuneet tässä? Minkälaista julkisuutta olette saaneet? Mitkä tekivät mielestäsi vaikuttavat median kiinnostukseen?
Tuottaako yhdistys itse julkaisuja/materiaalia – millaisia, miten jaellaan?
Mikä merkitys paikallisilla/kansallisilla/kansainvälisillä medioilla on toiminnassanne?

Taustatiedot
Syntymävuosi
Sukupuoli
Siviilisääty/perhetilanne

Koulutus
Ammatti
Puolue

Politicians

Grille thématique/politique et administration

Généralités

Quelles sont vos responsabilités dans la municipalité?
Quels sont les tâches principales de votre service?

Coopération avec le milieu associatif

Quelles associations/collectifs citoyens sont pour vous les plus proches (au niveau de la coopération) ?
Quelles tâches ont les associations dans votre champs de responsabilités?
Travaillez-vous en coopération avec des associations – sur quels sujets? Quelles associations?
Quelle importance a cette coopération à votre service?
Quel est le pouvoir d'influence, selon votre estimation, des partenaires associatifs dans la prise de décision?

Contacts et/ou coopération avec des citoyens

Quel types de voies les citoyens disposent/utilisent-ils pour vous contacter?
Les contacts sont-ils fréquents? De quoi s'agit-il par exemple?
Quelles sont, selon vous, les possibilités d'influence des citoyens aux décisions au niveau du quartier/l'arrondissement/la ville?
Qu'est-ce qui caractérise un citoyen actif? Passif?
Existe-t-il des différences entre les hommes et les femmes dans la citoyenneté ?
Que souhaiteriez-vous au mieux de la participation des citoyens?
Que voudriez-vous changer?

Coopération au sein de la politique et l'administration municipale

Comment sont les relations entre l'administration et la prise de décision à Lyon, de votre avis?
La gouvernance municipale fonctionne-t-elle d'une manière satisfaisante?
Que changeriez-vous dans les pratiques de la gouvernance?
Avez-vous remarqué des impacts dûs aux rapports sociaux de sexes dans ces pratiques? Les quels?

La démocratie locale

Qu'est-ce qui constitue la démocratie locale?

Quelle est son importance?

Quelles dont les pratiques mises en place dans le cadre de la démocratie de proximité dans votre service?

Les rapports sociaux de sexe jouent-ils un rôle dans le planning et/ou mise en place de ces pratiques? Si oui, quel type de rôle?

Quelles difficultés et/ou défis les pratiques de la démocratie locale font-elles face?

Selon vous, qu'est-ce qu'il faudrait faire pour améliorer la situation?

Comment voyez-vous la situation évoluée dans deux ans?

La sphère publique locale

Quel est le rôle des media dans la politique locale? Quels médias?

Quelle est l'importance des média dans la mise en place des projets de la démocratie de proximité?

Quel genre de publicité ont-ils eu par exemple les conceils de quartier ?

Quel genre de publicité souhaiteriez-vous avoir pour ces projets?

Quels sont les facteurs qui influencent la médiatisation ou non des activités venant de la part de la ville, selon vous?

Coopération extra-municipale

Avez-vous des responsabilités dans des structures inter-communales? Comment celles-ci ont-elles été organisées?

Quelles formes de coopération régionale/départementale/nationale existe-t-il dans votre service?

Existe-t-il de la coopération internationale dans votre service? Quel genre? Le dévéloppement de l'Union Européenne a-t-elle influencé ceci?

Comment choisit-on les représentants de la ville pour ces structures?

Parcours politique/professionnel

Comment êtes-vous arrivé à votre poste actuelle? Quand?

Le fait d'être un homme/une femme a-t-il influencé, selon vous, votre parcours?

Qu'aimez-vous le plus/le moins dans cette acivité?

Y-a-t-il eu des changements au cours des années?

Vos propres centres d'intérêt ont-ils changé?

Pouvez-vous mentionner l'une de vos actions qui vous a particulièrement satisfait?

Information personnel
Année de naissance
Sexe
Situation familiale
Formation
Structure
Parti

Haastattelurunko / poliitikot ja virkamiehet
Yleistä
Mitkä ovat yksikkösi / ryhmäsi keskeiset tehtävät?
Mitkä ovat omat tehtäväsi?

Yhteistyö kansalaisyhteiskunnan kanssa
Miten kuvaisit Helsingin kansalaistoimintakenttää?
Teetkö itse työssäsi / toiminnassasi yhteistyötä yhdistysten ja/tai kansalaisryhmien kanssa?
Minkä yhdistysten / kansalaisryhmien kanssa?
Mitä tehtäviä yhdistyksillä on omalla vastuualueellasi?
Mikä merkitys yhdistyksillä ja kansalaisryhmillä on oman työsi kannalta?
Minkälaista vaikutusvaltaa niillä on päätöksenteossa arviosi mukaan?

Yhteydet kansalaisiin
Miten kansalaiset ottavat yhteyttä – kuinka usein ja mitä koskien?
Minkälaisia ovat aktiiviset kansalaiset? Keitä he ovat? Onko naisten ja miesten välillä eroja osallistumisessa, aktiivisuudessa, tavoissa vaikuttaa?
Minkälaiset ovat mielestäsi kansalaisten vaikutusmahdollisuudet Helsingissä?
Millaista kansalaisten osallistuminen mielestäsi parhaimmillaan voisi olla? Mitä haluaisit muuttaa järjestelmässä / kansalaisten toimintatavoissa?

Poliittisen johdon ja hallinnon yhteistyö
Millainen on poliittisen johdon ja hallinnon suhde mielestäsi Helsingissä yleisesti ottaen? Entä oman toimialueesi kohdalla?
Toimiiko kunnallishallinto Helsingissä hyvin? Mitä muuttaisit siinä?

Paikallisdemokratia

Mistä paikallisdemokratia mielestäsi koostuu?

Mikä on sen merkitys?

Miten arvioisit helsinkiläisen paikallisdemokratian toimivuutta?

Kansalaisosallistumisen tärkeydestä puhutaan nykyään paljon. Millaisia käytäntöjä omalla toimialueellasi on käytössä sen lisäämiseksi / turvaamiseksi?

Miten toimivia ne ovat? Mitä kehitettävää niissä on? Miten arvioit tilanteen Helsingissä kehittyvän seuraavien viiden vuoden aikana?

Paikallisjulkisuus

Mikä on median rooli paikallisen politiikan / hallinnon / demokratian kannalta?

Mitkä ovat mielestäsi keskeisiä medioita Helsingissä?

Oma toiminta ja ura

Kerro ammatillisesta / poliittisesta taustastasi – miten olet päätynyt nykyisiin tehtäviisi?

Mikä on parasta / pahinta nykyisessä tehtävässäsi?

Henkilötiedot

Syntymävuosi

Sukupuoli

Elämäntilanne / perhe

Koulutus

Ammatti

Puolue

II Image material, copyrights and photographers (Chapter 4)

The image material consists of two sets of images. The first set was collected on several occasions in 2005–2007 mainly through two local activist portals, *Rebellyon* and *Megafoni*, through links followed from them, and from the sites of all the groups involved in the study. The final sample consists of 274 pictures from Helsinki and 232 from Lyon. The second set of images was collected from Lyon Citoyen and Helsinki-info, volumes 2004–2005 (and one issue from HI 2006). The primary data consisted of 607 images from the former, and 1833 from the latter. For the sake of manageability, I delimited the analyzed set of images to all cover page images, and all images from 4 issues (October and February 2004 and 2005) of each magazine. The final corpus consists of 208 city magazine images from Helsinki and 357 from Lyon.

I am deeply indebted and grateful to the photographers and copyright-holders of these images for giving me their permission to use their visual materials in this book (see list of Illustrations on pp. viii–ix).

Newspaper data

Cited articles / Helsingin Sanomat 2005

Original Article Headline (my translations):

HS01-09: 'The homeless will not have a shelter in Pitäjänmäki'
HS01-18: 'The Greens of Vantaa chafe at the falling down of the gas plant plans'
HS02-10: 'The railroad tunnel is being mined in eastern Vantaa'
HS02-16: 'The tenants of [the city of] Helsinki worry about their rights'
HS03-05: 'The airport's environment permit does not need to be changed'
HS03-09: 'There is a wish for clear calculations of the economies made by closing schools'
HS03-30: 'A golf course proposed for Turvesuo in Mankkaa'
HS04-27: 'The teachers' union would like to inspect the legality of the school savings in Vantaa'
HS05-12: 'The inhabitants of Ruoholahti gave advice to the planners of Jätkäsaari'
HS05-24: 'The inhabitants of Viherlaakso defended their library'

Cited articles / Le Progrès 2005

Original Article Headline (my translations):

LP03-06: 'The councilors answer to inhabitants. The general assembly of CIL [*Comité d'intérêt local*] of Montplaisir brought up several agendas including the A. Courtois market place, the project of the zone 30, the parking fees...'LP93 – 2005-01-16: 'Croix-Rousse and parking meters: 'refusing a fatality'
LP03-08: 'Parking: A neighborhood council brawls. Croix-Rousse: the parking meters will not pass'
LP03-13: '19 cameras of video surveillance installed at the Pavillons square'

LP03-16: 'The young and politics. For a few weeks, six young people from the Association of the Young of Lyon 7th have been carrying out a survey of the theme 'Youth and politics;'

LP04-21: 'Urban planning of Gerland: an encounter between inhabitants and councilors'

LP05-19: 'The demonstrators denounce an attack against the liberty of expression'

LP05-23: 'Petition against a deportation – the mobilization for Carnelle gains strength'

LP06-04: 'A small miracle to be done. They have come to the *Annonciation* church with their wheel chairs, their crutches, and their white sticks, not waiting for miraculous healing, but to show they exist'

Entries used in the digital archive search

LP: Citoyen, citoyenne, actif/active, activité/action citoyenne, participation citoyenne, démocratie locale, démocratie participative, démocratie de proximité, démocratie directe.

HS: Osallistuva demokratia, lähidemokratia, suora demokratia, paikallisdemokratia, paikallinen demokratia, kunnallinen demokratia, kuntademokratia, paikallinen kansalaisuus, kuntalaisuus, aktiivikansalaisuus, aktiivinen kansalaisuus, kansalaisaktiivisuus, kansalaistoiminta, demokratia, kansalaisuus, kuuleminen, kuulemistilaisuus

Notes

1 A Sociological Travelogue

1. During the fieldwork of this study, I lived in Lyon for seven months, and thereafter visited the field for shorter periods several times in 2005–2009. Before beginning this fieldwork, I had lived in France periodically and in different locations since my first stay in 1992, when I went to live in Paris as an au-pair. In the following years, I had short-term jobs in the country, as well as friends to visit. Since the beginning of my academic life, I've studied in France on several occasions both through exchange programs and on my own, and for the past fifteen years I've been engaged in various projects of Finnish–French cooperation, as well as comparative research projects (e.g. Holli *et al.* 2003). This is to say that even if my fieldwork period in Lyon was relatively short, the experience and knowledge I had acquired earlier of the French language and culture essentially helped me carry out this study.
2. Whether politicization is possible, and if so, what would be different in a non-democratic system is a complex question that will, however, not be considered further here.
3. The plural here is essential, as shown by Fraser (1992), 'the' public sphere is in fact always a multiplicity of conflicting, parallel, and hierarchical public arenas, some stronger, some weaker, some more central, some in the position of what she calls the subaltern counter-publics (ibid. 121, 132–3).
4. On the extensive debate concerning the public/private divide in democracy theories and its gender-related consequences in particular, see e.g. Fraser 1992.
5. The deliberative 'turn' in democracy theory was inspired by the 1960s social movements' ideals of inclusion on the one hand, and by the work of John Rawls and Jürgen Habermas respectively, on the other (Estlund 2002, 2–5). The overarching feature of the now rich and versatile field of study is a process-oriented definition of democracy, and an emphasis on democracy as something uncompleted and on-going (also Benhabib 1996; Fraser 1996; Mouffe 1999; Young 2000; Cohen 2002; Tilly 2007, 7–9).
6. In both France and Finland, the debate over the functioning of democracy has been vivid, as the encounter in the beginning of this chapter illustrates, and as becomes evident by examining the block of literature concerning democracy, and practices, procedures, tests, and other empirical phenomena of participative democracy, from various angles, published in both countries during recent years (e.g. Niemi-Iilahti 1999; Neveu C. 2003; Patomäki & Teivainen 2003; Setälä 2003; Rui 2004; Alapuro 2005a; Bacqué *et al.* (eds) 2005; Raevaara 2005; Carrel 2006; Leino 2006; Rosanvallon 2006, 2008; Suomen demokratiaindikaattorit [Finnish Democracy Indicators] 2006; Talpin 2006; Bäcklund 2007; Neveu C. (ed.) 2007; Revel *et al.* (eds) 2007; Sintomer 2007; Blondiaux 2008; ; Kettunen 2008; Ylä-Anttila 2010).

7. There is an evident resemblance between Rosanvallon's formulation of democracy and John Dewey's (1927) definition of the public. I will not treat this question further here, but I acknowledge that the borders between the key concepts I use are indeed blurred: they are all conceptions portraying different angles and aspects of the same general theme (see also, e.g. Chapter 5).
8. The currently most emphasized perspectives on citizenship take globalization as the starting point, instead of the more classical approaches such as citizenship as a membership category attached to nation states. The focus of these debates vary from citizenship (discourse) as an indicator of societal change to citizenship as a construct of multiple simultaneously significant layers (Mouffe 1999, 25; Yuval-Davis 1999: 120; Faulks 2000, 8). Furthermore, citizenship has been seen as the surface of intersections of different subjective identity positions and corporeal experiences, and as a question of human rights that stems from the worldwide increase in migration, to mention but a few approaches (e.g. Soysal 1994; Beasley & Bacchi 2000; Wind 2008–2009).
9. It should be noted that these situationally defined 'citizens-in-doing' are not mere momentary abstractions or reductions, but are instead flesh and blood, and in so being they are marked by different 'sediments' – identities that categorize them and structure their lives, and their accounts on citizenship – in multiple ways. The most salient one is gender. The perspective of citizenship as 'doing' is logically followed by an understanding of gender as not an essential category, but a complicated set of repeated acts and representations that constitute an all-encompassing social structure influencing all human action (de Lauretis 1987, 3–5; Butler 1990, 140–1). In this sense, gender is an inseparable dimension of citizenship, as well as the representations of a society or the processes of creating a public.
10. One of the most marked differences is that Finnish municipalities have traditionally had a wide autonomy from the state, whereas the autonomy of French local communities has been delimited by a strong, centralist state (Rosanvallon 1998; Alapuro 2005a; Stenius 2010). Still today, Finnish municipalities have considerably more power, more functions, and more important budgetary autonomy compared to the French.
11. Lyon is the third largest city in France, and with its 465 300 inhabitants (city agglomeration), only a little smaller than Helsinki (560 905 inhabitants). Lyon is the second largest metropolitan area in France and the capital of the Rhône-Alpes region (1 648 216 inhabitants). The Helsinki metropolitan area has approximatively 1 000 000 inhabitants. As the local civil society does not always respect the administrative frontiers of Lyon and Helsinki, this study does not narrowly follow them either, but extends to the urban community of Grand-Lyon with its 57 communes and the region of Rhône-Alpes with eight departments, of which Lyon is the capital, and the cities of Espoo and Vantaa that are part of the Helsinki metropolitan area (Lyon 2010; Helsinki 2010; Grand Lyon 2009; see also Bagnasco & Le Galès 2000, 6).
12. In Lyon, the council groups were the Socialists (Socialistes et Apparents; 25), Unir pour Lyon (Right Wing; 17), UMP (Right Wing; 14), the Communist Party (Communiste et Intervention Citoyenne 6), the Greens (5), the GAEC (Gauche Alternative, Ecologique, Citoyenne; extreme Left; 3) and

Radical group (extreme Left; 3). In Helsinki, the Council was composed of the National Coalition (Kokoomus; Right Wing; 25 seats), the Social Democrats (SDP; 21), the Green League (Vihreä liitto; 17), the Left League (Vasemmistoliitto; 8), the Swedish National Party (RKP; Right Wing; 6), the Center Party (Keskusta; Right Wing; 4), the Christian Democrats (Kristillisdemokraatit; Right Wing; 2), the True Finns (Perussuomalaiset; Right Wing; 1) and the Communist Party (SKP; 1).

13. The city mayors in Finland are usually officials, not political leaders, even though political power relations strongly define the position, as the City Council elects the mayor.
14. Citizen participation in urban communities has been promoted by the *Politique de la ville* (Politics of the city) program, resulting in a great variety of practices, policies and legislation, such as public inquiry and local referendum (Koebel 2006, 94–6, 101–6). Low turnouts, especially in the beginning of the 2000s, triggered yet a new effort to strengthen citizen participation, which resulted in the law on democracy of proximity in 2002. The so-called 'Vaillant law' instituted neighborhood councils in all cities with more than 80 000 inhabitants (relating to about 50 French cities), and presented other tools at different levels of public administration to boost civic involvement in decision-making (Deyon 1999, 17–19; Delbo 2005, 55–6, 88–91; Koebel 2006, 83–4).
15. The current Local Government Act obliges Municipal Councils to assure the participation of citizens in municipal decision-making, and includes for instance the possibility of a municipal referendum (The Local Government Act 395/1995 § 30–1; Bäcklund *et al.* 2006: 8;). The Act of Construction and the Use of Land (1999) is the strongest manifestation of the policy trend enhancing citizen participation (see Bäcklund *et al.* 2002). It decrees that citizens must be heard on all construction and zoning issues. Furthermore, the lowest turnout in Finland's elections since World War II, the Municipal elections of 2000, triggered 'The Citizen Participation Policy Program', a colossal inter-ministerial project during 2003–2007, with the purpose of evaluating and developing new participatory mechanisms.
16. All translations are by the author unless noted otherwise.
17. The French neighborhood councils always have councilor members, and they are led by a double presidency with one councilor and one layperson in the lead.
18. Thematic working groups aggregating councilors, professionals and others concerned (for example with preventing exclusion, or improving accessibility for the handicapped), the Lyonnais Council for Respecting Rights (CLRD, aggregating human rights associations and institutions), the Committee for Initiatives and Town Part Consultation (CICA, destined to enhance the participation of local associations in the municipal life), and the Council of Development of Grand Lyon.
19. Long-term participatory working groups have also existed in some neighborhoods, such as the Maunula District Forum that has organized occasions for inhabitants to deliberate on the future of the neighborhood (Kaupunginosat 2009).
20. Prior to 2009 when participation was for the first time emphasized in the Helsinki Strategy document, The City Council had never officially decided

on an issue concerning citizen participation or its enhancement directly (verbal information from City of Helsinki Urban Fact Centre's researcher, Pia Bäcklund).

21. *Contrat Premier Emploi*, the first employment contract; a bill destined, according to the Government, to reduce youth unemployment by rendering them more attractive to the employers. According to the protest movement, the bill would have exposed young employees at the mercy of employers, as it made firing them very easy. The bill did not pass in the orginally proposed form.
22. The revolutionary strike and consequent events lead to the abolition of the Estates and the creation of the Finnish Parliament, as well as the establishment of general suffrage in the country (Alapuro 1995; General Strike 2010).
23. For more details on each set of data presented, see Data Appendix.
24. As noted earlier, the Finnish Municipal Councils are not divided into a majority and an opposition, but the Finnish interviewees were both from the most powerful and from the smaller and less influential council groups. In the Finnish case, I also interviewed a few civil servants as, for example, the mayor is a civil servant in most Finnish municipalities.
25. Apart from the visual data, all the corpuses have required a lot of translating: all citations I use to illustrate my analyses have been translated into English from either French or Finnish. The translations are almost exclusively mine, and the task has been an extremely hard one. I have no other assurance of the final result but having tried my best to capture the tones and nuances, and to find the closest possible equivalents in English.

2 Group Styles of Local Collective Action

1. *Association pour la Taxation des Transactions financières pour l'Aide aux Citoyens*, the multi-national civic association founded originally in France in 1998 that has initiated or strongly influenced many of the Global Justice Movement's claims and actions, such as the World Social Forum (see ATTAC 2011).
2. Eliasoph and Lichterman have developed the approach based on their studies concerning the micro-level of collective and political action (Eliasoph 1996, 1998; Lichterman 1996). Leaning exclusively on ethnographic methods, they (2003; see also Lichterman 2002; Eliasoph 1996) have been critical of the use of thematic interviews, or other non-ethnographically produced material. I suggest, however, that the scope of application of the group styles can be widened, and that using it to analyze a more triangulated set of data, and drawing parallels between it and the mainstream social movement concepts results in a comparative understanding of local civic practices without reducing the sensitivity of the analysis. The cases of organizational styles I present in this chapter result from a triangulation of interviews, ethnographic observations, and institutional background information (see Chapter 1 and Data Appendix for details).
3. Group boundaries and their level of permeability are a part of an abundantly wide body of literature in sociology and social psychology (e.g. Lalonde *et al.* 1994; Lamont & Molnár 2002;). Eliasoph's and Lichterman's usage of the

boundary vocabulary falls in the category of symbolic boundaries, i.e. 'tools by which individuals and groups struggle over and come to agree upon definitions of reality' (Lamont & Molnár 2002, 168). However, the dimension of social boundaries, 'objectified forms of social differences manifested in unequal access to and unequal distribution of resources (material and nonmaterial) and social opportunities', is equally important in understanding how boundaries and boundary work shape the groups (ibid. 168).

4. The names of these institutions were often playful: Radio Canut owed its name to the silk weavers that first inhabited the district, called *Canuts* in French; the bar's name translates into 'The Red Ant', with probably a reference to the political color of the owner and most of the customers; and finally, the bookstore indicates in a humorous way that the store has more than one book, or more than one truth to offer, to put it simply.
5. All the names have been changed.
6. Thévenot's (2010) notion of commonplace refers to a (shared) emotional attachment to something – the something can be just as well a place, a song, a practice, or a habit – that makes people feel intimately engaged.
7. Cloé, an activist in her late twenties, was a very important interlocutor and a friend, who in many ways played the role of a gatekeeper in my fieldwork in Lyon, as she was extremely well known in the activist circles. She introduced me Lyonnais and groups, and often 'guaranteed' me before the activists who were sometimes suspicious of my research intentions. Conducting this study would have been very different, and for some parts impossible, without her help.
8. For parallel reflections from a very different environment, the Orthodox Jew community on Melrose in Los Angeles, see Tavory (2010a).
9. These three districts are closely tied to each other both geographically and imaginary-wise. They form the eastern part of downtown Helsinki.
10. The names cited here and above have the following meanings in English: Power (*Voima* magazine), Rhythm (*Rytmi* bar), and Chatter House (*Juttutupa* bar). Hakaniemi has no intentional political significance.
11. For instance, in recent years, squats were opened in a great variety of districts in Helsinki, and not in particular around these areas. There may be a spatial reason for this, too: According to statistics, in comparison to all of Finland, the inhabitants of Kallio live in the least square meters (Statistics Finland 2009a), so spaces big enough for squatting or other forms of collective living are a scarce resource. The *Elimäenkatu* squat (see section 3.2) was, however, located in a neighboring district Vallila at the immediate vicinity of the Kallio–Sörnäinen–Hakaniemi area.
12. In the center of Helsinki, a few rather exclusive and pricy farmers' markets contradict this claim, but they remain out of reach of the majority of people.
13. *Sörkka* is the inhabitants' nickname for Sörnäinen, one of the eastern downtown districts.
14. Associations have to be accepted by a state organ called the Patent and Register Committee, through a process in which the committee approves their application consisting of the name, the purpose, and the rules of the association. Furthermore, registered associations must report their yearly activities, make up a balance sheet, and write a plan for the upcoming year for the same official. This level of formality may sound peculiar, but the

practice is so common that not being registered is more of a peculiarity among Finnish activist groups. The status of a registered association makes things easier: it enables opening a bank account, buying a web domain, and the like. In particular, the status is the almost-non-exception requirement for the state or other public funding, which most associations depend on.

15. Contentious squatting movements were not unique to France: in the 1970s and 1980s, in many European cities the conflicts between squatters and police forces lead to 'urban wars' of various scales (see on Amsterdam Uitermark 2004).
16. This difference reflects national opinion polls in which the Finns express a high level of trust on the police (e.g. Poliisibarometri 2007).
17. The latest activity in the estate had been an industrial saw, from which the squat drew its name, The Sawmill.
18. Another point that stresses the continuity rather than abrupt change of repertoires in the Helsinki squatter movement is that, also the movement of the 2000s registered an association to deal with 'practicalities', the 'Free Roof association' [*Vapaa katto ry*].
19. The squat was named 'The Harbour' because of its vicinity to the old industrial port of Helsinki. The Satama story came to an end in 2011 when the squat was evicted after long and tense negotiations between the squatters, the Youth Board that mainly backed their claims, and the coalition between the Mayor and the Public Works Department. In addition to the plans of the latter to demolish the building, conflict arose from the Romany that the squatters allowed to camp in the squat's yard. After the Satama eviction, the movement continued squatting buildings, and even if the squatters' attitudes towards the establishment had probably hardened as a result of the Satama experience, mainstream news media was still just as welcome to the new squats as before (*Helsingin Sanomat*, the daily newspaper, reported on the issue for instance in June 25, 26 and 27, 2011).
20. I did, unfortunately, not manage to be around for any of the house meetings, and am thus relying on others' descriptions.
21. The emphasis here indicates here that the interviewee used the English word in her speech.
22. This characteristic resembles historical accounts of Finnish associational culture that can be traced back to the 18th century (Stenius 1987; 1988). Yet, it would be incautious to resume to local group in question into a mere 'representative' of a Finnish tradition.
23. In a sense, also the current squatters voluntarily positioned themselves under the category of *youth* activities, which proved strategically successful, as they thus gained the support of the City Council's Youth Board and the Youth Department. I am grateful to Veikko Eranti for pointing this out.
24. In addition to the power company, Helsinki Port (*Helsingin Satama*), the local water company (*Helsingin Vesi*), and the public transportation company (*HKL*) functioned as semi-privatized companies. Since their semi-privatization, their profits and losses had not been spelled out in the balance sheet or in the city budget. Instead, they accounted a standard annual sum to the city. For the power company, the sum had been around 50 million Euros. The remaining profits, regardless their quantity, were reserved for the independent use of the company and were handled as profits in the private sector, e.g. in investments.

In the case of the power company, then, the city did not benefit from the large profits resulting from high electricity prices (see Forssell 2005).

25. Finnish municipalities have heavy legal obligations for organizing and assuring several social, health, and education services, many of which are considered citizens' subjective rights (cf. the Municipal Act).
26. The leading Finnish Right-wing party.
27. In Raevaara's analysis of the Parliament discussions concerning the gender quotas in political organs, expertise was the most prevalent – and successful – line of argumentation both for those supporting, and those opposing the quotas in Finland. In her study, the French MPs rooted their arguments in the notions of the Republic, and democracy.

3 Citizenship and Gender in Local Activism

1. This comparison has an asymmetrical starting point: the influence of the French revolution, and political thought concerning citizenship is widespread, whereas the Finnish concept and debates are historically and conceptually peripheral. While the French debates and conceptions have also influenced the Finnish debates and conceptions, the Finnish ones, in turn, are largely ignored outside the country. Juxtaposing citizenship in these contexts is therefore simultaneously an analysis of asymmetric conceptual power relations, not a comparison of 'similar cases' (Stenius 2002, 309).
2. Finland has a tradition of extremely strict immigration legislation, and the country's refugee intake, for example, remains one of the smallest in Europe (see, e.g. Eurostat 2010; Maahanmuuttovirasto 2010; Tilastokeskus 2010;).
3. Stenius (2002) provides a lengthy analysis concerning the disputes over the word that will not be summarized in detail here – there were several options of which *kansalainen* finally proved the most successful.
4. Other axes of comparison, naturally, exists and have been studied as well, such as social policy issues, particularly childcare, security and violence against women, gender divisions of the labor market, and so on (see e.g. Heinen *et al.* 2004).
5. Finland was, together with New Zealand, the first country in the world to realize a universal suffrage that granted the right to vote to men and women equally in 1906. French women were granted the right to vote in 1947.
6. This trend would most likely to be different today, as in the 2011 Parliamentary elections the extreme right party Perussuomalaiset (The True Finns) became the third biggest party of the Parliament with an explicitly anti-immigration campaign, and thus immigration and immigrant rights have become topical in the public debate in unforeseen ways.
7. These names have been changed as well. They are all women's names.
8. See La Gryffe 2010.

4 Visual Frames of the Local Society

1. I am deeply indebted to the photographers and publishers of these images, and thankful for the permission to use their work in illustrating my analysis. In the case of the Lyonnais activist images, the majority of the images were

'copy-left' publications, i.e. not granted with a copyright, and the names of the photographers were impossible to trace. The webmasters in charge of the websites did, however, grant me the right to republish the photos, to the extent of their own right to do so. In the case of the Finnish activist images, some photographers wanted their names to appear, some did not, and I have followed their wishes (see List of Illustrations, pp. viii–ix). The editors of both Lyonnais and Helsinki city information magazines kindly permitted the use of the materials.

2. Louis Althusser (1984) described ideology as appellations of recognition: as the combination of rituals and practices of social institutions in and through which norms and habits are defined and reproduced. Ideology functions through the recruitment of concrete subjects to recognize themselves as subjects, through the learning process in which norms and habits – learned ways of doing the right thing and acting in the proper way – become internalized (ibid. 129). Thus, in this context the question is what kinds of 'visual appellations' take part in the local definition struggles (cf. Williamson 1978). I interpret, however, the Althusserian concept of ideology in wider terms: in my reading, there is no one source or structure 'putting out' an ideology, but all actors engaged in the definition struggles of the public sphere are ideological actors, and ideology thus is not a structure, but a process of defining and redefining the terms of the struggle.
3. The same applies, in some cases even more, to email lists. They are, however, both less accessible and less public. Regarding more 'traditional' alternative media, there is no comprehensive 'activist journal' in Helsinki, whereas in Lyon, 'Potpourri' bullet in is published rather frequently, but the web sites gathered a far wider range of different activist groups than the bulletin published by a small collective of people and distributed in few places.
4. I collected the images on several occasions in 2005–2007. The final sample consists of 274 pictures from Helsinki and 232 from Lyon.
5. See Megafoni (2009) and Rebellyon (2010). Their names make reference to a loudhailer for the former, and to rebellion fused with the name of the city, Lyon for the latter.
6. Since then, new local 'umbrella' sites have been established in Helsinki.
7. The names of the magazines translate to Lyon Citizen and Helsinki Information.
8. 2004–2005 (one issue of HI 2006). The primary data consisted of 1833 from Lyon Citoyen and 607 images from Helsinki-Info. For the sake of manageability, I limited the analyzed set of images to all cover page images, and all images from 4 issues – those of October and February 2004 and 2005 – of each magazine (*Lyon Citoyen* N=357; *Helsinki-info* N=208).
9. Also, *Lyon Citoyen* is published 10 times a year with approximately 45 pages, whereas *Helsinki-info* appears once every two months with a standard of 24 pages, even if bigger in size due to the newspaper format. Another difference between the magazines is that *Helsinki-info* is bilingual – every issue has a story or two in Swedish, the second official language of Finland, although the magazine is primarily in Finnish – whereas *Lyon Citoyen* is published entirely in French.
10. Indeed the captions were often important in defining the frames, a feature that shows how the visual frame analysis method 'imitates' the reading of the images

by the people they address, and thus the production of meaning that occurs in the two-way negotiations between the image and the viewer. Analyzing images 'in their social context' requires evidently including caption and other texts in the analysis, as in this sense captions are part of the representation, not separate from it (for more discussion on the topic, see Luhtakallio 2003).

11. Both during the procedures of counting and writing the qualitative interpretations, there is no denying that visual representations are subject to multiple 'translations', as is probably always more or less the case in a sociological analysis of any kind of empirical material. These translations are verbalizations and numerical representations, but also, as in the following tables, re-visualizations. The debate concerning these translations, and more generally the relationship between images, words, numbers, and so on, is extensive and far-reaching (see e.g. Benjamin 1936/1989, 149; Barthes 1977, 38–41; Mitchell 1986, 42–74; 1994, 111–17;). At this point, however, I only note that these imperfections should not hinder sociological analysis of the visual culture. I believe that analyzing visual representations with the best possible tools results in significant new insights concerning the local public spheres, although certainly not in the whole 'truth' about these images.
12. The dominant frames in both Table 4.1 and 4.2 are presented in the order of their average amount of representations in the two contexts.
13. See Finlandization 2010.
14. Features of ethnicity, for example, in addition to being often extremely difficult to pinpoint and define, were not strongly emphasized in the activist imageries and will, therefore, not direct the analysis strongly.
15. For technical reasons, not all caption texts are visible on the Illustrations.
16. Naturally, the mother–child portrait dates back way further to the foundations of Western art and art history, and the Christian visual traditions.

5 Framing Democracy

1. An earlier version of the analysis in this chapter has been published in Luhtakallio, E. 2010. 'Perceptions of Democracy in Helsinki and Lyon.' In Stenius, Henrik & Alapuro, Risto (eds) *Nordic Associations in a Comparative Perspective*. Baden-Baden: Nomos Verlagsgesellschaft, 281–306.
2. Alapuro (2005a, 379) highlights especially the French universal suspicion towards both particularity and all mediating structures between the citizens and the state in contrast to the Finnish principle of associations representing people's interests for the good of the nation. In France, group representation was, and partly still is, problematic, due to the republican ideal of universalism that rejected all organized mediation between the state and the citizens. In Finland, by contrast, associations were historically crucial pillars in building the state and creating a political culture marked by the idea of group representation. At the local level, associations brought together different layers of people, including local officials, and formed an ideologically constricted, but efficient intermediate-level machinery of the national imperative (Rosanvallon 1998; Stenius 2010).
3. With politicians, I refer both to councilors and officials, in terms of fluency, but also because I regard these actors as representatives of the local political

institutions even though their way of attachment to it differs (a similar solution in Bäcklund 2007). The statuses are, however, indicated in the citations. Unlike with the activists, I've chosen to keep the politicians 'anonymous' in the sense of calling them only by their statuses (naturally, the activists are not referred to by their real names either). This solution corresponds, in my view, correctly to their position in this study: they were interviewees I mainly met only once, I did not follow their actions, nor get acquainted with them the way I did with the activists.

4. The interviewee used the word *kuntalainen*, inhabitant of a municipality (*kunta*), whose full significance cannot be translated – it was used frequently alongside with *kansalainen* (citizen) and *asukas* (inhabitant), the latter being perhaps the term most frequently in the Finnish politicians' use. It is noteworthy that there is no equivalent term in French: *citadin* and *villageois*, a city and village dweller may be the closest corresponding words, but they were rarely used. Instead, the French politicians used most commonly *citoyen-ne* (citizen), and at times, *habitant-e* (inhabitant). The differences in the traditions of local autonomy, and political culture more in general, thus echoed also in the use of words.

6 Justifying in the Local Public Sphere

1. See Chapter 1 and the Data Appendix for more information on the two newspapers.
2. Headlines of the cited articles are listed in Data Appendix.
3. As shown in Table 6.1, many claims included several justifications, and thus combinations and overlapping of more than one justification principle. Therefore, the proportions stand for 'appearance 'in the ensemble of the claims, and do not result in a total of 100%.
4. In the case Eric Neveu (2003) analyzes, the conflict is between a local movement of farmers and a somewhat faceless EU whose regulations were located, if anywhere, in Brussels far from the local context, a feature that he also recognizes as an influential one regarding the coverage of the conflict in the media (ibid. 452).
5. This claim comes up in innumerable other studies as well, whenever activists are asked about mainstream media policies – and apart from the activists themselves, this idea is often shared by researchers of social movements, see e.g. Gamson 1995.
6. Furthermore, it is most telling that Boltanski and Thévenot were also confronted with this phenomenon when writing *De la justification*: they had to choose a foreign manual as the empirical basis to build the constitutive example of the market worlds, as they could find none in France.
7. In 2008–2009, 26 France Télécom employees killed themselves within eighteen months.

Methods Appendix

1. The methodological apparatus has been developed with the help of numerous discussions with Laurent Thévenot, Risto Alapuro, Julien Charles, and

Markku Lonkila, as well as of data sessions with under-graduate students at our seminar, in particular Veikko Eranti and Suvi Huikuri, all to whom I am deeply indebted to.

2. This application can also be used in a more statistical analysis when the data and study question require it, as in Ylä-Anttila (2010).
3. The division of the worlds stem from texts in the history of Western political philosophy: St Augustin's *Cité de Dieu* (world of inspiration), Bossuet's *Politique* (domestic world), Thomas Hobbes' *Leviathan* (world of renown/opinion), Jean-Jacques Rousseau's *Contrat Social* (civic world), Adam Smith's *Wealth of Nations* (market world), and Saint-Simon's *Système Industriel* (industrial world) (Boltanski & Thévenot 1991, 27). According to the authors, the ecological world has no particular philosophical founding, as its emergence on the public sphere is more recent: it is a result of the post-1960s environmental movement (Lafaye & Thévenot 1993).
4. The emphasis on common humanity means that there are no such figures of greatness that would lean on an idea of fundamental differences in the value of human life, or equality in birth – racism is, in Boltanski's and Thévenot's reading, thus comparable to violence, that is, non-justifiable. This feature of the theory would certainly merit more discussion than is possible to fit in here – racist arguments are by far not unknown to for example French and Finnish public debate, nor is violence self-evidently absent from justifying acts, at least if applying a definition of violence that takes into account acts of symbolic violence, such as silencing another, not listening to another's justifications, forcing another to justify (as is often done in public meetings, sometimes in rather violent ways, like banging one's fist on the table), and so on (see Charles 2010; Ylä-Anttila 2010; see however Boltanski & Thévenot 1991, 41721).

Bibliography

Abbott, Andrew 1995. 'Things of Boundaries.' *Social Research* 6:4, 857–82.

Abèles, Marc 1989. *Jours tranquilles en 89. Enthnologie politique d'un département francais*. Paris: Editions Odile Jacob.

Abèles, Marc 1990. *Anthropologie de l'État*. Paris: Armand Colin.

Alapuro, Risto & Henrik Stenius 1987. 'Kansanliikkeet loivat kansakunnan' [Popular Movements Created a Nation]. In Alapuro, Risto (ed.) *Kansa liikkeessä*. Helsinki: Kirjayhtymä, 7–52.

Alapuro, Risto 1989. 'Finnish Demonstrations as Confrontations.' Paper prepared for the Finnish–Bulgarian symposium 'Perspectives on the contemporary culture in small countries,' University of Jyväskylä, May 24.

Alapuro, Risto 1997. *Suomen älymystö Venäjän varjossa* [Finnish Intelligentsia in the Shadow of Russia]. Helsinki: Tammi.

Alapuro, Risto 2003. 'Finlande. Citoyen; kansalainen. Citoyenneté; kansalaisuus.' In *Cahiers Européens d'Houjarray* no. 6. Publication Internet de l'Association Jean Monnet. www.cahierseuropeens.net

Alapuro, Risto 2005a. 'Associations and Contention in France and Finland: Constructing the Society and Describing the Society.' *Scandinavian Political Studies* 28: 4, 377–99.

Alapuro, Risto 2005b. 'Voluntary Associations and the State.' In Landgrén, Lars-Folke & Pirkko Hautamäki (eds) *People Citizen Nation*. Helsinki: Renvall Institute.

Alapuro, Risto 2007. 'La representation, les associations et la culture politique en Finlande et en France.' Paper presented in Colloque franco-finlandais Malaise dans la démocratie, Institut finlandais, Paris, December 7.

Alapuro, Risto & Markku Lonkila 2010. 'Political Culture in Russia in a Local Perspective.' Unpublished article manuscript presented at the *Spaces of Democracy* seminar, Department of Sociology, University of Helsinki.

Alapuro, Risto & Markku Lonkila 2012. 'Political Culture in Russia from a Local Perspective.' In Alapuro, Risto, Arto Mustajoki & Pekka Pesonen (eds) *Understanding Russianness*. London & New York: Routledge.

Alasuutari, Pertti 2006. 'Suunnittelutaloudesta kilpailutalouteen: Miten muutos oli ideologisesti mahdollinen' [From Planning Economy to Competition Economy: How the Change Became Ideologically Possible]. In Risto Heiskala & Eeva Luhtakallio (eds) *Uusi jako: miten Suomesta tuli kilpailukyky-yhteiskunta?* Helsinki: Gaudeamus.

Albert, Pierre 1998. *La presse française*. Paris: Presses universitaires de France.

Althusser, Louis 1984. *Ideologiset valtiokoneistot* [Ideological State Machinery]. Tampere: Vastapaino.

Anderson, Benedict 1983. *Imagined Communities. Reflections on the Origin and Spread of Nationalism*. London: Verso.

Anttila, Erkko 2004. 'Paikallisyhteisöllisyys ja sen katoaminen Helsingin seudun työläisesikaupungeissa' [Local Communality and Its Disappearance in Helsinki Region Working Class Suburbia]. *Sosiologia* 41: 3, 181–94.

Anttonen, Anneli (1998). 'Vocabularies of Citizenship and Gender: Finland.' *Critical Social Policy* 18 (3): 355–73.

Bacchi, Carol Lee 1999. *Women, Policy and Politics. The Construction of Policy Problems*. London, Thousand Oaks & New Delhi: Sage Publications.

Bäcklund, Pia 2007. *Tietämisen politiikka. Kokemuksellinen tieto kunnan hallinnassa* [The Politics of Knowing. Experience-based Knowledge in Municipal Governance]. Helsinki: Helsingin kaupungin tietokeskus.

Bäcklund, Pia & Jouni Häkli & Harry Schulman 2002. 'Osallisuuden jäljillä' [Tracing Participation]. In Bäcklund, P. & J. Häkli & H. Schulman (eds) *Osalliset ja osaajat – kansalaiset kaupungin suunnittelussa*. Gaudeamus: Helsinki.

Bäcklund Pia, Anna Kuokkanen & Riikka Henriksson 2006. *Kuntalaisten ja hallinnon vuorovaikutuksen käytännöt Helsingissä* [The Practices of Interaction of Municipal Citizens and Governance in Helsinki]. Helsinki: Helsingin kaupungin tietokeskus.

Bacqué, Marie-Hélène, Henri Rey & Yves Sintomer (eds) 2005. *Gestion de proximité et démocratie participative. Une perspective comparative*. Paris: Editions La Découverte.

Bagnasco, Arnaldo & Patrick Le Galès 2000. *Cities in Contemporary Europe*. Cambridge: Cambridge University Press.

Baiocchi, Gianpaolo 2005. *Militants and Citizens: The Politics of Participatory Democracy in Porto Alegre*. Stanford: Stanford University Press.

Baker, Keith Michael 1992. 'Defining the Public Sphere in Eighteenth-Century France: Variations on a Theme by Habermas.' In Calhoun, Craig (ed.) *Habermas and the Public Sphere*. Cambridge, Massachusetts & London: The MIT Press, 181–211.

Bakhtin, Mikhail 1987. *Problems of Dostoevsky's Poetics*. Minneapolis: University of Minnesota Press.

Balibar, Étienne 2001. *Nous, citoyens d'Europe? Les frontières, l'État, le people*. Paris: La Découverte.

Barthes, Roland 1977. *Image–Music–Text*. London: Fontana.

Beasley, Chris & Carol Bacchi 2000. 'Citizen Bodies: Embodying Citizens – a Feminist Analysis.' *International Feminist Journal of Politics* 2: 3, 337–58.

Benford, Robert & David Snow 2000. 'Framing Processes and Social Movements: an Overview and Assessment.' *Annual Review of Sociology* 26, 611–39.

Benhabib, Seyla 1996. 'Toward a Deliberative Model of Democratic Legitimacy,' In Benhabib, Seyla (ed.) *Democracy and Difference. Contesting the Boundaries of the Political*. Princeton, New Jersey: Princeton University Press, 67–94.

Benjamin, Walter (1936/1989). 'Taideteos teknisen uusinnettavuutensa aikakaudella' [The work of art in the age of mechanical reproduction]. In Benjamin, W. *Messiaanisen sirpaleita. Kirjoituksia kielestä, historiasta ja pelastuksesta*. Eds Koskinen M., K. Rahkonen & E. Sironen. Translated into Finnish by Raija Sironen. Helsinki: Kansan sivistystyön liitto/Tutkijaliitto, 139–73.

Bennett, Lance W. 2003. 'New Media Power: The Internet and Global Activism.' In Couldry Nick & James Curran (eds) *Contesting Media Power*. Lanham: Rowman and Littlefield.

Benson, Rodney & Daniel C. Hallin 2007. 'How States, Markets and Globalization Shape the News. The French and US National Press 1965–97.' *European Journal of Communication* 22:1, 27–47.

Berger, John 1972. *Ways of Seeing*. London: British Broadcasting Corporation and Penguin Books.

Berger, Mathieu 2009. *Répondre en citoyen ordinaire. Enquête sur les engagements profanes dans un dispositif d'urbanisme participatif à Bruxelles*. PhD thesis. Brussels: Institut de Sociologie, Université Libre Bruxelles.

Blondiaux, Loïc 1999. 'Représenter, déliberer ou gouverner? Les assises politiques fragiles de la démocratie participative de quartier.' In *La démocratie locale. Représentation, participation et espace public*. CURAPP & CRAPS. Amiens, Lille, Paris: Presses Universitaires de France, 367–404.

Blondiaux, Loïc 2008. *Le nouvel esprit de la démocratie. Actualité de la démocratie participative*. Paris, Éditions du Seuil, coll.'La république des idées'.

Boltanski, Luc & Laurent Thévenot 1991. *De la justification. Les économies de la grandeur*. Paris: Éditions Gallimard.

Boltanski, Luc & Laurent Thévenot 1999. 'The Sociology of Critical Capacity.' *European Journal of Social Theory* 2: 3, 359–77.

von Bonsdorff, Johan 1986. *Kun Vanha vallattiin* [The Occupation of the Old Student House]. Helsinki: Tammi.

Braconnier, Céline & Jean-Yves Dormagen 2007. *La démocratie de l'abstention*. Paris: Éditions Gallimard.

Brémond, Janine 2004. 'La concentration dans les médias en France.' In (OFM) 14 avril 2004: Analyse de l'OFM. http://www.observatoire-medias.info/article.php3?id_article=103

Breviglieri, Marc 2009. *'L'insupportable. L'excès de proximité, l'atteinte à l'autonomie et le sentiment de violation du privé' – Sens critique, sens de la justice*. Paris: Economica.

Breviglieri, Marc & Claudette Lafaye & Danny Trom 2009. *Compétences critiques et sens de la justice. Colloque de Cerisy*. Paris: Economica.

Brubaker, Rogers 1992. *Citizenship and Nationhood in France and Germany*. Cambridge, Massachusettes: Harvard University Press, 1992.

Burawoy, Michael 1998. 'The Extended Case Method.' *Sociological Theory* 16: 1, 4–33.

Butler, Judith 1990. *Gender Trouble. Feminism and the Subversion of Identity*. New York & London: Routledge.

Calhoun, Craig 1992a. 'Introduction: Habermas and the Public Sphere.' In Calhoun, C. (ed.) *Habermas and the Public Sphere*. Cambridge, Massachusetts & London: The MIT Press, 1–50.

Calhoun, Craig 1992b. (ed.) *Habermas and the Public Sphere*. Cambridge, Massachusetts & London: The MIT Press.

Camus-Vigué, Agnès 2000. 'Community and Civic Culture: the Rotary Club in France and the United States.' In Lamont, Michèle & Laurent Thévenot (eds) *Rethinking Comparative Cultural Sociology. Repertoires of Evaluation in France and the United States*. Cambridge: Cambridge University Press.

Carrel, Marion 2003. 'Susciter un public local. Habitants et professionnels du transport en confrontation dans un quartier d'habitat social.' In Barril C., M. Carrel., J-C Guerrero & A. Marquez (eds) *Le public en action. Usages et limites de la notion d'espace public en sciences sociales*. Paris: L'Harmattan, 219–40.

Carrel, Marion 2006. 'Politisation er publicisation: Les effets fragiles de la délibération an milieu populaire.' *Politix: Revue des sciences sociales du politique* vol.19: 75, 33–51.

Carrel, Marion 2007a. 'Pauvreté, citoyenneté et participation. Quatre posititions dans le débat sur la 'participation des habitants."' In Neveu C. (ed.) *Cultures et pratiques participative. Perspectives comparatives*. Paris: L'Harmattan.

Carrel, Marion 2007b. 'La citoyenneté urbaine du point de vue des gouvernés.' In Neveu Catherine, Jacques Ion, Marion Carrel, Claire Gillio, François Menard, Nicole Rousier, Pascal Lemonnier & Patrice Aubertel (eds) *La citoyenneté urbaine: formes d'engagement et enjeux de solidarité*. Paris: Ministère l'Emploi, de la Cohésion sociale et du logement Ministère des Transports, de l'Equipement, du Tourisme et de la Mer, DGUHC / PUCA.

Castoriadis, Cornelius 1975. *L'institution imaginaire de la société*. Paris: Éditions du Seuil.

Cefaï, Daniel 2002. 'Qu'est-ce qu'une arène publique? Quelques pistes pour une approche pragmatiste.' In Cefaï, D & I. Joseph (eds) *L'Héritage du pragmatisme*. Paris: Éditions de l'Aube, 2002, 51–82.

Charles, Julien 2009. 'The Participant. Personal Requirements and Promises within Participatory Democracy.' Presentations at the 5th ECPR Potsdam. Panel: Ordinary citizens and politics.

Charles, Julien 2010. *Ce que la participation fait à la personne*. Unpublished PhD thesis manuscript. Louvain-La-Neuve: Université catholique de Louvain.

Charles, Julien 2011. 'Des savoirs citoyens au raisonnement démocratique: La compétence politique à l'heure de la démocratie participative.' In *Gouverner les mémoires. Le témoin, l'archive et le réseau*, V. Tournay, F. Cantelli, and C. Routelous (eds). Presses Universitaires de Rennes. Forthcoming.

de Certeau, Michel, Luce Giard & Pierre Mayol 1994. *L'invention du quotidian. 2. Habiter, cuisine*. Paris: Editions Gallimard.

Cohen, Joshua 2002. 'Deliberation and Democratic Legitimacy.' In Estlund, David (ed.) *Democracy*. Malden & Oxford: Blackwell Publishers Inc, 87–106.

Collet, Serge 1982. 'La manifestation de rue comme production culturelle militante.' *Ethnographie francaise*, XII: 2, 167–76.

Cortese, Anthony J. 1999. *Provocateur. Images of Women & Minorities in Advertising*. Rowman & Littlefield Publishers.

Cowie, Elizabeth 1994. *Sociology and Visual Representation*. London & New York: Routledge.

Craig, Steve (ed.) 1992. *Men, Masculinity and the Media*. London & Delhi: Sage.

Crettiez, Xavier & Isabelle Sommier (eds) 2002. *La France Rebelle. Tous les mouvements et acteurs de la contestation*. Paris: Editions Michalon.

Croteau, David & William Hoynes 2003. *Media Society. Industries, Images, and Audiences*. Third Edition. Thousand Oaks, London & New Delhi: Sage Publications/Pine Forge Press.

Dahlgren, Peter 2003. 'A la recherche d'un public parlant. Les médias et la démocratie deliberative.' In Cefaï, Daniel &Dominique Pasquier (eds) *Les sens du public: Publics politiques, publics médiatiques*. Paris: PUF.

Dahlgren, Peter 2005. 'The Internet, Public Spheres, and Political Communication: Dispersion and Deliberation.' *Political Communication* Vol. 22:2, pp. 147–62.

Dahlgren Peter & Colin Sparks (eds) 1991. *Communication and Citzenship. Journalism and the Public Sphere*. London & New York: Routledge.

Delbo, Robert 2005. *La décentralisation depuis 1945*. Paris: Librairie Générale de Droit et de Jurisprudence.

Dewey, John 1927. *The Public and Its Problems.* Ohio: Swallow Press, Ohio University Press, Athens.

Deyon, Pierre 1999. 'Le long refus de la démocratie locale.' In *La démocratie locale. Représentation, participation et espace public.* CURAPP & CRAPS. Amiens, Lille, Paris: Presses Universitaires de France, 13–20.

Doidy, Eric 2005a. 'L'économie politique de la proximité. Des outils pragmatiques pour penser la mise en valeur du proche dans le champ politique.' In Le Bart, C. & R. Lefebvre (eds) *La proximité en politique. Usages, rhétoriques, pratiques.* Rennes. Presses Universitaires de Rennes, 33–44.

Doidy, Eric 2005b. '(Ne pas) juger scandaleux. Les électeurs de Levallois-Perret face au comportement de leur maire.' In *Politix* 71, 165–89.

Duchesne, Sophie 1997. *Citoyenneté à la française.* Paris: Presses de Sciences Po.

Eley, Geoff 1992. 'Nations, Publics, and Political Cultures: Placing Habermas in the Nineteenth Century.' In Calhoun, C. (ed.) *Habermas and the Public Sphere.* Cambridge, Massachusetts & London: The MIT Press, 289–339.

Eliasoph, Nina 1996. 'Making a Fragile Public: A Talk-Centered Study of Citizenship and Power.' *Sociological Theory,* 14: 3, 262–89.

Eliasoph, Nina 1998. *Avoiding Politics. How Americans Produce Apathy in Everyday Life.* Cambridge: Cambridge University press.

Eliasoph, Nina 2004. 'Can We Theorize the Press Without Theorizing the Public?' *Political Communication 21,* p. 297–303.

Eliasoph, Nina 2009. 'Local Organization, Global Comparison: Top Down Efforts at Promoting Participatory Democracy.' Presentation in The Social Science History Association conference November 12–15, 2009, Long Beach, California, USA.

Eliasoph, Nina 2011. *Making Volunteers. Civic Life After Welfare's End.* Princeton: Princeton University Press.

Eliasoph, Nina & Paul Lichterman 1999'"We Begin with Our Favorite Theory...': Reconstructing the Extended Case Method.' *Sociological Theory* 17:2, 228–34.

Eliasoph, Nina & Paul Lichterman 2003. 'Culture in Interaction.' *American Journal of Sociology* 108: 4, 735–94.

Eräsaari, Leena 2002. *Julkinen tila ja valtion yhtiöittäminen.* [Public Space and the Hiving Off of the State]. Helsinki: Gaudeamus.

Estlund, David 2002. 'Introduction.' In Estlund, D. (ed.) *Democracy.* Malden & Oxford: Blackwell Publishers, 1–28.

Faulks, Keith 2000. *Citizenship. Key Ideas.* London & New York: Routledge.

Forssell, Eveliina 2005. *Kansalaisliike kunnallisen päätöksenteon areenoilla: Tapaustutkimus Pro kuntapalvelut -liikkeen toiminnasta Helsingissä* [A Social Movement on the Arenas of Municipal Decision-Mt. Helsinki: University of Helsinki, Department of Political Science.

Franguiadakis, Spyros 1997. 'Affichage humanitaire: Témoigner des 'blessures qui se voient et aussi de celles ne se voient pas".' In Ion, J. & M. Peroni (eds) *Engagement public et exposition de la personne.* La Tour d'Aigues: Éditions de L'Aube.

Franguiadakis, Spyros 2001. 'Le réseau 'Tibérius Claudius' à Lyon: L'obligé de l'etranger et le militantisme désincarné.' In Ion J. (ed.) *L'engagement au pluriel.* Saint-Étienne: Publications de l'Université de Saint-Étienne.

Fraser, Nancy 1992. 'Rethinking the Public Sphere: A Contribution to the Critique of Actually Existing Democracy.' In Calhoun, C. (ed.) *Habermas and the Public Sphere.* Cambridge, Massachusetts & London: The MIT Press, 109–42.

Fraser, Nancy 1996. 'Gender Equity and the Welfare State: A Postindustrial Thought Experiment.' In Benhabib, S. (ed.) *Democracy and Difference. Contesting the Boundaries of the Political.* Princeton, New Jersey: Princeton University Press, 218–42.

Fyfe, Gordon & John Law 1988. *Picturing Power: Visual Depiction and Social Relations.* London: Routledge.

Gamson, William 1995. 'Constructing Social Protest.' In Johnston, Hank/Bert Klandermans (eds) *Social Movements and Culture.* Minneapolis: Minnesota University Press.

Garnham, Nicolas 1992. 'The Media and the Public Sphere.' In Calhoun, Craig (ed.) *Habermas and the Public Sphere.* Cambridge, Massachusetts & London: The MIT Press, 359–76.

Giugni, Marco 1998. 'Was it Worth the Effort? The Outcomes and Consequences of Social Movements.' *Annual Review of Sociology* 98: 371–93.

Goffman 1967 [1972]. *Interaction Ritual. Essays on Face-to-Face Behaviour.* Middlesex & Ringwood: Penguin Books.

Goffman, Erving 1974. *Frame Analysis. An Essay on the Organization of Experience.* Boston: Northeastern University Press.

Goffman 1979. *Gender Advertisements.* Cambridge, MA: Harvard University Press.

Gordon, Tuula 2005. 'Kaupunkikansalaisuus ja kansallisuuden paikallisuudet.' [Urban Citizenship and the Localities of Nationality]. In Hirsiaho A., M. Korpela, L. Rantalaiho (eds) *Kohtaamisia rajoilla.* Helsinki: SKS, 55–70.

Gordon, Tuula 2006. 'Gender and Citizenship.' In Skelton C., B. Francis, L. Smulyan (eds) *The Sage Handbook of Gender and Education.* London, Thousand Oaks, New Delhi: Sage Publications Ltd.

Gronow, Antti 2011: *From Habits to Social Structures. Pragmatism and Comtemporary Social Theory.* Frankfurt Am Main: Peter Lang.

Giugni, Marco & Florence Passy 2006. *La citoyenneté en débat.* Paris: L'Harmattan.

Gupta, Akhil 2006. 'Blurred Boundaries: The Discourse of Corruption, the Culture of Politics, and the Imagined State.' In Sharma, Aradhana & Akhil Gupta (eds) *The Anthropology of the State. A Reader.* Oxford: Blackwell Publishing.

Habermas, Jürgen 2004 [1962]. *Julkisuuden rakennemuutos. Tutkimus yhdestä kansalaisyhteiskunnan kategoriasta* [Strukturwandel der Öffentlichkeit. Untersuchungen zu einer Kategorie des bürgerlichen Gesellschaft]. Translated into Finnish by Veikko Pietilä. Tampere: Vastapaino.

Hall, Stuart 1997a. 'Introduction.' In Hall, Stuart (ed.) *Representation. Cultural Representations and Signifying Practices.* London, Thousand Oaks & New Delhi: Sage Publications, 1–12.

Hall, Stuart 1997b. 'The Work of Representation.' In Hall, Stuart (ed.) *Representation. Cultural Representations and Signifying Practices.* London, Thousand Oaks & New Delhi: Sage Publications, 13–74.

Hall, Stuart 1997c. 'The Spectacle of the "Other".' In Hall, Stuart (ed.) *Representation. Cultural Representations and Signifying Practices.* London, Thousand Oaks & New Delhi: Sage Publications, 223–79.

Hamidi, Camille 2006. 'Élements pour une approche interactionniste de la politisation. Engagement associatif et rapport au politique dans des associations locales issues de l'immigration.' *Revue française de science politique,* vol. 56:1, 5–25.

Hamidi, Camille 2010. *La société civile dans les cites. Engagement associative et politisation dans desassociations de quartier.* Paris: Economica.

Hamilton, Peter 1997. 'Representing the Social: France and Frenchness in Post-War Humanist Photography.' In Hall, Stuart (ed.) *Representation. Cultural Representations and Signifying Practices.* London, Thousand Oaks & New Delhi: Sage Publications, 75–150.

Hantrais, Linda 2009. *International Comparative Research: Theory, Methods and Practice.* Basingstoke: Palgrave Macmillan.

Harinen, Päivi 2000. *Valmiiseen tulleet. Tutkimus nuoruudesta, kansallisuudesta ja kansalaisuudesta* [Ready-Made Futures. A Study of Youth, Nationality and Citizenship]. Nuorisotutkimusseura, julkaisuja 11/2000. Helsinki: Nuorisotutkimusseura.

Heinen, Jacqueline & Alisa del Re 1996. *Quelle citoyenneté pour les femmes? La Crise des États-providence et de la representation politique en Europe.* Paris: L'Harmattan.

Heinen, Jacqueline & Lieber, Marylène & Gubin, Eliane & Pereira, Bérèngere Marques & Holli, Anne Maria & Luhtakallio, Eeva & Raevaara, Eeva & Cettolo, Hélène & Gaspard, Françoise & Kergoat, Michelle & Lépinard, Eléonore & Le Quentrec, Yannick & Rieu, Annie & Pantelidou Maloutas, Maria & Del Rei, Alisa & Longo, Valentina & Sebastiani, Chiara & Siebert, Renate & Cova, Anne & Viegas, José Manuel Leite & Elgan, Elisabeth & Ostberg, Kjell 2004. *Genre et gestion locale du changement dans sept pays de l'Union européenne: rapport final de recherche. Partie 1: Rapport transversal.* Luxembourg: La Commission Européenne, 2004.

Heiskala, Risto 1997. *Society as Semiosis. Neostructuralist Theory of Culture and Society.* Helsinki: Research Reports No. 231, Department of Sociology, University of Helsinki.

Heiskala Risto & Eeva Luhtakallio 2000. 'Sukupuolen julkisivu: sukupuoli suomalaisten aikakauslehtien kansissa 1950- luvulta 1990-luvulle' [The Front Page of Gender: Gender in Covers of Finnish Magazines from the 1950s to the 1990s]. *Naistutkimus-Kvinnoforskning* 13: 3, s. 4–25.

Hoikkala, Tommi & Mikko Salasuo (eds) 2006. *Prekaariruoska? Portfoliopolvi, perustulo ja kansalaistoiminta* [The Portfolio Generation, Basic Income and Civic Activity]. Nuorisotutkimusverkosto, verkkojulkaisusarja. Helsinki: Nuorisotutkimusseura.

Holli, Anne Maria 2003. *Discourse and Politics for Gender Equality in Late Twentieth Century Finland.* Department of Political Science, Acta Politica 23, Helsinki University Press, Helsinki 2003. 202 pp.

Holli, Anne Maria, Eeva Luhtakallio & Eeva Raevaara 2003. ' Maailman huonoin laki"? Kunnallispolitiikka, kiintiöt ja vastarinta' ['The Worst Law in the World'? Municipal Politics, Gender Quotas, and Resistance]. *Naistutkimus – Kvinnoforskning* 16:4, 1–15.

Holli, Anne Maria, Eeva Luhtakallio & Eeva Raevaara 2004. 'Gender and Local Management of Change: National Report of Finland.' In Jacqueline Heinen & Marylène Lieber (eds) *Genre et gestion locale du changement dans sept pays de l'Union européenne : rapport final de recherché. Partie 2 : Rapport nationaux.* Luxembourg: La Commission Européenne.

Holli, Anne Maria, Eeva Luhtakallio & Eeva Raevaara 2006. 'Quota Trouble. TalkingAbout Gender Quotas in Finnish Local Politics.' *International Feminist Journal of Politics,* 8:2, 169–93.

Holli, Anne Maria, Eeva Luhtakallio & Eeva Raevaara 2007. *Sukupuolten valtakunta. Politiikka, muutos ja vastarinta suomalaisissa kunnissa* [Politics, Transformation, and Resistance in Finnish Municipalities]. Tampere: Vastapaino.

Homanen, Riikka fortcoming. 'Internetin sikiökuvat: tieteellisen tutkimuksen tulos, poliittinen subjektifiointi ja fetissiobjekti' [Internet Fetus Images: The Result of a Scientific Investigation, Political Subjectivation, and the Fetich Object]. *Media ja Viestintä*, 2011.

Jepperson, Ronald L. 2002. 'Political Modernities: Disentangling Two Underlying Dimensions of Institutional Differentiation.' *Sociological Theory* 20:1, 61–85.

Joseph, Lauren, Matthew Mahler & Javier Auyero 2007. *New Perspectives in Political Ethnography*. Berlin: Springer.

Juntti, Eira 1998. 'Moderni kansakunta ja puuttuvat sukupuolet' [The Modern Nation and the Absent Genders]. *Politiikka* 40:2, 105–19.

Kantola, Johanna 2007. 'The Gendered Reproduction of the State in International Relations.' *The British Journal of Politics & International Relations*, vol 9: 2, 270–83.

Keränen, Marja 2001. 'Vertaileva ja poikkikulttuurinen tutkimus. Kaksi tapaa lähestyä muita maita' [Comparative and Transcultural Research. Two Ways to Approach Other Countries]. In *Politiikka* 43:2, 82–92.

Keränen, Marja 2007. 'Poliittisen osallistumisen epäpolitisoituminen' [The De-politicization of Political Participation]. In Tapani Kaakkuriniemi & Juri Mykkänen (eds) *Politiikan representaatio. Juhlakirja Kyösti Pekoselle hänen 60-vuotispäivänään*. Helsinki: Valtiotieteellinen yhdistys, 193–221.

Keskinen, Suvi, Anna Rastas & Salla Tuori 2009. *En ole rasisti, mutta... Maahanmuutosta, monikulttuurisuudesta ja kritiikistä* [I'm Not a Racist, But... On Immigration, Multiculturality, and Critique]. Tampere: Vastapaino.

Kettunen, Pauli 1997. *Työjärjestys: tutkielmia työn ja tiedon poliittisesta historiasta* [Working Order: Studies on the Political History of Work and Knowledge]. Helsinki: Tutkijaliitto.

Kettunen, Pauli 2004. 'The Nordic Model and Consensual Competitiveness in Finland.' In Castrén, Anna-Maija, Markku Lonkila & Matti Peltonen (eds) *Between Sociology and History. Essays on Microhistory, Collective Action, and Nation Building*. Studia Historica 70. Helsinki: SKS/Finnish Literature Society.

Kettunen, Pauli 2008. *Globalisaatio ja kansallinen me. Kansallisen katseen historiallinen kritiikki* [Globalization and the National We. The Historical Critique of the National Gaze]. Tampere: Vastapaino.

Kilpinen, Erkki 2000. *The Enormous Fly-Wheel of Society: Pragmatism's Habitual Conception of Action and Social Theory*. Helsinki: University of Helsinki, Department of Sociology.

Koebel, Michel 2006. *Le pouvoir local ou la démocratie improbable*. Collections de l'association Raisons d'agir. Bellecombe-en-Bauges: Éditions du Croquant.

Kolářová, Marta 2004. 'Gender Representation of the Anti-Globalisation Movement in the Alternative Media.' *Sociologický časopis/Czech Sociological Review* 40:6, pp. 851–68.

Konttinen, Esa & Jukka Peltokoski 2000. 'Ympäristöprotestin neljännen aallon sielunmaisema' [The Mindscape of the Fourth Wave of Environmental Protest]. *Sosiologia* 37: 2, 111–29.

Koopmans, Ruud & Dieter Rucht 1999. 'Introduction to Special Issue; Protest Event Analysis – Where to Now?' *Mobilization: An International Quarterly* Volume 4, Number 2. pp. 123–30.

Koopmans, Ruud & Dieter Rucht 2002. 'Protest Event Analysis.' In Klandermans, Bert & Suzanne Staggenborg (eds) *Methods of Social Movement Research.* University of Minnesota Press.

Koopmans, Ruud & Paul Statham 1999. 'Political Claims Analysis: Integrating Protest Event and Political Discourse Approaches.' *Mobilization: An International Quarterly* 4: 2, 203–21.

Koopmans, Ruud, Paul Statham, Marco Giugni & Florence Passy 2006. *Contested Citizenship. Immigration and Cultural Diversity in Europe.* Minneapolis & London: University of Minnesota Press.Korvajärvi, Päivi 199. 'Reproducing Gendered Hierarchies in Everyday Work: Contradictions in an Employment Office.' *Gender, Work & Organization* 5: 1, pp. 19–30.

Koveneva, Olga 2010. 'Vivre ensemble dans la nature et dans la ville: Capacités et expériences de la mise en commun en France et en Russie.' In Thévenot, Laurent (ed.) *Des liens du proche aux lieux du public. Russie – France, regards croisés.* Paris : Groupe de Sociologie Politique et Morale.

Krause, Peter & Petteri Pietikäinen 2009. 'Reshaping Europe: Migration and Its Contexts in Austria and Finland.' Introduction to Finnish Journal of Ethnicity and Migration Special Issue. *Finnish Journal of Ethnicity and Migration* Vol. 4, No. 2, 2–3.

Lafaye, Claudette & Laurent Thévenot 1993. 'Une justification écologique? Conflits dans l'aménagement de la nature.' *Revue française de sociologie* XXXIV, 495–523.

Laine, Sofia 2009. 'Contestatory Performative Acts in Transnational Political Meetings.' *Societies Without Borders*, Vol 4: 3, 398–429.

Lalonde, Richard N. & Randy A. Silverman 1994. 'Behavioral Preferences in Response to Social Injustice: The Effects of Group Permeability and Social Identity Salience'. *Journal of Personality and Social Psychology*, vol. 66: 1, pp. 78–85.

Lammert, Christian & Katja Sarkowsky 2010. *Travelling Concepts: Negotiating Diversity in Canada and Europe.* Wiesbaden: VS Verlag für Sozialwissenschaften.

Lamont, Michèle & Virág Molnar 2002. 'The Study of Boundaries in the Social Sciences.' *Annual Review of Sociology*, vol. 28, pp. 167–95.

Lamont, Michèle & Laurent Thévenot (eds) 2000. *Rethinking Comparative Cultural Sociology*. Repertoires of Evaluation in France and the United States. Cambridge: Cambridge University Press.

Landman, Todd 2000. *Issues and Methods in Comparative Politics: An Introduction.*
Oxford & New York: Routledge.

de Lauretis, Teresa 1987. *Technologies of Gender. Essays on Theory, Film, and Fiction.* Indiana University Press.

Lehti, Martti & Janne Kivivuori 2009. 'Kuolemaan johtanut väkivalta' [Lethal Violence]. In *Rikollisuustilanne 2008. Rikollisuus ja seuraamusjärjestelmä tilastojen valossa.*

Oikeuspoliittisen tutkimuslaitoksen tutkimuksia 247, Helsinki: Oikeuspoliittinen tutkimuslaitos, pp. 43–6.

Leino, Helena 2006. *Kansalaisosallistuminen ja kaupunkisuunnittelun dynamiikka. Tutkimus Tampereen Vuoreksesta* [Citizen Participation and the Dynamics of Urban Planning. A Study of the Tampere Vuores]. Acta Universitatis Tamperensis 1134. Tampere: Tampere University Press.

Lepola, Outi 2000. *Ulkomaalaisesta suomenmaalaiseksi. Monikulttuurisuus, kansalaisuus ja suomalaisuus 1990 – luvun maahanmuuttopoliittisessa keskustelussa*

[From a Foreigner to a Finlander. Multiculturality, Citizenship, and Finnishness in the 1990s Debate on Immigration Politics]. Helsinki: SKS.

Lichterman, Paul 1996. *The Search for Political Community: American Activists Reinventing Commitment*. Cambridge & New York: Cambridge University Press.

Lichterman, Paul 2002. 'Seeing Structure Happen: theory-driven Pparticipant Observation'. In Klandermans, B. & Suzanne Staggenborg (eds) *Methods of Social Movement Research*. Minneapolis: University of Minnesota Press.

Lichterman, Paul 2005. *Elusive Togetherness: Church Groups Trying to Bridge America's Divisions*. Princeton, NJ: Princeton University Press.

Lichterman, Paul 2006. 'Social Capital or Group Style? Rescuing Tocqueville's Insights on Civic Engagement.' *Theory and Society* 35: 529–63.

Lichterman, Paul & Daniel Céfaï 2006. 'The Idea of Political Culture.' In Goodin, Robert E. & Charles Tilly (eds) *The Oxford Handbook of Contextual Political Analysis*. Oxford: Oxford University Press.

Lindström, Samu 2009. *Demokratian kuokkavieraat. Kuokkavierasjuhlat yhteiskunnallisen keskustelun kohteena 1997–2007*. Master's thesis. Helsinki: Department of Sociology, University of Helsinki, e-thesis: http://urn.fi/URN:NBN:fi-fe200910202266

Lister, Ruth 2003. *Citizenship: Feminist Perspectives*. Second Edition. New York: New York University Press.

Lonkila, Markku 2011. 'Yhteisyyden kieliopit helsinkiläisessä ja pietarilaisessa kaupunkiaktivismissa' [Grammars of Communality in Urban Activism in Helsinki and Piertari]. *Sosiologia* 48(2011):1, pp. 22–33.

Luhtakallio, Eeva 2003. *Julkinen nainen ja mies: sukupuolirepresentaatiot suomalaisten ja ranskalaisten aikakauslehtien kansikuvissa 1955, 1975 ja 1995* [Public Women and Men: Gender Representations in Finnish and French Magazine Covers in 1955, 1975, and 1995]. Master's thesis. Helsinki: Department of Sociology, University of Helsinki.

Luhtakallio, Eeva 2005. 'Kehysanalyysi mediakuvien sukupuolirepresentaatioiden tutkimuksessa' [Frame Analysis in the Study of Gender Representations in Media Images]. *Sosiologia* 42 (2005): 3, pp. 189–206.

Luhtakallio, Eeva 2007. 'Kansalaistoiminnan ulottuvuudet.' [Dimensions of Civic Action]. In Holli, Anne Maria, Eeva Luhtakallio & Eeva Raevaara (eds)*Sukupuolten valta/kunta. Politiikka, muutos ja vastarinta suomalaisissa kunnissa*. Tampere: Vastapaino, 167–206.

Luhtakallio, Eeva 2009. 'Visual Orders of Democracy: Representations of the Local Society in Activist Websites and City Magazines.' Paper presented on February 27 at the Emory S. Bogardus Research Colloquium. Department of Sociology, University of Southern California, Los Angeles Ca.

Luhtakallio, E. 2010. 'Perceptions of Democracy in Helsinki & Lyon.' In Stenius, Henrika & Alapuro, Risto (eds) Nordic Associations in a Comparative Perspective. Baden-Baden: Nomos Verlagsgesellschaft, 281–306.

Luhtakallio, Eeva & Risto Alapuro 2008. 'Vaalidemokratia, vastademokratia ja politiikan paluu. Johdatusta Pierre Rosanvallonin ajatteluun' [Election Democracy, Counter-Democracy, and the Return of Politics. Introduction to the Thinking of Pierre Rosanvallon]. In Rosanvallon, Pierre *Vastademokratia. Politiikka epäluulon aikakaudella*. Translated into Finnish by Tapani Kilpeläinen. Tampere: Vastapaino, 7–17.

Luhtakallio, Eeva & Nina Eliasoph (2012). 'Ethnography of Politics and Political Communication: Studies in Sociology and Political Science'. In Kenski, Kate & Kathleen Hall Jamieson (eds) *The Oxford Handbook of Political Communication.*

Luhtakallio, Eeva & Tuomas Ylä-Anttila 2011. 'Julkisen oikeuttamisen analyysi sosiologisena tutkimusmenetelmänä'.[The Public Justifications Analysis as a Sociological Method]. *Sosiologia* 48: 1, 34–51.

Luostarinen, Heikki & Turo Uskali 2006. 'Suomalainen journalismi ja yhteiskunnan muutos' [Finnish Journalism and Societal Change]. In Heiskala, Risto & Eeva Luhtakallio (eds) *Uusi jako: miten Suomesta tuli kilpailukyky-yhteiskunta?* Helsinki: Gaudeamus.

Mahler, Matthew 2006. 'Politics as a Vocation: Notes Toward a Sensualist Understanding of Political Engagement.' *Qualitative Sociology* (2006) 29: 281–300.

Manning, Philip 1992. *Erving Goffman and Modern Sociology*. Polity Press, Cambridge.

Marsh, Robert M. 1967. *Comparative sociology: A Codification of Cross-societal Analysis*. New York: Harcourt, Brace and World.

Marshall, T. H. 1950. *Citizenship and Social Class and Other Essays*. London & New York: Cambridge University Press.

Martinez, Caroline 2003. *D'un collectif à l'autre: Étude de la mouvance féministe radicale lyonnaise*. Thèse de DEA. Lyon: Université Lyon 2.

Marx Ferree, Myra, William Gamson, Jürgen Gerhards & Dieter Rucht 2002a. 'Four models of the Public Sphere in Modern Democracies.' *Theory and Society* 31: 289–324.

Marx Ferree, Myra, William Gamson, Jürgen Gerhards & Dieter Rucht 2002b. *Shaping the Abortion Discourse. Democracy and the Public Sphere in Germany and the United States*. Cambridge, New York, Melbourne, Madrid & Cape Town: Cambridge University Press.

McNair, Brian 2000. *Journalism and Democracy. An Evaluation of the Political Public Sphere*. New York & London: Routledge.

Mikkelsen, Flemming & Rene Karpantscho 2001. 'Youth as a Political Movement: Development of the Squatters' and Autonomous Movement in Copenhagen'. *International Journal of Urban and Regional Research* 25: 3, pp. 593–608.

Mikola, Elina 2008. *Toisenlainen tila on mahdollinen! Etnografinen tutkielma Helsingin talonvaltauksista*. [Another Space is Possible! An Ethnographic Study of Squatting in Helsinki]. Master's thesis. University of Tampere, epartment of Sociology. http://tutkielmat.uta.fi/pdf/gradu02558.pdf

Mitchell, W.J.T 1986. *Iconology. Image, Text, Ideology*. Chicago: The University of Chicago Press.

Mitchell, W.J.T 1994. *Picture Theory. Essays on Verbal and Visual Representation.* Chicago & London: University of Chicago Press.

Morales, Laura 2009. *Joining Political Organisations. Institutions, Mobilisation and Participation in Western Democracies*. Essex: ECPR Press.

Morreale, Joanne 1991. *A New Beginning. A Textuel Frame Analysis of the Political Campaign Film*. Albany: State University of New York Press.

Mouffe, Chantal 1999. 'Deliberative Democracy or Agonistic Pluralism?' *Social Research,* Vol. 66, Issue 3.

Murard, Numa & Étienne Tassin 2007. 'Les engagements des citoyens de "non,"' In Daum, Christophe (ed.) *Citoyenneté, engagements publics et espaces urbains.* L'Homme et la Société n°160. Paris: L'Harmattan.

Näre, Lena 2008. 'Ylirajaiset hoivajärjestykset. Puolalaisten naisten kokemuksia koti- ja hoivotyöstä Napolissa' [Polish Women's Experiences of Home and Care Work in Naples]. In Tolonen, T. (ed.) *Yhteiskunta ja sukupuoli*. Tampere: Vastapaino.

Näre, Lena forthcoming. 'Empowerment, Survival and Everyday Life Struggles – Ukranian and Polish Care Workers in Naples.' In Saarinen, A. & M. Calloni (eds.) *Eastern European Migrants as 'Builders' of a 'New Europe'. Gender Experiences and Perspectives in European Trans-Regions*. Helsinki: Kikimora Publications.

Nash, Kate 2010. *Contemporary Political Sociology. Globalization, Politics and Power.* Oxford: Wiley–Blackwell.

Neveu, Catherine 2003. *Citoyenneté et espace public. Habitants, jeunes et citoyens dans une ville du Nord*. Villeneuve d'Ascq : Presses Universitaires de Septentrion.

Neveu, Catherine 2004. 'Les enjeux d'une approche anthropologique de la citoyenneté.' *Revue Européenne des Migrations Internationales*, vol. 20, no. 3, pp. 89–102.

Neveu, Catherine (ed.) 2007. *Cultures et pratiques participatives. Perspectives comparatives*. Paris: L'Harmattan.

Neveu, Eric 2003. 'Engagement et distanciation. Le journalisme local face à un movement social.' In Cefaï, Daniel &Dominique Pasquier (eds) *Le sens du public: Publics politiques, publics médiatiques*. Paris: PUF.

Niemi-Iilahti Anita 1999. *Kansalaisten ja hallinnon vuorovaikutus. Helsingin paikallisagendaprosessin arviointia* [Interaction of Citizens and Governance. Evaluation of the Helsinki Local Agenda Process]. Helsinki: Helsingin kaupungin tietokeskus.

Nixon, Sean 1997. 'Exhibiting masculinity.' In Hall, Stuart (ed.) (1997) *Representation: Cultural Representations and Signifying Practices*. London, Thousand Oaks & New Delhi: Sage, 291–330.

Offerlé, Michel 1998. 'La nationalisation de la citoyenneté civique en France à la fin du XIXè siècle.' In Romanelli, Raffaele (ed.) *How Did They Become Voters? The History of Franchise in Modern European Representation*. The Hague: Kluwer Law International.

Oliver, Pamela E. & Daniel J. Myers 1999. 'How Events Enter the Public Sphere: Conflict, Location, and Sponsorship in Local Newspaper Coverage of Public Events.' *American Journal of Sociology* Vol. 105:1, 38–87.

Overney, Laetitia, Rémi Elicabe, Amandine Guilbert, Anne-Sophie Haeringer & Yannis Lemery 2008. 'Ressaisir la citoyenneté aux bords du politique.' Presentation at PUCA/ La citoyenneté Urbaine seiries; 'Le regard des chercheurs et visibilité des phénomènes observes' Coordination: Jacques Ion. October 23, Paris.

Palonen, Kari 2003. 'Four Times of Politics: Policy, Polity, Politicking, and Politicization.' *Alternatives* 28, 171–86.

Palonen, Kari 2002. 'Politiikka.' [Politics]. In Hyvärinen, Matti, Jussi Kurunmäki, Kari Palonen, Tuija Pulkkinen ja Henrik Stenius (eds) *Käsitteet liikkeessä. Suomen poliittisen kulttuurin käsitehistoria*. Tampere: Vastapaino.

Papacharissi, Zizi 2002. 'The Virtual Sphere.The Internet as a Public Sphere.' *New Media & Society*, Vol. 4: 1, 9–27.

Patomäki, Heikki & Teivainen, Teivo 2003. *Globaali demokratia* [Global Democracy]. Helsinki: Gaudeamus.

Pernaa, Ville, Mari K. Niemi & Ville Pitkänen 2009. *Politiikan journalismin tila Suomessa* [The State of Political Journalism in Finland]. Turun yliopisto: Kirja-Aurora.

Perrineau Pascal & Henri Rey 2002. 'Crise urbaine et citoyennete.' In *Agora débats/jeunesse* no. 30 (132 p.), pp. 28–4.

Peräkylä, Anssi 1990. *Kuoleman monet kasvot: identiteettien tuottaminen kuolevan potilaan hoidossa* [The Multiple Faces of Death: Production of Identities in the Care of a Dying Patient]. Tampere: Vastapaino.

Perälä, Riikka 2009. 'Huumeidenkäyttäjien terveysneuvontakoulutukset liberaalina hallintakäytäntönä: etnografinen analyysi huumeongelmien uusista hallintastrategioista' [The Health Counselling Events for Drug Users as a Liberal Governance Practice. An Ethnographic Analysis of the New Strategies of Governing the Drug Problem]. *Sosiologia* 46:2, 111–26.

Pollitt, Christopher & Geert Bouckaert 2004. *Public Management Reform. A Comparative Analysis*. Oxford: Oxford University Press.

della Porta, Donatella & Mario Diani 2006. *Social Movements. An Introduction.* Second Edition. Malden, Oxford & Carlton: Blackwell Publishing.

Purhonen, Semi, Tommi Hoikkala & J.P. Roos (eds) 2008. *Kenen sukupolveen kuulut? Suurten ikäluokkien tarina* [Whose Generation Do You Belong To? The Story of the Great Age Classes]. Helsinki: Gaudeamus.

Putnam, Robert D. 2000 *Bowling Alone. The Collapse and Revival of American Community*. NY, London, Toronto & Syndey: Simon & Schuster.

Raevaara, Eeva 2005. *Tasa-arvo ja muutoksen rajat. Sukupuolten tasa-arvo poliittisena ongelmana Ranskan parité- ja Suomen kiintiökeskusteluissa* [Equality and the Limits of Change. Gender Equality as a Political Problem in the French Parité and the Finnish Quota Debates]. TANE-julkaisuja 2005:7. Helsinki: Sosiaali- ja terveysministeriö, tasa-arvoasian neuvottelukunta.

Ragin, Charles C. 1987. *The Comparative Method: Moving Beyond Qualitative and Quantitative Strategies*. Berkeley & Los Angeles: University of California Press.

Rättilä, Tiina 2001. 'Kansalaistuva politiikka? Huomioita kuntalaisaktiivisuudesta poliittisena toimijuutena' [Politics Gone Citizen? Observations on Municipal Activeness as Political Action]. *Politiikka* 43: 3, s. 190–207.

del Re, Alisa & Jacqueline Heinen 1996. *Quelle citoyenneté pour les femmes?: La crise des États-providence et de la représentation politique en Europe*. Bibliothèque du féminisme. Paris: L'Harmattan.

Revel, Martine, Cécile Blatrix, Loïc Blondiaux, Jean-Michel Frouniau, Bertrand Hériard Dubreuil & Rémi Lefebvre (eds) 2007. *Le débat public: une experience française de démocratie participative*. Paris: la Découverte.

Ricoeur, Paul 1991. *From Text to Action. Essays in Hermeneutics*, II. Translated by Kathleen Blamey and John B. Thompson. Evanston: Northwestern University Press.

Ricoeur Paul 1995. *Le Juste*. Paris: Editions Esprit.

Robbe, François 2007. 'Démocratie representative et participation.' In Robbe, François (ed.) *La démocratie participative*. Paris: L'Harmattan.

Rosanvallon, Pierre 1998. *Le peuple introuvable. Histoire de la représentation démocratique en France*. Paris: Gallimard.

Rosanvallon, Pierre 2006. *La contre-démocratie. La politique à l'âge de la défiance*. Paris: Éditions du Seuil.

Rosanvallon, Pierre 2008. *La légitimité démocratique. Impartialité, réflexivité, proximité*. Paris: Éditions du Seuil.

Rose, Gillian 2001. *Visual Methodologies. An Introduction to the Interpretation of Visual Materials*. London, Thousand Oaks, New Delhi: Sage.

Rossi, Leena-Maija 2003. *Heterotehdas: televisiomainonta sukupuolituotantona* [The Hetero Factory: TV Commercials as Gender Production]. Helsinki: Gaudeamus.

Roy, Arundhati 2009. *Listening to Grasshoppers. Field Notes in Democracy*. London: Penguin Books.

Rui, Sandrine 2004. *La démocratie en débat. Les citoyens face à l'action publique*. Paris: Armand-Colin.

Ryan, Mary P. 1992. 'Gender and public access: women's politics in nineteenth century America.' In Calhoun, C. (ed.) *Habermas and the Public Sphere*. Cambridge, Massachusetts & London: The MIT Press, 259–88.

Salamon, Lester M. & Helmut K. Anheier 1998. 'Social Origins of Civil Society: Explaining the Nonprofit Sector Cross-Nationally.' *Voluntas* 9, 213–48.

Salasuo, Mikko 2006. 'Smash Asem. Kansalaistarkkailu metodina ja pohdiskelun pontimena' [Smash Asem. Civic Control as a Method and a Reflection]. In Hoikkala & Salasuo (eds) *Prekaariruoska? Portfoliopolvi, perustulo ja kansalaistoiminta*. Nuorisotutkimusverkosto, verkkojulkaisusarja. Helsinki: Nuorisotutkimusseura. www.nuorisotutkimusseura.fi/smashasem.pdf

Salmenniemi, Suvi 2005. 'Civic Activity – Feminine Activity? Gender, Civil Society and Citizenship in Post-Soviet Russia'. *Sociology* (Journal of the British Sociological Association) Vol. 39:4, 735–53.

Salmenniemi, Suvi 2008. *Democratization and Gender in Contemporary Russia*. London: Routledge.

Schnapper, Dominique 1994. *La communauté des citoyens*. Paris: Éditions Gallimard.

Sennett, Richard 2007. *The Culture of New Capitalism*. Yale: Yale University Press.

Seppänen, Janne 2001. *Katseen voima. Kohti visuaalista lukutaito*. [The Power of Gaze. Towards Visual Literacy]. Tampere: Vastapaino.

Seppänen, Janne 2002. Valokuvaa ei ole [Photograph Is Not]. Helsinki: Musta Taide & Suomen valokuvataiteen museo.

Seppänen, Janne 2005. *Visuaalinen kulttuuri. Teoriaa ja metodeja mediakuvan tulkitsijalle* [Visual Culture. Theory and Methods for Interpreters of Media Images]. Tampere: Vastapaino.

Setälä, Maija 2003. *Demokratian arvo. Teoriat, käytännöt ja mahdollisuudet* [Democracy's Worth. Theories, Practices and Possibilities]. Helsinki: Gaudeamus.

Sharma Aradhana & Akhil Gupta 2006. *Anthropology of the State. A Reader*. Oxford: Blackwell Publishing.

Siisiäinen, Martti 1992. 'Social Movements, Voluntary Associations and Cycles of Protest in Finland 1905–91.' *Scandinavian Political Studies* 15: 1, pp. 21–40.

Siisiäinen, Martti 2002. 'Yhdistysten nykytila ja kehityksen suunnat' [The Current State and Future Directions of Associations]. In Riikonen, Virve & Martti Siisiäinen (eds) *Yhdistystoiminnan uusjako*. Helsinki: Opintotoiminnan keskusliitto.

Silber, Ilana Friedrich 2003. 'Pragmatic Sosiology as Cultural Sosiology. Beyond Repertoire Theory?' *European Journal of Social Theory* 6(4): 427–99.

Silverman, Kaja 1983. *The Subject of Semiosis*. NY & Oxford: Oxford University Press.

Sineau, Mariette 2005. 'Vote et participation politique.' In Margaret Maruani (ed.) *Femmes, Genre et société. L'état des saviors*. Paris: La Découverte.

Sintomer, Yves 2007. *Le pouvoir au peuple. Jurys cityoens, tirage au sort et démocratie participative*. Paris: La Découverte.

Snow, David & Benford, Robert 1988. 'Ideology, Frame resonance, and Participant Mobilization'. *International Social Movements Research* 1, s. 197–218.

Soysal, Yasmine Nuhoglu 1994. *Limits of Citizenship*. Chicago: University of Chicago Press.

Standifird, Stephen S. 2001. 'Conceptual Bonds: Network Analysis as a Way of Understanding Institutional Rigidity.' *Emergence* 3 (3): 7–21.

Steinberg, Marc W. 1998. 'Tilting the Frame: Considerations on Collective Action Framing from a Discursive Turn.' *Theory and Society* 27: 845–72.

Stenius, Henrik 1987. *Frivilligt, jämlikt, samfällt: föreningsväsendetsutveckling i Finland fram till 1900-talets början med speciell hänsyn till massorganisationsprincipens genombrott*. Helsingfors: Svenska litteratursällskapet i Finland.

Stenius, Henrik 1988. In Stenius, Henrik & Tigerstedt, Christoffer (red.). *Brandkårsliv: festskrift till Helsingfors FBK:s 125 års jubileum*. Helsingfors: Helsingfors FBK.

Stenius, Henrik 2002. 'Kansalainen' [Citizen]. In Hyvärinen, Matti, Jussi Kurunmäki, Kari Palonen, Tuija Pulkkinen ja Henrik Stenius (eds) *Käsitteet liikkeessä. Suomen poliittisen kulttuurin käsitehistoria*. Tampere: Vastapaino.

Stenius, Henrik 2010. 'Nordic Associational Life in European and Inter-Nordic Perspectives.' In Alapuro, Risto & Henrik Stenius (eds) *Nordic Associations in a Comparative Perspective*. Nomos.

Stranius, Leo & Mikko Salasuo (eds) 2008. *Talonvaltaus liikkeenä – miksi squat ei antaudu?* [Squatting as a Movement]. Nuorisotutkimusverkosto Verkkojulkaisuja 19. Helsinki: Nuorisotutkimusseura.

Strömbäck, Jesper & Daniela V. Dimitrova 2006. 'Political and Media Systems Matter. A Comparison of Election News Coverage in Sweden and the United States.' *Press/Politics* 11:4, 131–47.

Suomen demokratiaindikaattorit 2006. [Finnish Democracy Indicators]. Helsinki: Oikeusministeriö.

Swidler, Ann 1986. 'Culture in Action: Symbols and Strategies.' *American Sociological Review* Vol. 51, 273–86.

Sztompka, Piotr 1999/2006. *Trust. A Sociological Theory*. Cambridge.: Cambridge University Press.

Tallberg, Teemu 2009. *The Gendered Social Organisation of Defence: Two Ethnographic Case Studies in the Finnish Defence Forces*. Economics and Society, 193. Helsinki: Hanken School of Economics.

Talpin, Julien 2006. 'Jouer les bons citoyens. Les effets contrastés de l'engagement au sein de dispositifs participatifs.' *Politix: Revue des sciences sociales du politique* vol.19: 75, 13–31.

Tavory, Iddo 2010a. *Off Melrose: Orthodox Life in Secular Space*. Unpublished PhD Dissertation. Los Angeles: University of California, Los Angeles.

Tavory, Iddo 2010b. 'The Hollywood Shtetl: From Ethnic Enclave to Religious Destination.' *Ethnography*, 11(1).

Taylor, Charles 2004. *Modern social imaginaries*. Durham & London: Duke University Press.

Thévenot, Laurent 2006. *L'action au pluriel. Sociologie des régimes d'engagement*. Paris: Éditions la Découverte.

Thévenot, Laurent 2007. 'The plurality of cognitive formats and engagements: moving between the familiar and the public.' *European Journal of Social Theory* 10, 409–23.

Thévenot, Laurent 2010. 'Bounded Justifiability. Assurance and Oppression in Securing Life Together with Binding Engagements.' Spaces of Democracy Workshop, Helsinki Research Group for Political Sociology, University of Helsinki, June 14–15, 2010. Available at http://blogs.helsinki.fi/politicalsociology/files/2011/06/spaces_thevenot.pdf.

Thévenot, Laurent, 2011. 'Oikeutettavuuden rajat. Yhteiselämää koossa pitävät sidokset ja niiden väärinkäyttö.' Translated from English by Veikko Eranti *Sosiologia* 48:1, pp. 7–21.

Thévenot, Laurent, Michael Moody & Claudette Lafaye 2000. 'Forms of Valuing Nature: Arguments and Modes of Justification in French and American Environmental Disputes.' In Lamont, Michelle & Laurent Thévenot (eds) *Rethinking Comparative Cultural Sociology. Repertoires of Evaluation in France and the United States.* Cambridge: Cambridge University Press.

Tilly, Charles 1978. *From Mobilization to Revolution.* New York: Random House.

Tilly, Charles 2007. *Democracy.* Cambridge: Cambridge University Press.

Törrönen, Jukka 1999. *Juomisen vapaus ja vastuu. Sosiosemioottinen analyysi alkoholipoliittisesta liberalismista maallikkoajattelussa* [The Liberty and Responsibility of Drinking. A Socio-semiotic Analysis of Liberalism in Lay Thinking of Alcohol Politics]. Sosiologian laitoksen tutkimuksia No. 234. Helsinki: Helsingin yliopisto.

Tremblay, M, Th.-H. Balmer-Cao, B. Marques-Pereira, M. Sineau (eds) 2007. *Genre, citoyenneté et représentation.* Sainte-Foy: Presses Universitaires de Laval.

Tuominen, Laura 2008. *Sorkkaraudalla kotiin: Freda 42 suomalaisena talonvalta-usliikkeenä vuosina 1986–1988* [Claw Bar as Home Keys: Freda 42 as a Finnish Squatting Movement in 1986–1988]. Master's thesis. Helsinki: University of Helsinki.

Uitermark, Justus 2004. 'Framing Urban Injustices: The Case of the Amsterdam Squatter Movement.' *Space and Polity*, 8: 2, 227–244.

Valenius, Johanna 2004. *Undressing the Maid: Gender, Sexuality and the Body in the Construction of the Finnish Nation.* Helsinki: SKS.

Verdery, Katherine 1996. *What Was Socialism, What Comes Next?* Princeton, Chichester: Princeton University Press.

Walby, Sylvia 1997. *Gender Transformations.* London: Routledge.

Warren, Dorian 2009. 'Studying Politics with an Ethnographic and Historical Sensibility.' *Qualitative & Multi-Method Research* Vol. 7: 2, 44–8.

Weber, Max 1992 [1921]. *Kaupunki* [Die Stadt]. Translated into Finnish by Tapani Hietaniemi. Tampere: Vastapaino.

Weber, Max 2009 [1919]. *Tiede ja politiikka ammattina ja kutsumuksena.* [Politik aus Beruf]. Translated into Finnish by Tapani Hietaniemi. Tampere: Vastapaino.

Williamson, Judith (1978/1988). *Decoding Advertisements. Ideology and Meaning of Advertisement.* London: Boyars.

Wind, Marlene 2008–2009. 'Post-National Citizenship in Europe: The EU as a Welfare Rights Generator.' *The Columbia Journal of European Law*, Special Issue: European Citizenship at Center-Stage, Vol 15:1, 239–64.

Ylä-Anttila, Tuomas 2010. *Politiikan paluu. Globalisaatioliike ja julkisuus Suomessa* [The Return of Politics. The Globalization Movement and the Public in Finland]. Tampere: Vastapaino.

Young, Iris Marion 1996. 'Communication and the other: Beyond deliberative democracy.' In Benhabib, Seyla (eds) *Democracy and Difference. Contesting the boundaries of the political*. Princeton, NJ: Princeton University Press, 120–36.

Young, Iris Marion 2000. *Inclusion and Democracy*. Oxford & New York: Oxford University Press.

Yuval-Davis Nira 1999. 'The "multi-layered citizen": citizenship in the age of "glocalization".' *International Feminist Journal f Politics* 1:1, 119–36.

Online sources

The Act of Construction and the Use of Land 1999. http://www.finlex.fi/fi/laki/ajantasa/1999/19990132

ATTAC 2011. http://www.attac.org/en

APUS 2010. http://www.millenaire3.com/Affichage_de_la_ressou.69+M55dde8bf248.0.html

Cabiria 2010. http://www.cabiria.asso.fr/

Centre d'histoire de la Résistance et de la deportation 2010. http://www.culture.lyon.fr/culture/sections/fr/musees__expositions/

Citizen Participation Policy Programme 2007. http://www.om.fi/en/Etusivu/Ajankohtaista/Arkistoidutsisallot/Kansalaisvaikuttamisenpolitiikkaohjelma

Eurostat 2010. Immigration statistics in EU-countries.

http://europa.eu/rapid/pressReleasesAction.do?reference=STAT/09/175

Finlandization 2010. http://en.wikipedia.org/wiki/Finlandization

Grand Lyon 2009 http://www.grandlyon.com/

La Gryffe 2010. http://lagryffe.net/

HELKA 2010. http://helka.net/

Helsinki 2009. www.hel.fi

http://www.hel.fi/osallistuminen

www.hel.fi/wps/wcm/resources/file/eb948e456eda1ee/Helsinki_vaalitilinpaatos.pdf

http://nk.hel.fi/hna/

http://www.kaupunginosat.net/maunula/asuminen/aluefoorumi_esittely.htm

Hesan Nuorten Ääni 2008. http://nk.hel.fi/hna/

KMT Lukija S08/K09 / TNS Gallup. Reader Statistics of Finnish newspapers. www.ts.fi/yritysasiakkaat/mediatiedot/103071.pdf

The Local Government Act 1995. http://www.finlex.fi/fi/laki/ajantasa/1995/19950365

Lyon 2009. www.lyon.fr

http://www.lyon.fr/vdl/sections/fr/vie_democratique/democratie_de_proxim

http://www.tns-sofres.com/etudes/dossiers/muni2001/muni2001_lyon.htm

Lähiradio 2010. http://www.kansanradioliitto.fi/index2.htm

Maahanmuuttovirasto 2010. Immigration statistics in Finland. http://www.migri.fi/netcomm/content.asp?article=2560

Marsura, Evelyne 2004. 'Lyon 'Capitale de la Résistance' Quelle est l'origine de l'expression?' http://www.memoire-net.org/article.php3?id_article=129

Megafoni 2009. http://megafoni.kulma.net/

Non à Big Brother 2008. http://nonabigbrother.free.fr/

Nordic Countries 2010. http://en.wikipedia.org/wiki/Nordic_countries

Oranssi ry 2009. http://www.oranssi.net/

Poliisibarometri 2007. http://www.poliisi.fi/julkaisu/poliisi042008

Pro Kuntapalvelut 2009 http://capsicumguys.com/~prokunta/index.php, checked February 23, 2009

Radio Canut 2010. http://radio.canut.free.fr/

Rebellyon 2010. http://rebellyon.info/

Statistics Finland 2009. Statistics on Habitation. http://www.stat.fi/til/asas/index_en.html

Statistics Finland 2009. Statistics on population. http://www.stat.fi/til/vaerak/2008/vaerak_2008_2009-03-27_kuv_006_fi.html

Tilastokeskus 2010. Statistics on municipal elections 2008. http://pxweb2.stat.fi/Dialog/varval.asp?ma=630_kvaa_2008_2009-10-30_tau_139_fi&ti=Kunnallisvaalit+2008%2C+valittujen+lukum%E4%E4r%E4&path=../Database/StatFin/vaa/kvaa/2008_05/&lang=3&multilang=fi

Voima 2010. http://www.voima.fi/

World Value Survey 2004. ASEP/JDS Databank http://www.jdsurvey.net/bdasepjds/Question.jsp Checked May 27, 2008

Index